Second Edition

Patently Persuasive

Strategies for Influencing Judge and Jury

Karen Lisko, PhD, and Kevin Boully, PhD

AMERICAN BAR ASSOCIATION
Intellectual Property Law Section

Cover design by Jill Tedhams/ABA Design

Printed in the United States of America.

29 28 27 26 25 5 4 3 2 1

A catalog record for this book is on file with the Library of Congress.

Contents

Acknowledgments

We are grateful to so many people for their help and support in completing the second edition of this book. The words and ideas stem from our decades of work in patent litigation and with many amazing trial lawyers and patent litigation clients with whom we have collaborated and from whom we have learned. You will see many of their names and their wisdom throughout this book. We are grateful for all those opportunities and for the many to come. It is the source of our inspiration and a great gift to developing new and creative ideas!

Perkins Coie LLP is an incredibly supportive law firm filled with great patent minds. We owe our gratitude to Perkins and the leadership who has supported us as we finished work on this updated edition, as well as numerous trial lawyers who have supported and contributed to our knowledge along the way and in specific parts of this book. We are also thankful for the support (including gratitude for the nudges, believe it or not) from Jeff Salyards with the American Bar Association. We could not have completed this book without each of you.

Completing the first edition would not have been possible without the support of Holland & Hart LLP and our colleagues at Persuasion Strategies. We are especially grateful to Dr. Shelley Spiecker, Dr. Ken Broda-Bahm, Nick Bouck, and Jason Bullinger from Persuasion Strategies for their help and support of ideas and content in this book. We also want to acknowledge Jill Kustner from IMS Services, who helped us develop graphics and visual ideas presented in this book. You'll see mention of all of them throughout this book for good reason.

Finally, this book would never have been written without the love and patience of our families. Their support during the years of work and many late nights required to make this book a reality has been unconditional and inspiring. Thank you Brian, Elena, Alex, and Nika. Thank you Lauren, Arden, and Afton.

We love you.

About the Authors

Dr. Karen Lisko has more than 30 years of experience in courtroom persuasion in intellectual property litigation and is a senior litigation consultant at the law firm Perkins Coie LLP. She strategizes with sophisticated patent litigators nationwide on persuasive arguments in arbitrations and bench and jury trials. She holds a doctorate in legal communication, a specialized degree held by only a few consultants in the nation, and is past president of the American Society of Trial Consultants (ASTC), and a recipient of its highest honor of the ASTC Lifetime Achievement Award. Karen has consulted on high-profile patent cases beginning with the landmark AZT patent litigation in the mid-1990s and carrying on to numerous patent cases involving well-known technologies, consumer products, and pharmaceuticals. She has conducted numerous mock arbitrations, mock jury trials, and mock *Markman* hearings for those cases, and has assisted in selecting numerous juries for patent trials. She is also a frequent speaker on the topic of intellectual property litigation.

When not working to meet book deadlines and provide case strategy on patent cases, she works out to keep up with her three active children and husband.

Dr. Kevin Boully is a senior litigation consultant with the international law firm Perkins Coie LLP. He has bachelor's degrees in psychology and crime and delinquency studies, a master's degree in forensic psychology, a doctoral degree in legal communication, and has been actively consulting with and assisting attorneys and companies in litigation since 2001. He is past president of the ASTC, as well as the former associate editor of the *Jury Expert*, and has spoken nationwide on topics ranging from jury selection to anti-corporate bias to persuasion in patent litigation.

Kevin is also a published poet, a television writer for an award-winning late-night format comedy show, and a co-author of feature-length screenplays and sitcom pilot episodes for television. He is an avid outdoorsmen, hiker, and fly fisherman who loves to hang with his wife, Lauren, their two daughters Arden and Afton, and a variety of pets from dogs to chickens to turtles and beyond.

More information about these authors is available at https://perkinscoie.com/.

About the Authors

CHAPTER 1

Introduction

"Preparing a patent case for trial is like setting up a Christmas tree while trying to convince your extended family not to hang all of their cherished but ugly ornaments on it."

—Tom Millikan, patent litigator, Perkins Coie

I. Introduction

Persuasion in any litigation is multilayered but the complexity of patent litigation demands a different level of persuasive techniques. In this book, we aim to dissuade any temptation to tell your fact finder, "This case is complex." Effective persuasion simplifies. We rely on decades of research with district court judges, administrative patent judges, and juries. The approaches we have developed represent the accumulation of their wisdom that we will share with you in this book.

In this edition, we focus on persuading juries and judges, including administrative patent judges. Chapter 1 sets the stage by comparing findings regarding judges and juries. Chapters 2 and 3 address judicial persuasion in *Markman* hearings and Patent Trial and Appeal Board (PTAB) proceedings. In Chapters 4 and beyond we turn to jury persuasion, introducing the context for jury decision-making today (Chapter 4), and jury selection techniques (Chapter 5). Then, we discuss persuading judge and jury about infringement/noninfringement issues (Chapter 6), patent validity/invalidity (Chapter 7), and patent damages (Chapter 8). We provide in Appendix A a brief description of a sample fact pattern that we use throughout the chapters. Finally, Appendices B, C, and D contain samples of juror questionnaire items you can use to create juror questionnaires tailored to your case.

II. Are Different Patent Fact Finders Persuaded Differently?

Let us start this edition with an admittedly contradictory statement. Different fact finders in patent cases (juries, district court judges, and administrative patent judges) make sense of patent cases differently and use different terminology when discussing the case, *yet* significant research finds that juries and district court judges share far more similarities in the ways they are persuaded.

Consider the data on case outcomes. First, outcomes of patent claims by jury are statistically different from outcomes of patent decisions by a federal judge. Judges' decisions at the summary judgment stage favor defendants about 80% of the time in claims terminated from 2011 to 2021, four times more than they favor the claimant.[1] In more than 1,700 patent claims in that same period, defendants were 136 times more likely to win judgment on the pleadings and nearly twice as likely to win judgment as a matter of law. In those contexts, patent infringement defendants do quite well.

So why do patentees continue to file patent infringement lawsuits? It is an easy answer, supported by our experience with nationwide research of jury-eligible Americans as well as trends in patentee win rates in jury trials. Despite the "loss rates" when judges evaluate claims at the summary judgment, trial, and appellate stages, patentee plaintiffs from 1998–2017 had much greater success in jury trials than in bench trials, winning about three-fourths of jury trials compared to around half of bench trials. The differences are more pronounced in cases involving non-practicing entities (NPEs), who prevailed in just 36% of bench trials compared to 72% of jury trials from 1998–2017.[2] Differences in median damages awards are also significant: $10.2 million for juries and $1.9 million for judges during the years 2013–2017. These statistics support the conclusion that disposition of patent cases resolved by jury trial is substantially different from that of patent cases resolved by the court. Different results suggest different processes. This assumption requires a closer look, starting with perceptions of the U.S. Patent and Trademark Office (USPTO).

A. Comparing Juries' and District Court Judges' Rankings of the USPTO Among Government Agencies

How does the USPTO's credibility fare with judges and juries? Consider the fact that the American public reports declining faith and trust in government officials and many government agencies tasked with fulfilling the mandates of the U.S. government.[3] In 2020, the Persuasion Strategies National Juror Survey results showed just 52% of jury-eligible Americans had positive views of government agencies in general, significantly fewer than their positive views of

1. *See* LEX MACHINA, https://lexmachina.com/ (last visited Feb. 5, 2025).

2. *See* LANDAN ANSELL ET AL., PwC, 2018 PATENT LITIGATION STUDY (2018), https://www.ipwatchdog.com/wp-content/uploads/2018/09/2018-pwc-patent-litigation-study.pdf.

3. See, for example, the Gallup poll results showing that trust in federal and state government reached all-time lows in September 2010, with 46% of Americans reporting a fair amount or a great deal of trust in federal government to handle domestic problems and 51% reporting a fair amount or a great deal of trust in state government to handle state problems. Lydia Saad, *Americans Trust U.S. More on Foreign Than on Domestic Affairs*, GALLUP (Sept. 23, 2010), http://www.gallup.com/poll/143195/Americans-Trust-Foreign-Domestic-Affairs.aspx; Jeffrey M. Jones, *In U.S., Trust in State Government Sinks to New Low*, GALLUP (Sept. 10, 2009), http://www.gallup.com/poll/122915/Trust-State-Government-Sinks-New-Low.aspx.

medical device companies (81%) and insurance companies (62%).[4] In 2023, Pew Research Center found just 16%—a nearly 70-year low percentage of Americans—said they trust the government just about always or most of the time.[5] The shift coincides with increasing political polarization, declining public opinions about our recent presidents, and the consequences of government involvement in some of the most significant and most public events of our lifetimes—the terrorist attacks of September 11, the devastation of Hurricane Katrina, and numerous instances of corporate corruption, collapse, and massive bailouts by the federal government, not to mention the coronavirus pandemic of 2020.

The result? Jurors no longer see the same shine on the government's seal as they once did. They do not place the same level of trust in the average government official they did even a decade ago. Where the government is involved in the facts of a lawsuit, jurors are inherently skeptical of work ethic, productivity, and even motive—with one important exception. Jurors still place great faith and trust in the USPTO, as demonstrated in the following figure.

Favorable Opinions of Government Agencies

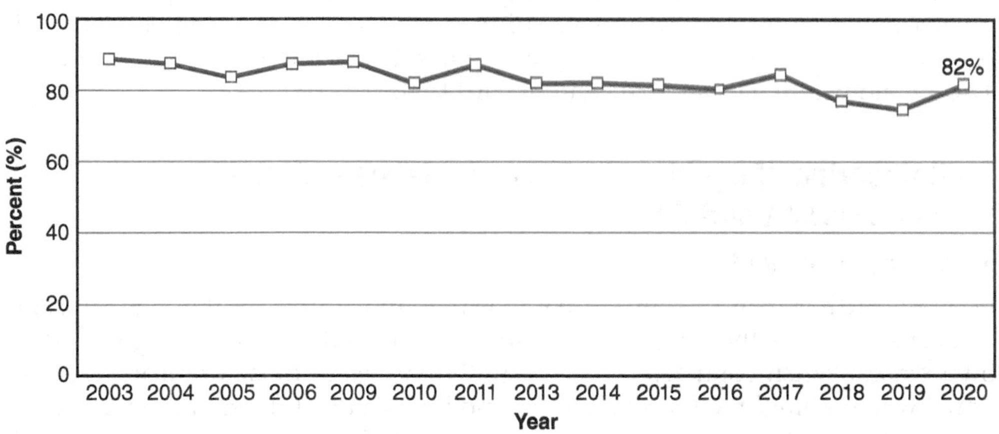

Source: Persuasion Strategies, National Juror Survey 2003–2020 (N=6,022)

Of all the government agencies both Perkins Coie's litigation consulting group and Persuasion Strategies' litigation consulting group have asked about in the past decade, nationwide jury-eligible Americans consistently rate the USPTO as the most credible. While the percentage of potential jurors rating the USPTO as credible has declined slightly since 2006 (when favorability was at a high of 88%), it is still the most favorably rated agency, with more than four of

4. Persuasion Strategies National Juror Survey is an annual survey of jury-eligible Americans regarding opinions of litigation and focused types of litigation including intellectual property and patents. Before joining Perkins Coie, the authors co-designed the survey research alongside the current consultants who remain at Persuasion Strategies, a service of Holland & Hart LLP.

5. *See Public Trust in Government: 1958–2024*, Pew Rsch. Ctr. (June 24, 2024), https://www.pewresearch.org/politics/2024/06/24/public-trust-in-government-1958-2024/.

five potential jurors surveyed voicing favorable opinions of the agency.[6] Interestingly, in our 2008 survey of 105 district court judges, judges also rated the USPTO as the most credible government agency, with 82% reporting favorable opinions, compared to 60% noting favorable opinions of the Food and Drug Administration (FDA) and just 55% expressing favorable opinions of the Bureau of Land Management (BLM).[7]

Today's views have already changed compared with the early 2000s. Then, potential jurors' generally positive opinions of government regulatory agencies meant that jurors saw agency standards as benchmarks by which they could evaluate litigants' conduct.[8] If a heated dispute over a failed telecommunications merger ended up in the courtroom, jurors placed great weight in Securities and Exchange Commission standards and any evidence proving either party met those standards. Now, our mock trial research (conducted from 2006 to 2021) and trial court experience reveal that a party that meets government standards is less meaningful to jurors. Jurors give *decreasing* weight to the persuasive impact of meeting *minimum* standards and greater persuasive weight to contemporaneous evidence that one party has *exceeded* government standards, has created and met its own higher standards, and/or generally has treated other parties with a greater and more subjective measure of respect.[9] Meeting required obligations is less meaningful than just ten or 15 years ago, so the requirements also mean less. This phenomenon has held true with regard to the USPTO.

B. Comparing "Cognitive Processing" Between Juries and District Court Judges

1. Shared Cognitive Biases

Look no further than the current composition and rulings of the U.S. Supreme Court to recognize that judges (and justices) come to decision-making with their own biases. When comparing their cognitive biases to those of jurors, conventional wisdom might tell us that judges and juries have different biases by virtue of education and experience. To a limited extent, that is true. But solid research that compares judges to juries finds that judges learn new case details similarly to how jurors learn them.[10] Researcher Brian Bornstein summarizes the most comprehensive research conducted on this topic, noting:

---

6. Persuasion Strategies, Holland & Hart LLP, National Juror Survey (2020).

7. Persuasion Strategies, Holland & Hart LLP, Persuasion Strategies Federal Judge Survey (2008).

8. Both authors observed these opinions in numerous mock trials and focus groups conducted in the first half of the decade, and prior Persuasion Strategies National Juror Surveys showed that a majority of potential jurors had favorable opinions of government officials and government agencies, compared to recent data showing increased negative perceptions of government officials and government agencies.

9. For instance, mock jurors give the benefit of the doubt to a company that has enacted its own internal standard that meets or exceeds the standard created by the governing regulatory agency.

10. Chris Guthrie et al., *Inside the Judicial Mind*, 86 Cornell L. Rev. 777 (2001).

> The most comprehensive such study, conducted by Chris Guthrie and colleagues, assessed whether judges were susceptible to five different "cognitive illusions" to which laypeople (including jurors) are generally susceptible: anchoring (making estimates based on normatively irrelevant starting points, such as an ad damnum); framing (treating economically equivalent gains and losses differently); hindsight bias (perceiving events to have been more probable after one knows the event has occurred, also referred to as the "knew-it-all-along" effect); the representativeness heuristic (undervaluing relevant background statistical information, or base rates); and egocentric biases (overestimating one's own abilities). They found that judges were just as susceptible as laypeople to three of the five illusions; they were less susceptible to the other two (framing and representativeness), though they were still not completely immune to their effects.[11]

Looking more closely at the three cognitive biases that judges have been found to possess just as equally as laypeople, Guthrie et al.'s research finds:

Hindsight Bias	A researcher aptly described hindsight bias as one where people overestimate their own ability to have predicted the past and believe others should have been able to predict events better than was possible.[12] Past studies have found that hindsight bias affects judges' assessments of negligence and recklessness.[13] In addition, another study found judges exhibit hindsight bias in procedural contexts, such as judgments regarding whether Rule 11 sanctions should be imposed. These researchers found that "24 percent of the judges in our study made a different choice because of hindsight bias."[14]
Anchoring Effects	An anchoring effect is one in which a fact finder bases a damages award based on the "anchor" or base number provided, even when the logic for the number is suspect. Judges are as likely as jurors to be influenced by the anchor number, reducing awards by 29% when the anchor number is lower.[15]
Egocentric Bias	An egocentric bias is one where a person overestimates his or her own abilities. In their study, Guthrie et al. found that 56% of judges underestimated their own reversal rates on appeal and 88% overestimated the reversal rates of their peers.[16]

Other studies have obtained comparable results. Judges, as human beings, are not very successful at ignoring information they have been told to disregard,[17]

11. Brian H. Bornstein, *Judges v. Juries*, 43 CT. REV. 56 (2006).

12. Baruch Fischhoff, *For Those Condemned to Study the Past: Heuristics and Biases in Hindsight*, *in* JUDGMENT UNDER UNCERTAINTY: HEURISTICS AND BIASES 335, 341 (Daniel Kahneman et al. eds., 1982).

13. John C. Anderson et al., *Evaluation of Auditor Decisions: Hindsight Bias Effects and the Expectation Gap*, 14 J. ECON. PSYCH. 711, 726–27 (1993); W. Kip Viscusi, *How Do Judges Think About Risk?*, 1 AM. L. & ECON. REV. 26 (1999).

14. *See* Guthrie et al., *supra* note 10.

15. *See id.*

16. *See id.*

17. Stephan Landsman & Richard F. Rakos, *A Preliminary Inquiry into the Effect of Potentially Biasing Information on Judges and Jurors in Civil Litigation*, 12 BEHAV. SCI. & L. 113 (1994); Andrew J.

and they actually make decisions based on factors other than those that they believe influence their decisions.[18]

2. Shared Need for Case Knowledge

Yes, judges generally are more trained and conversant with the law. However, they, like jurors, will always have *far* less time with your case facts than you do. They need to understand early and often your key themes, story, and arguments. That context helps them understand your more detailed argumentation. If your judge must work hard to understand your arguments, you run the risk that she will decide to work elsewhere. In our past mock *Markman* hearings, mock arbitrations, and mock bench trials, we have been repeatedly struck by the fact that judges pay close attention to the parties' behavior in addition to the claim language, much like juries do. And we have often seen retired federal judges "fill in the blanks" of the evidence as well as regale one another with their own personal experiences during the mock deliberative process, much like juries do. These mock judges are people with great litigation savvy. Still, their decision-making is influenced by their humanity—something trial counsel should not overlook in brief writing or in oral argumentation.

Of course, there are differences between the ways judges and juries process the evidence. However, patent judges and juries are far more similar to one another in processing the evidence than you might think. Despite the perception that patent juries face overly complex tasks and often fail to meet the expectations associated with their task, there is limited evidence that judges can and do perform any better than jurors in complex cases. To the contrary, most research evidence suggests judges are vulnerable to the same cognitive biases and information processing limitations as the rest of us. In most instances, only one judge determines your case outcome, contrasted with six to 12 jurors, a significant increase in the number of people considering the decision and hedging the effect of human biases. These biases suggest similarities in juror and judicial decision-making that transcend case type. Yet there is also evidence that district court judges may not be better equipped than jurors when dealing specifically with patent disputes. Some research shows district court judges make claim construction errors on as many as 33% of patents, and the Federal Circuit reverses or vacates those appealed claim constructions 27% of the time.[19] This provides strong evidence that district court judges can and do struggle with the complexities of patent language that frame a given dispute.

Just like jurors, judges look hard for tiebreakers in close cases, often studying the parties' behavior and motives surrounding the invention and the claim language. Few judges are scientists. Few are inventors. Even in the Court of

---

Wistrich et al., *Can Judges Ignore Inadmissible Information? The Difficulty of Deliberately Disregarding*, 153 U. Pa. L. Rev. 1251 (2005).

18. Ebbe B. Ebbesen & Vladimir J. Konecni, *Decision Making and Information Integration in the Courts: The Setting of Bail*, 32 J. Personality & Soc. Psych. 805 (1975).

19. Kimberly Moore, *Are District Court Judges Equipped to Resolve Patent Cases?*, 15 Harv. J.L. & Tech. 1 (2001).

Appeals for the Federal Circuit, only roughly one in three judges has a technical or scientific background. While we have anecdotally observed these similarities over the years, we now can cite to side-by-side comparisons of these fact finders based on a national survey we conducted in 2008 and again in 2011.

Judges and Juries on the Patent Process and Competition

Knowing that the monopolistic nature of a patent is a strategy often emphasized by counsel at trial, we decided to ask jurors and judges about their views. They were quite aligned in their support of patents and the role they play in healthy competition.

Percentage of Judges and Jurors Who Believe the Patent Process Helps Competition

Jurors (2011):	69%
Judges (2008):	70%

Source: Persuasion Strategies/K&B National Research, National Juror Survey (2011) (N=400); Persuasion Strategies, Holland & Hart LLP, Persuasion Strategies Federal Judge Survey (2008) (N=105)

Judges and Juries on Obtaining (and Keeping) Patent Protection

At the same time, and of particular note for when considering claims of patent invalidity, judges and juries do tend to differ on their views of *obtaining* patents. Specifically, our survey research and experience support the conclusion that judges hold a less glorified view of the process of getting a patent, positioning jurors as potentially better fact finders for parties asserting an invalidity claim.

Percentage of Judges and Jurors Who Believe Patents Are Easy to Obtain

Jurors (2011):	26%
Judges (2008):	45%

Source: Persuasion Strategies/K&B National Research, National Juror Survey (2011) (N=400); Persuasion Strategies, Holland & Hart LLP, Persuasion Strategies Federal Judge Survey (2008) (N=105)

Percentage of Judges and Jurors Who Believe It Is Easy to Mislead the Patent Office During the Patent Approval Process

Jurors (2011):	37%
Judges (2008):	50%

Source: Persuasion Strategies/K&B National Research, National Juror Survey (2011) (N=400); Persuasion Strategies, Holland & Hart LLP, Persuasion Strategies Federal Judge Survey (2008) (N=105)

Interestingly, while the majority of judges and jurors are aligned in their opinions that patent exclusivity in the range of 15 to 20 years is "just right," judges are more at peace with the status quo.

Judges' and Jurors' Perceptions of Patent Holders' Having Exclusive Rights for 15–20 Years

Jurors (2011):	23% too short; 57% just right; 20% too long
Judges (2008):	7% too short; 76% just right; 17% too long

Source: Persuasion Strategies/K&B National Research, National Juror Survey (2011) (N=500); Persuasion Strategies, Holland & Hart LLP, Persuasion Strategies Federal Judge Survey (2008) (N=105)

Judges and Juries on Views of NPEs

Jurors and judges differ significantly on their views of NPEs that acquire patent rights for the purpose of suing alleged infringers. Jurors are far less likely to be familiar with these parties, often derogatorily called "patent trolls." Once we provided a neutral description of NPEs to both judges and jurors, jury fact finders expressed stronger criticism of these entities.

Percentage of Judges and Jurors Who Believe NPEs Are Less Deserving of Money Damages Than an Original Inventor

Jurors (2011):	57%
Judges (2008):	47%

Source: Persuasion Strategies/K&B National Research, National Juror Survey (2011) (N=400); Persuasion Strategies, Holland & Hart LLP, Persuasion Strategies Federal Judge Survey (2008) (N=105)

C. "Teaching the Technical" to Fact Finders

"My brain was hurting after I heard the first presentation. It was way too technical."

—Patent mock juror

"Basically, what I am saying is that they need to somehow simplify that language. Put that language in lay terms. They have the winning argument, if you can understand it."

—Patent mock arbitrator

1. Patent Litigators Speak from Technical Expertise

Given the nature of patents and the law that governs them, it is no surprise that attorneys specializing in patent law often have training and experience in a technical field. For instance, more than 84% of patent attorneys' nonlegal education majors were in a scientific or technical field.[20] While many administrative patent judges have some type of technical background, not all do and certainly far fewer district court judges share a technical education with patent attorneys.

For those lacking technical education, many possess the inclination and detail orientation to handle the typical combination of technology and technicality. These positive skills come with a flip side. It is human nature to develop abilities consistent with our interests, but developing one set of abilities usually means minimizing the development of others. Communication philosophers have termed this inherently human limitation "occupational blindness."[21] By virtue of focusing our energy and abilities on a specific field or specialization, we narrow our ability to perform as effectively outside those areas. Through no fault of his, her, or their own, the technically proficient and detail-oriented patent attorney can often have difficulty communicating at a far less technical level that jurors need.

Jurors are not the only fact finders who struggle to grasp the technical components of the case. Just as the quotes above indicate, judges and arbitrators typically lag trial counsel in understanding the nuances of the case. Mock bench trials or mock arbitrations with retired judges who share a similar background to the actual fact finder can make a significant difference in gauging effective arguments at the necessary level of detail.

2. Patent Juries Need Teachers, Not Technicians

> *"This evidence that we're looking at here is just mind-boggling as hell."*
>
> —Patent mock juror

A patent litigator's technical proficiency does not always speak to the average juror. The average American juror is high-school educated, watches 28 hours of TV per week,[22] has thousands of dollars of credit card debt, and perceives jury duty as a substantial sacrifice. The average juror has neither training nor specialized knowledge of the patent system. She has never had a single interaction or experience with the USPTO, patents, or inventions, outside of hearing her distant relative describe his "invention" for a new way to turn on his lawn mower with a screwdriver. Jurors' reactions to complex case facts and complicated attorney presentations reflect their experiences and limited facility with

---

20. *See* Ralph D. Clifford et al., *A Statistical Analysis of the Patent Bar: Where Are the Software-Savvy Patent Attorneys?*, 11 N.C. J.L. & Tech. 223 (2010).

21. *See, e.g.*, Kenneth Burke, Permanence and Change: An Anatomy of Purpose (3d ed. 1984) (including references to Thorstein Veblen and his concept of trained incapacity). The relevant concept is that a person's skills and abilities can also serve as a blindness—in this case, a patent attorney's ability to excel in the world of technical detail can create a blindness to the bigger picture jurors need to understand to render fully informed decisions.

22. *See* Nielsen, A2/M2 Three Screen Report: 1st Quarter 2009 (2009), https://www.nielsen.com/wp-content/uploads/sites/2/2019/04/nielsen_threescreenreport_q109.pdf.

technical concepts. They own up to being nontechnical and are frustrated by a presenting attorney who fails to recognize most jurors are neither technical geniuses nor uneducated imbeciles.

While it may sometimes take a rocket scientist with a law degree to understand the technology and the law that applies to a patent-in-suit, it usually takes an effective teacher to score persuasive points with a jury of laypeople—who are highly capable of understanding complexity when well-taught. Astute litigators know patent litigation is not only for engineer-lawyers and scientists-turned-litigators. Indeed, patent juries long for counsel who can speak simply and unscientifically to help them absorb the complex and difficult concepts nearly every patent case brings to the courthouse. Clear and persuasive communication is paramount. In addition, you will find us repeating the critical reality that fact finders of all types need clear stories that focus on the key parties' behaviors, even more so than grasping the claim language. Poor comprehension is almost always the fault of the teacher, not the student.

3. Patent Judges Need Teachers Too!

"The vast majority of district court judges, and their law clerks, are generalists without technical training. Judges, with their busy dockets, simply do not have the time to invest in learning complex technologies, let alone to stay abreast of the latest technological and scientific developments."

—Neil Smith, former PTAB judge

Judges are more educated than the average juror, with some estimates as high as 66% of judges and magistrate judges having doctoral education (predominantly law degrees, of course), and 9% having postdoctoral training.[23] But the typical judge lacks technical training. Even district court judges frequently presiding over patent trials have difficulty with the technical details of new technology and specific inventions. Do not presume that judges are any more proficient with the technical details of your case than jurors would be. You have been living your case many more months or even years than your fact finder has. Listen to a judge speak at a conference or on a web meeting and you will notice that even those with dozens of patent trials under their belts do not speak with highly technical knowledge. These judges still remind patent trial attorneys to keep it simple. They lack the technical expertise and want you to make your case straightforward and clear. (See Chapters 2 and 3 for more on persuading judges and other non-jury fact finders.)

Most litigators realize the need to simplify the case for juror comprehension, but too often this understanding is only at the intellectual level. You must constantly remind yourself that jurors face an uphill battle against understanding

---

23. See the most common education levels for judges and magistrates, at *Judges, Magistrate Judges, and Magistrates*, MYFUTURE, https://myfuture.com/career/judges-magistrate-judges-and-magistrates (last visited Feb. 5, 2025).

the technical facts of your case. Look no further than the jury sitting in front of you to recall the need to simplify, simplify, simplify. Use focus groups and mock trials to gauge your fact finder's starting point of comprehension. The same goes for judges who are not as adept at decoding technical details and technology jargon as you may think. In the chapters that follow, we provide specific examples and demonstrate concrete ways to turn understanding into habit. (See Chapter 6 for persuasive infringement/noninfringement arguments and Chapter 7 for persuasive invalidity/validity arguments.)

CHAPTER 2

Persuasion in the *Markman* Process

"'Get to the Point!' Lawyers spend way too much time doing the wind up and then do not often enough make clear what relief it is that they are seeking. I would start with telling the judge what you want him [or her] to do, give a little background as to why, ask the Court if he has any questions, then close by repeating exactly what it is that the lawyer wants."[1]

—Judge Alan Albright, U.S. District Court—Western District of Texas

I. Our Research in Patent Litigation with Judges

A. Comparing Judges to Juries

When you couple the complexities of patent law with the wide variance of patent litigation experience on the district court bench, you could find yourself with either a judge who shares a lay jury's level of patent sophistication or one who has strong experience in this area of law. Throughout our many mock *Markman* hearings, mock bench trials, and mock arbitrations in patent cases, we have interviewed a great number of retired federal judges and senior litigators who have made us smarter through the rare opportunity of having a front-row seat into their decision-making processes.

"They have the winning argument if you can only understand it."

—Mock judge in mock *Markman* hearing

In one memorable encounter with a mock hearing panel of three mock judges, the standout response was that the defendant company had a winning claim construction position if they could only make it clear enough to the court.

1. Personal Communication with the Authors (2022).

This takeaway that parties need to simplify, even with sophisticated judges, is something we continue to find and communicate in our advice to patent litigators.

We have encountered similar patterns of judicial decision-making that were sometimes surprising and always thought-provoking. This chapter draws from that experience in our discussion of claim construction briefs and *Markman* hearings.

II. Persuasion in the Claim Construction Process

A. Persuasion in Claim Construction Briefing

"If I were writing briefs . . . again, I would go to great lengths to try to make the arguments simpler and clearer, the briefs shorter and much easier to read and reread at a high speed."[2]

—Ret. Chief Circuit Judge Paul R. Michel

Of course, you assume your brief will be your golden opportunity to get the judge's undivided attention. You spend hours at your computer writing the language just so, citing the correct law, and your verbiage begins to grow. However, there comes a point when your own prose can be your biggest enemy, when more input from more people during the writing process seems invariably to turn into more pages (and often less persuasively phrased throughout the "drafting by committee" process). More pages risk losing the undivided attention of the reader and watering down the persuasiveness of the document.

1. Components of a More Persuasive Claim Construction Brief

Eleven key factors guarantee a more persuasive claim construction brief, including:

1. Accurately identify your central reader(s).
2. Frontload what the judge need *not* do.
3. Frontload *exactly* what you want the judge to do.
4. Integrate your theme throughout your brief.
5. Make story order a central organizational mechanism for your factual background.
6. Use headings to draw your argumentative conclusions up front.
7. Have the courage to cut less critical details and arguments from your brief.
8. Include demonstratives throughout your brief.
9. Include videotaped deposition excerpts or animated/videotaped demonstrations where possible.

---

2. Pamela Banner Krupka, *An Interview with Chief Circuit Judge Paul R. Michel*, LANDSLIDE, Sept./Oct. 2009, at 18.

10. Provide the court with an effective joint claim construction chart.
11. Get feedback to your *Markman* brief in time to do something with what you learn.

Across all of these factors, what you choose to exclude from your brief is often as important as what you decide to keep. Too many briefs throw in everything, which waters down the key "things." It takes courage to determine what to choose, but it is courage well spent. It also takes time. As many well-known writers and orators will tell you, it takes more time and focus to write a shorter brief. It is time well spent.

a. Accurately Identify Your Central Readers

The Honorable Roderick McKelvie (ret.) has aptly made the point that your brief is likely to have two key readers, varying in influence. The first reader may be the law clerk or magistrate assigned to the case. The second reader is your judge. Know everything you can about the law clerk and their level of sophistication in patent law. Learn the same about your judge. Aim your arguments and language toward the *less* sophisticated of the two readers. The more sophisticated of the two readers will have the luxury of feeling knowledgeable and in control of the arguments raised. The less sophisticated will feel empowered with the teaching and story you provide in your brief.

b. Frontload What the Judge Need *Not* Do

The judge has plenty on her plate to decide. When you can remove from her plate the extraneous information she need not consider, you create some psychological motivation (and perhaps relief) to streamline what really matters. In its *Markman* brief in the case of *Function Media, L.L.C. v. Google, Inc.*, counsel for Google, Inc. utilized the precious focus that accompanies every first line of a brief by stating, "To clarify the issues for the Court, Google begins with the points of *agreement* between Google and Function Media ("FM"). . . ."[3] Counsel then cited what Google defined as the three key areas of agreement in a presumed attempt to "clear the decks" for the judge to focus on the critical areas of disagreement. Instead of beginning with predictable focus on the contentious disagreements in the case, she chose to facilitate a narrowing of the judge's focus.

Several lines later, she then inserted motivation to narrow that focus even more finely:

> Thus, of the myriad claim construction disputes, the court may be well advised to focus initially on the five independent claims that have been asserted, as all five have common issues that could dispose of this case outright *without requiring the substantial amount of work that is necessary to contend with all 84 asserted claims*.[4]

3. Google Inc.'s *Markman* Brief at 1, Function Media, L.L.C. v. Google, Inc., No. 2:07-CV-279 (E.D. Tex. May 15, 2009) (emphasis added).
4. *Id.* at 2 (emphasis added).

c. Frontload Exactly What You Want the Judge to Do

> *"When writing a brief, a lawyer should step back and read it from the perspective of the audience. Is it clear? Does it fairly identify the matters in issue? Does it identify the decisions the judge needs to make and explain why particular results make sense? In this context, the biggest mistake lawyers made in* Markman *briefs is in failing to focus on what it is the judge needs to decide."*
>
> —Honorable Roderick R. McKelvie (ret.),
> U.S. District Court—District of Delaware[5]

In the *Markman* process, it may seem obvious to you (and therefore, you believe, to your judge) why you want the judge to construe the disputed claim terms your way. However, we have repeatedly heard judges and arbitrators bemoan the fact that litigators presume too much case-specific knowledge on the judge's part when arguing their position. In addition, many judges and arbitrators say that they often have to work too hard in reading the brief to understand exactly what the party wants them to decide and why. Explain overtly why your claim construction makes sense in the bigger picture. That context may provide the necessary clarity to help construction on a given term go your way.

d. Integrate Your Theme *Throughout* Your Brief

Too often, litigators narrow their use of themes to trial or, even more narrowly, just to juries. Some of these attorneys argue that judges neither want them nor need them. Wrong. In fact, a great many judges say they *do* want themes in briefs. We have found this to be the case in mock briefs exercises and in a national survey our firm conducted in 2008. Federal judges had this to say about briefs *with* themes versus *without* them:

Percentage of Federal Judges and Magistrate Judges Who Believe Written Briefs Containing Themes Compared to Briefs Without Themes Are:

Less Persuasive:	12%
More Persuasive:	88%

Source: PERSUASION STRATEGIES, HOLLAND & HART LLP, PERSUASION STRATEGIES FEDERAL JUDGE SURVEY (2008) (N=105).

Why would a theme matter? If you think about it, the right theme is a mechanism for focusing the judge on your key case strengths (and/or on your opponent's key case weaknesses). The right theme should be something you can return to repeatedly throughout your brief. Too often, attorneys use otherwise great themes just like keynote speakers use the obligatory opening joke in a speech. The speaker starts off with great wit and then, much to the audience's

5. Personal Communication with Roderick McKelvie (2011).

disappointment, the humor (or, in this case, the theme) disappears for the duration of her remarks. Like good humor in a speech, your written theme in your brief should be designed so well as to be referenced throughout your brief rather than simply at the beginning.

For example, the patent holder may choose a simple analogy to a recipe:

> [The accused infringer] creates from scratch a new required element that is nowhere in the plain and obvious recipe—the language of the claim. To do so would add ingredients never intended.

Is it a little cheesy? Perhaps. However, many a litigator knows the simpler themes with vivid imagery tend to stick. The key then becomes to reuse this theme and recipe analogy elsewhere in the brief.

Attorneys Mark Nelson and Eric Cernyar make a persuasive argument for framing introductory arguments with themes in mind:

> Frame introductory argument(s) in terms of simple, unifying themes. "Every brief should make its primary point within 90 seconds."[6] Too often, claim construction briefs fail to make a primary point at all, let alone to do it in 90 seconds. The reason for this failure is unclear. It may be that patent attorneys get so caught up in the minutia of arguing each individual claim term that they forget about the bigger picture. To be persuasive, however, a claim construction brief, like any brief, must be clear and cohesive. It needs a central theme or themes that glue the respective arguments together and provide an overall reason why the court should adopt your side's position.
>
> In claim construction briefs, these themes may be legal. Compare, for example, these themes relating to the use of the specification:
>
> - Ignoring both the specification and the plain and ordinary meaning plaintiff time and again proposes overly broad constructions in a blatant attempt to ensnare the accused device, or
> - Defendant, not surprisingly, attempts to read-in non-existent limitations from the specification at every opportunity in hopes of avoiding infringement.
>
> Or, these themes may be technical. Either way, establishing and maintaining clear and cohesive themes is necessary both to hold the brief together and to provide the judge with the legal and moral authority to decide the claim construction issues in your client's favor.[7]

6. Bryan A. Garner, The Winning Brief 175 (2004) (quoting Jacques Barzun, Teacher in America 47 (1945)).

7. Mark C. Nelson & Eric W. Cernyar, How to Draft a Persuasive Markman Brief, State Bar of Texas Continuing Legal Education Seminar, Second Annual Advanced Patent Litigation Course: Fast-Track Litigation (2006).

e. Make Story Order a Central Organizational Mechanism for Your Factual Background

> *"Your table of contents should read like maybe a script for a movie would read—the snippets that take me through the entirety of the scene of the production."*[8]
>
> —U.S. Circuit Judge Jimmie V. Reyna

Litigators and trial consultants have long known that the use of story in jury trials transforms good but disparate facts into a more persuasive case.[9] Jurors are better able to tie together the evidence through their placement in story order, whether that story "begins at the beginning" or at the climax of the action. Not only does the story teach key case facts well, it makes the evidence inherently more interesting. Granted, there is no jury to engage throughout the claim construction process. For a smart, learned judge, does story order really matter that much? Even worse, could its use insult the intelligence of a judge who should, by rights, be able to make sense of legal argument via a topical structure? We have conducted many mock hearings and mock bench trials with retired federal court judges who repeatedly tell us that trial attorneys take "much too much" for granted when it comes to the trial court's understanding of the case facts and key arguments. They tell us that, no matter how experienced they might be, their learning curve on a specific case or new technology can be steep. Learning the case in a story format can shorten their learning curve and, more important, tilt the case in your favor. We conducted a mock arbitration in a significant patent matter and used the mock panel's input to revise the brief into a more user-friendly story. After our client won the actual arbitration, the lead arbitrator commented, "You had the better story—and it started with your brief."

One client began its brief by combining the chronological history with a brief tutorial about the prior art and the problem that needed to be solved by the present invention:

8. Jimmie V. Reyna, *quoted in* Dani Kass, *You Want Judge Reyna to Have Coffee with Your Brief*, LAW360 (Feb. 16, 2024), https://www.law360.com/articles/1788639/you-want-judge-reyna-to-have-coffee-with-your-brief.

9. Shelley C. Spiecker & Debra L. Worthington, *The Influence of Opening Statement/Closing Argument Organizational Strategy on Juror Verdict and Damage Awards*, 27 LAW & HUM. BEHAV. 437 (2003); W. LANCE BENNETT & MARTHA S. FELDMAN, RECONSTRUCTING REALITY IN THE COURTROOM (1981); Nancy Pennington & Reid Hastie, *Explaining the Evidence: Tests of the Story Model for Juror Decision Making*, 62 J. PERSONALITY & SOC. PSYCH. 189 (1992).

Put Your Story in Your Brief

BACKGROUND

A. **Random Versus Registered Graphics**

Through the 1980's, disposable diapers and training pants generally contained random graphics, so-called because those graphics were wallpaper-like in that they appeared on products in a completely random fashion. Examples of products containing random graphics are shown to the right, while the products shown below contain registered graphics. The left-most products are "taped" diapers,

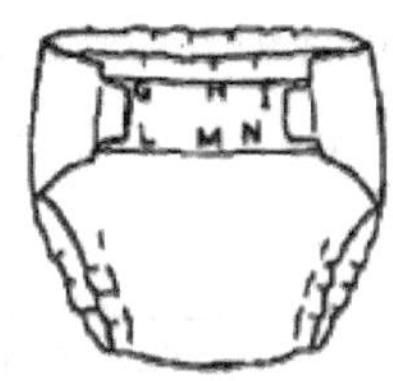

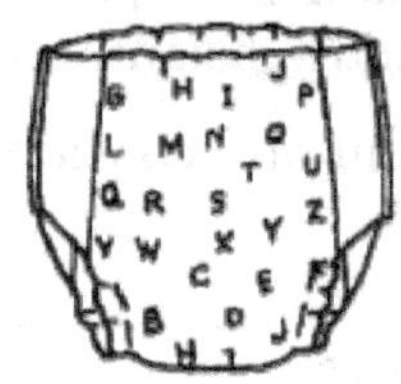

where the tapes are either adhesive or mechanical, and the products to the right are training

pants, generally used by toddlers and younger children engaged in potty training. Training pants are pulled on and off like underwear.

Attorney Steve Hansen addressed the importance of and possibilities for including story in the claim construction brief:

> If you haven't read a claim construction brief lately, they tend to be incredibly dry. . . . Part of the difficulty is that the courts focus (often exclusively) on the intrinsic evidence of claim meaning—the patent and prosecution history—and this evidence does not include the parties' respective stories and themes that brought them to court in the first place. . . .
>
> However, claim construction briefs can be improved. There is often a story to be told based on the intrinsic evidence. It can be included in a background or statement of facts section in the brief. The patent and the prosecution history can be used to put together a narrative that fits each party's claim construction theories. The result is a far more compelling and persuasive brief. . . .
>
> The key is to build a narrative that supports your position. In other words: *Create a narrative from the intrinsic evidence by using the claim terms in a manner that is consistent with your constructions and inconsistent with your opponent's constructions.* This will leave the reader with the feeling that your constructions are right simply by reading your story.[10]

10. Steve Hansen, *Tell Me a Story About Claim Construction*, Hansen IP L. PLLC (Apr. 23, 2012), http://hanseniplaw.com/tell-me-a-story-about-claim-construction/.

f. Use Headings to Draw Your Argumentative Conclusions Up Front

The talented patent litigator Mark Banner, of the firm Banner & Witcoff, was a strong proponent of using headnotes and subheadings to introduce an argumentative point. Retired Chief Circuit Judge Paul R. Michel once referred to his observation of Banner's practice when they were both on the faculty at John Marshall Law School in this way:

> I was very interested in the emphasis [Mark Banner] correctly placed on the value of headnotes and subheadings scattered throughout the brief to summarize the argument and make it easy to see where the argument was headed. I'd pay much more attention to the summary of the argument and substantive headnotes and much less on long legal exposition.[11]

For example, consider the contrast between two approaches to framing headings:

Neutral Heading	Conclusory Heading
"Infringement of the Patent '000"	"Defendants Infringed Patent '000 via Three Avenues"
"Invalidity via Obviousness"	"The Claimed Inventors Relied on Obvious Rather Than Novel Processes to Acquire Their Patent"
"Inequitable Conduct During Patent Prosecution"	"Counsel for Z Company Actively Set Out to Deceive the Patent and Trademark Office and Succeeded"

g. Have the Courage to Cut Less Critical Details and Arguments from Your Brief

Again, citing the wisdom of Retired Chief Circuit Judge Michel:

> [T]ry to exercise extreme amounts of courage to just cut stuff out—cut out facts, cut out case citations, cut out quotes, cut out long discussions, cut out anything that wasn't absolutely necessary to get the result that you're trying to get. . . . I'm not happy with what seems to be the product of committee writing. I would much rather have a five-page brief written in hand on yellow sheets than to have a 14,000-word brief written by a committee that's diffuse, unfocused, and detailed on points that will not matter at all.[12]

Drafting briefs by committee waters down persuasion. Everyone's well-intentioned words and additions routinely muddy up otherwise clear waters of argumentation. So how, then, do you determine what matters at all? Perhaps that is exactly why you invited a committee to your brief drafting in the first place. However, the one who matters is your judge. Wonderful books have spoken eloquently on writing tight, persuasive briefs.[13] We will not try to replicate those treatises here. Rather, the angle we suggest you consider is one that takes some of the guesswork out of what you think will persuade your judge. Rather than guess at what matters to the judge, some of our clients are increasingly

---

11. Krupka, *supra* note 2, at 18.
12. *Id.*
13. Bryan A. Garner, Garner on Language and Writing (2008).

turning to mock brief assessment exercises. In those exercises, we follow these seven steps across three discrete roles we ask the mock judges to play:

Mock Briefs Assessment

Fact-Finder Phase

Step One: Learn as much as possible about the actual judge's (or special master's) decision-making style and legal background, specifically with regard to patent experience and academic training.[14]

Step Two: Match and recruit retired judges or senior attorneys (typically three) without immediately disclosing the sponsoring side of the research. (We litigation consultants communicate as third parties with the mock judges on behalf of our client.)

Step Three: Have mock judges review your draft brief as well as an actual version or mocked-up draft for the other side. Collect their leanings via a tailored questionnaire that guides the specific input we wish to receive.

Critic Phase

Step Four: Bring the panel together in one location and collect their critiques via (1) an additional written questionnaire and then (2) verbally in a focused group interview (*still* before disclosing the identity of the client).

Strategist Phase

Step Five: Disclose the identity of the client and lead the mock panel through a strategy interview to brainstorm ideal approaches to the brief's content.

Step Six: Revise the written draft based on the exercise.

Step Seven: Return the revised version to the mock panel within a few days' time to determine how/if those revisions meet their criteria for clarity and persuasiveness.

The outcome of this mock exercise always results in a much tighter, more persuasive document. When the outcome of your case hinges on an important brief, consider this approach to briefs assessment. In addition, the feedback you get from your mock judges will likely prove helpful in getting an outsider's view of your case merits above and beyond your written brief.

h. Include Demonstratives Throughout Your Brief

As with themes, too frequently litigators reserve demonstratives for trial and/or for juries. As early as your first brief for your *Markman* hearing, consider the

---

14. One patent litigator with whom we have worked notes that he has found a great deal of variance among judges in the view they take on patents. He found one patent judge to be seemingly focused on cutting back the scope of overly broad patents issued by the U.S. Patent and Trademark Office. He found another judge in a different jurisdiction to be much more "by the book" in interpreting the claim language within its plain meaning, which also led to a more narrow claim interpretation.

teaching impact your key points can concretely have with demonstratives compared to a more abstract, purely narrative description. And yes, we checked this advice with current federal judges. Their preferences are:

Perception of Federal Judges Who Believe Briefs Containing Visual Elements Compared to Briefs Without Visual Elements Are:

Less Persuasive:	11%
More Persuasive:	89%

Source: Persuasion Strategies, Holland & Hart LLP, Persuasion Strategies Federal Judge Survey (2008) (N=105)[15]

When you consider incorporating demonstratives into your brief, be thoughtful about the number and type you use. We suggest no more than one demonstrative every few pages to avoid saturating your document. As to type, if it feels logical to include figures from the patents in dispute, perhaps you should.

In addition, think beyond the four corners of the patent. For example, the following is a visualization of the process, terms, and relationships involved in a method for reducing deposits in fuel ethanol plants.[16] The graphic simply and clearly gives the reader a memorable and easily referenced map of the key elements in the method to increase comfort and fluency necessary to consider and apply the more technical claims and elements.

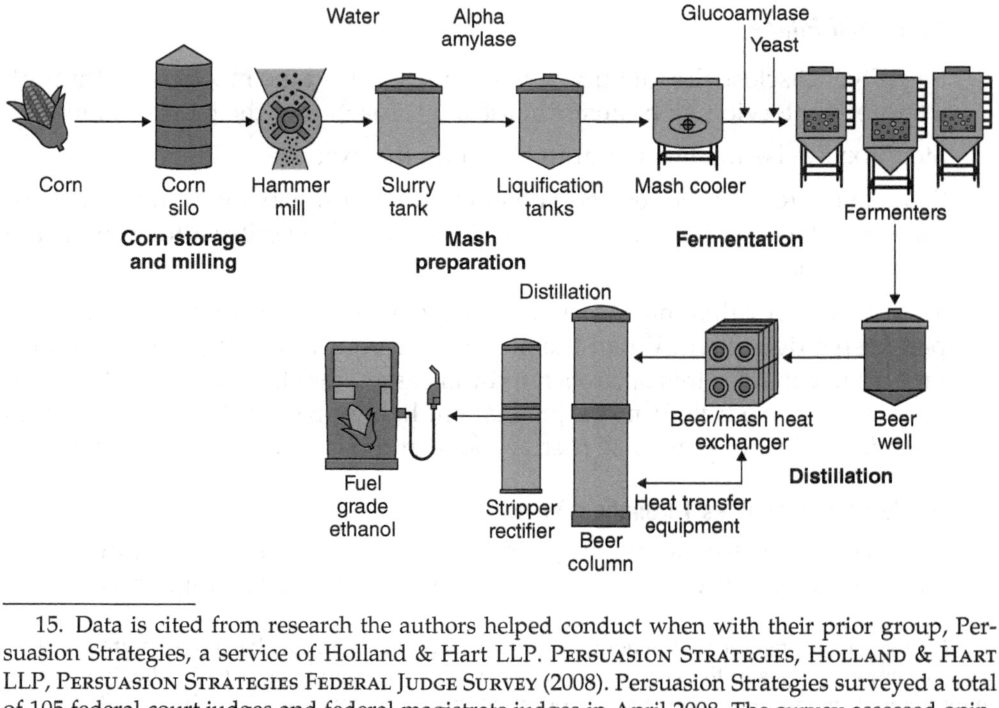

15. Data is cited from research the authors helped conduct when with their prior group, Persuasion Strategies, a service of Holland & Hart LLP. Persuasion Strategies, Holland & Hart LLP, Persuasion Strategies Federal Judge Survey (2008). Persuasion Strategies surveyed a total of 105 federal court judges and federal magistrate judges in April 2008. The survey assessed opinions of attorneys, attorney performance, corporations, litigation, and the patent system.

16. Special thanks to Perkins Coie partner Michelle Kemp for providing this example.

Of course, you can also include a well-done timeline to make a powerful point in a summary judgment brief, especially because your judge can spend time reviewing the elements (in comparison with the elaborate timelines prepared for trial whose volume of entries require shrinking font sizes to the point of being unreadable for the fact finder unless he is in possession of a powerful magnifying glass).

i. Consider Video Excerpts or Animated/Video Tutorials

The proliferation of electronic briefing has created opportunity to use technology more liberally, including the potential for embedded video in a brief. While still exceedingly rare, our anecdotal research suggests increasing this practice may be popular among many judges.[17] The visual makes the abstract more concrete, leaving your judge's interpretation of the point much less to chance. Hearing and seeing the words of the witness gives that witness's testimony greater emphasis than reading a summary will accomplish. Cognitive research finds that the more senses a person engages (e.g., visual, auditory, sensory), the more the message will embed in memory.

j. Provide the Court with an Effective Joint Claim Construction Chart

Claim construction charts are now quite common these days, and with good reason. They provide a handy summary to which the judge can refer in defining each party's proposed construction of disputed terms. At a minimum, most charts include the following:

Typical Claim Construction Chart

Claim Term	Plaintiff's Proposed Construction	Defendant's Proposed Construction

One more detailed example of that approach is the "Krieger Chart," created and required for use in her *Markman* hearings by Colorado Federal District Court Judge Marcia Krieger:

Judge Marcia Krieger's Claim Construction Chart

Claim Term	Plaintiff's Proposed Construction	Support for Plaintiff's Proposed Construction	Plaintiff's Extrinsic Evidence	Defendant's Proposed Construction	Support for Defendant's Proposed Construction	Defendant's Extrinsic Evidence

17. Check with your judge's clerk to determine his use of electronic briefs and linked material. Some judges still read off hard copies printed from the electronic file and/or express a lack of interest in linked material.

k. Get Feedback to Your *Markman* Brief in Time to Do Something with What You Learn

The easiest, most time-efficient way to get feedback on your brief is to ask someone else on your team to review and comment. But be careful; your team colleague is likely well-versed on the technology and arguments. Such review often allows a brief to leave your office still filled with technical definitions and arguments that could confound a judge new to your patent(s) and case facts. The second easiest (and better) way to get feedback is to ask a colleague *not* involved in your case to review it. Choose a colleague or mentor who is similar in technical background and patent litigation sophistication *to your judge* (and/or clerk), and, even more important, choose someone who will be brutally honest with you rather than someone who will give you a "feel good" reaction to your draft. The least easy (and best) way to get feedback is to ask someone outside both the case and your firm to comment. Hiring a panel of blindly recruited mock judges to review your brief is a superior way to get feedback that will most closely mirror your actual judge's response to what he reads. An experienced trial consultant can also give you feedback about the persuasive appeal of your brief's theme and story.

B. Persuasion in the *Markman* Hearing

"Even with all the rules about claim construction, there is plenty of room for good lawyering over the 'ordinary meaning' of a claim term to a person of skill in the particular art."[18]

*"*Markman *hearings provide a litigator an early opportunity to shape the entire case."*[19]

1. *The Importance of the* Markman *Hearing*

One rationale for the birth of the *Markman*[20] hearing was to enable trial counsel to try the case with a firm idea of claim construction, thereby "eliminating the need to propose alternative claim constructions to the jury and reducing the expense and complexity of the trial."[21] The complexity of the claim construction process certainly makes a persuasive case for putting those determinations before the court.

A Federal Judicial Center survey found that judges estimated that claim construction was key to the resolution of their patent cases in almost 94% of

18. Thomas Selby, *A Primer on Litigating Patent Infringement Claims*, 34 LITIGATION 15 (2007).

19. *Id.*

20. Markman v. Westview Instruments, Inc. (*Markman I*), 52 F.3d 967, 989 (Fed. Cir. 1995) (Mayer, J., concurring).

21. MANUAL FOR COMPLEX LITIGATION, FOURTH § 33.223 (2004).

their cases.[22] If that statistic fails to put the significance of the *Markman* hearing into context, nothing does. As Pamela Banner Krupka aptly noted in this book's first edition, the *Markman* determination can be case dispositive.

2. *Preparing for the* Markman *Hearing*

Given the importance of the *Markman* hearing, it behooves you to take your preparation for this phase as seriously as if you were preparing for trial. Consider the following six steps in your preparation:

1. Learn about the judge's technical background and learning style.
2. Learn about the timeliness of your judge's patent law knowledge and litigation experience.
3. Recommend an advance tutorial to the judge, assuming that clarity regarding the technology in the case works to your benefit.
4. Determine the strong claim terms to pursue in oral argument.
5. Practice your oral argument in front of a *relevant* audience.
6. Persuade as a teacher, *not* as a technical colleague.

a. Learn About the Judge's Technical Background and Learning Style

If your own background is in engineering or some other technical field, it is easy to forget that mere mortals (including judges) may never understand (nor be motivated to understand) technology as you do. Many judges have told us that attorneys presume too much knowledge and technical sophistication on their part, making it difficult for them to follow technical arguments and definitions. Even judges with significant patent litigation experience need to be taught in a fresh way about the specific technology in your dispute. (Judges with little patent litigation experience will also need to be taught the machinations of patent law, something we have also heard from retired federal judges who have participated in our mock *Markman* hearings and mock bench trials.) Learn what you can about the judge's technical background to determine where your starting point should be in translating technical concepts. Remember, it is the rare judge who will be insulted by you giving a *brief* tutorial regarding the technology in your case.

In addition, determine what you can about the judge's learning style. Some judges need to read and digest what you are presenting to fully appreciate your position. Others need demonstratives to picture either a technical aspect of the claimed invention or to see why your claim interpretation makes more sense. While some judges disagree, most federal judges with whom we have consulted lament the fact that trial counsel use too few demonstratives when the adjudicator is a judge.

Finally, research whether your judge learns by questioning counsel a little or a lot during the hearing. The best thing you can determine is the judge's typical bandwidth for allowing oral argument before interrupting you with her first question. If you know you have two minutes versus ten before the first

---

22. Rebecca N. Eyre et al., Federal Judicial Center, Patent Claim Construction: A Survey of Federal District Court Judges (2008).

interruption is likely to occur, your first few minutes will need to be structured far differently. Learn what you can about your judge's preferences in prior hearings.

b. Learn About the Timeliness of Your Judge's Patent Law Knowledge and Litigation Experience

The incredibly diverse array of patent experience among judges makes them tough to gauge when you decide how much detail to include in your briefs and in your argument about the rules of claim construction. When in doubt, include more detail, if only by way of review for the more seasoned jurist. Even if your judge has been involved in past *Markman* hearings, her experience could be dated. Even if you did a brilliant job describing the significance of *Phillips*[23] in your written brief, do not assume she is current in the latest changes to the rules of claim interpretation at the time of the *Markman* hearing.

c. Recommend an Advance Tutorial to the Judge, Assuming That Clarity Regarding the Technology in the Case Works to Your Benefit

In her book *The Patent Litigator's Job: A Survival Guide*, Jennifer Dzwonczyk makes the point that "some courts may also invite the parties to prepare a technology 'tutorial' to present to the court early on in the *Markman* process, either live or on recorded media, to assist the court to better understand the technology and the subject matter in dispute in the context of the *Markman* process."[24] When time is short, your judge may be more willing to permit a tutorial if she can watch a video outside the courtroom. If your judge has no such procedure in place, by all means recommend it. If your judge says no, try again with the next judge on your next case. This critical teaching of the technology could serve as a strong filter for the judge's interpretation of your claims. By taking the initiative in creating this tutorial, you gain a strategic advantage in defining the technology at issue.

In addition, attorneys Nelson and Cernyar offer sound advice on using the technology tutorial as a persuasive device whether the tutorial occurs within or apart from your brief:

> The most important purpose of a technology tutorial is to advance your client's claim construction position. That's right—tutorials are advocacy pieces cleverly disguised as objective scientific teaching aids.
>
> Designing an effective tutorial is, therefore, an art, and a lot of work. To be persuasive, the tutorial needs to work seamlessly with the main themes of the party's claim construction position. Indeed, if the tutorial is presented prior to the briefing, it should introduce some of the main claim construction themes and preemptively rebut our opponent's expected themes. But, it must do so in an objective way. For example, if the accused device uses a type of technology that was not available at the time of the invention (e.g., a digital television signal), the defendant

23. Phillips v. AWH Corp., 415 F.3d 1303 (Fed. Cir. 2005).
24. Jennifer L. Dzwonczyk, The Patent Litigator's Job: A Survival Guide (2010).

may advance a claim construction that seeks to limit the scope of the claims to analog television signals. An important precursor to this argument would be to establish that digital signals were not contemplated at the time of the invention. To do so, the defendant might include in the tutorial a story depicting the evolution of the television signal beginning with its early analog days—including the state of the art at the time of the invention and the invention itself—and concluding with the advent of the digital television signal. The tutorial might continue by describing the accused device as the next technological leap. Although appearing objective, such a tutorial subtly advances one of the main themes of defendant's argument—that the claims should be construed to exclude a digital television signal.

The tutorial can also be used to rebut the expected themes of your opponent. Referring to the previous example, a plaintiff-slanted tutorial might focus on the evolution of the concepts contained in the patent instead of dwelling on the analog/digital distinction. The timeline might highlight the conceptual problem solved by the invention and stress that the same problem exists no matter the signal type. The patent holder could use such a tutorial to carefully, and seemingly objectively, further explain the patent in such a way that it, at least conceptually, appears identical to the accused device, which might remain nameless—the elephant in the room.

Another theme commonly advanced by the plaintiff/inventor is that the invention is pioneering—created by a hero, a true innovator. One persuasive way to preemptively rebut such a theme is to create a tutorial with a timeline depicting the prior art as a series of minor improvements with the invention being just the next, obvious step in implementing an already well-known concept. This theme also sets the stage for later summary judgment motions.

Finally, the claim construction tutorial is a great place to test out possible demonstrative exhibits to be used at trial. If the judge "gets it" during the claim construction hearing, such demonstrative can then be slightly tweaked to be reused during trial. Conversely, if the judge cannot follow your tutorial, chances are very good that a jury will not be able to follow it later.[25]

d. Determine the Strong Claim Terms to Pursue in Oral Argument

The claim terms you choose to have construed must be considered from two perspectives—from a legal one and from a persuasive one. Given the bent of this book, our focus here is on the latter perspective. Once you identify the claim terms you want to include in your claim construction, ask yourself four questions from a persuasion standpoint:

---

25. Nelson & Cernyar, *supra* note 7.

Persuasive question one: Is the volume of claim terms so high as to water down our ability to focus and persuade the judge on the key ones that matter most?

Persuasion question two: Does the volume of claim terms hurt our credibility if it conveys a message that we are making a grab for every advantage we can out of desperation rather than out of a legitimate need to construe so many claims?

Persuasion question three: In construing the claim terms themselves, do we create an unintentional pattern that conveys an attempt to stray from rather than stay close to the intended meaning of the term?

And, most important for the big picture of your case:

Persuasion question four: Are we seeking to have claims construed in a way that will be consistent with our stand on the infringement and invalidity claims, among others?

> *"These strategic questions are the most important part of preparation for the* Markman *hearing. You need to know your case—and your ultimate strengths and weaknesses—before you go into claim construction. If you know your case, you know which terms are important and you can focus on those. You have to know your 'make or break' terms and put those front and center, figuring out how to structure a theme that interweaves a story interrelated among the key terms. That way, your argument on one term will reinforce the argument on the other."*
>
> —James Hartley, Holland & Hart LLP[26]

In addition, when more than one patent is involved in the claim construction process, consider the order in which you would prefer to discuss the patents in your brief. The patent with the lower patent number is not necessarily your first, best one to discuss. You are likely to feel that one patent has stronger claim terms for you in the construction process. This also applies to the terms within a patent. As one Perkins Coie patent litigator, Joe Reid, put it, "I've seen instances where we've been very successful by putting the other side's worst argument or our best argument first, building momentum and damaging their credibility."[27]

However, many judges now require the parties to get together to create a joint submission of terms to be construed, which will dictate the order in which they will be considered by the court. Therefore, once you determine your preferred order, next consider how you can sell that order to opposing counsel. Put yourself in their shoes. How can you make your preferred order palatable to them? In what way could they benefit from the order you seek? Making your case for your preferred progression may be a tall order if it is apparent that it helps you much more than it helps the other side. However, it is at least worth a try to negotiate a logical compromise on the flow of the patents.

---

26. Personal Communication with James Hartley (2012).
27. Personal Communication with Joseph Reid (Mar. 2023).

e. Practice Your Oral Argument in Front of a *Relevant* Audience

No oral argument rehearsal should end with practice in front of a mirror. The mirror may tell you if your collar is askew, but it will not give you in-depth feedback and questions that a well-chosen audience could provide. For litigation where the *Markman* phase is crucial, bring in a panel of mock judges to hear your argument. If possible, bring in at least one mock judge who is conversant with the questioning and decision-making style of your actual judge. Then bring in two other judges who closely match the educational background and patent litigation sophistication of your actual judge. Your goal in this exercise is not to predict the actual judge's ruling in the *Markman* phase; rather, it is to determine how best to teach and persuade the judge about your position on claims interpretation (including identifying areas of confusion that bear more discussion with the court).

A sample schedule for a single-day mock *Markman* hearing appears in the following table. Prior to the day of the mock *Markman* hearing, provide your mock judges with copies of all parties' *Markman* briefs. Ask them to complete a brief written questionnaire that allows you to gather individual feedback to your written arguments before they meet at the mock hearing.

Mock *Markman* Hearing Schedule

Fact Finder/Critic Phase (Identity of Client Is *Not* Disclosed)	
8:30 a.m.–8:45 a.m.	Mock judges' orientation
8:45 a.m.–9:45 a.m.	Plaintiff's summary argument (including questioning by the panel)
9:45 a.m.–10:10 a.m.	Completion of questionnaire A/break
10:10 a.m.–11:25 a.m.	Defendant's summary argument (including questioning by the panel)
11:25 a.m.–11:45 a.m.	Completion of questionnaire B
11:45 a.m.–12:00 p.m.	Plaintiff's rebuttal
12:00 p.m.–1:00 p.m.	Completion of questionnaire C/lunch
1:00 p.m.–2:45 p.m.	Mock judges deliberate
Strategist Phase (Identity of Client Is *Now* Disclosed)	
3:00 p.m.–4:00 p.m.	Post-decision interview with trial consultant
4:00 p.m.–4:30 p.m.	Mock judges debrief with attorneys
4:30 p.m.	Mock judges dismissed

If you hire a trial consultant experienced in patent litigation to run the mock exercise, you will incur some additional cost, but it will typically be a worthwhile investment. The trial consultant can (1) contact and recruit the mock judges so these mock fact finders can be blind to the identity of the client; (2) advise you on persuasive argumentation to test; (3) collect advance feedback to the *Markman* briefs from the mock panel; (4) design the mock panel's individual written questionnaires and interviewing protocol; (5) facilitate the exercise (including initial debriefing with the mock judges); and (6) provide key strategy recommendations regarding effective oral argument for the actual *Markman* hearing.

f. Persuade as a Teacher, *Not* as a Technical Colleague

Picture your role as that of a teacher. *Do not* worry about insulting the intelligence of the judge. *Do* worry about wasting the judge's time. If you simply reiterate the points made in your brief (presuming your judge has read the brief), you are likely to frustrate your judge. Use your oral argument to supplement and expand upon the concepts covered in your brief. If you learned from practice that a particular concept or claim term is dense, spend your energy and demonstrative design time there. While there is no jury at a *Markman* hearing, your judge shares more in common with juries when it comes to the need for orientation and teaching than you might think.[28]

3. *Persuasive Arguments for* Markman *Hearings*

a. Find the Right Theme and Stick with It

Whether your opponent is arguing for a narrow or broad interpretation of the claim language, the key to persuading the judge is to point out that your opponent's claim interpretation is a departure from the intent of the language. Contrary to our advice in litigating patent cases to juries, we find that *Markman* hearings are best organized by *first* pointing out your opponent's flaws in its claim interpretations, *followed by* your more reasonable interpretation (or, on occasion, by your point that no interpretation is necessary). Examples of themes follow in the next section.

b. Interpretation of Claim Terms

As you well know, you face strategic choices in how to argue claim terms, including whether the term should be interpreted broadly, narrowly, or even at all.

(1) Argument *for* a Broad Interpretation of a Claim Term

In *Markman* hearings, you may expect the rule of thumb to be that the patent holder will argue for broad definitions that cast a wider net of patent protection via claims interpretation. Even if the broad interpretation of certain claim language is more traditionally the plaintiff's purview, this theme can be adapted for the defendant's use, as follows:

> Your honor, this inventor held up his end of the bargain by disclosing everything in the patent. He earned the full protection of the Patent and Trademark Office for his full disclosure. The defendant's more narrow interpretation of the claim language grants the inventor only partial protection that fully and unfairly preserves defendant's position.

---

28. Kimberly Moore, *Are District Court Judges Equipped to Resolve Patent Cases?*, 15 Harv. J. L. & Tech. 1 (2001).

(2) Argument *Against* a Broad Interpretation of a Claim Term

Choose your theme carefully, because it should have relevant appeal throughout your argument. For example, consider:

> Your honor, what plaintiff, in essence, is asking you to do is to act as a patent examiner rather than as a judge. Why do I say that? Because, in fact, plaintiff's interpretations of its claims create a broader, different patent than what exists now. They truly are trying to reinvent their own wheel.
>
> Plaintiff invented its own concept. Plaintiff wrote its own patent language. It was given neither word limits nor page restrictions at the time. To go back and ask for broader, different interpretations of its own language after the fact is too much, too late.

(3) Argument for *No* Interpretation of a Claim Term

Of course, you will encounter claims where you wish to argue that no interpretation is necessary because the claim language speaks for itself. Consider the following argument, especially for an adjudicator less experienced in patent law:

> The prior art language tells us what the patent is not.
>
> The specification language tells us what the patent is.
>
> The law tells us the boundary lines for interpreting the claims—and we believe the law coupled with the patent language in this case make it quite clear that the patent language "as is" suffices for interpreting the claim.

c. Create a Persuasive Yet Flexible Structure

The best-laid structures often get eviscerated by a "hot bench," where the judge asks many questions throughout your oral argument. However, even an active judge appreciates the fact that you have specific points to make. The more you can solve the judge's problem of which claim construction to choose (and in a way that does not simply repeat your points in the brief), the more you will have his ear. There are at least three ways you can increase your chances that you will get your key point across.

(1) "Story-ize" Your Structure

Certainly the *Markman* hearing is about claim construction, but the mere words in your construction will not stick together without context. Judges tell us they struggle when counsel fails to provide that critical context. Consider your story the glue of your argument. Most learners need to understand the *significance* of claim language to provide good interpretation. The story provides the significance. If you engage your judge in a story order (or, at a minimum, in a hybrid chrono-topical structure), you may increase the chances she will stick with you and wait for the completion of your tale.

Structuring Your Oral Argument for the *Markman* Hearing

Classic Topical Structure (Patent Infringement Plaintiff)	More Persuasive Story Structure (Patent Infringement Plaintiff)
I. The Invention II. Claim Language III. Prosecution History IV. Their Construction V. Our Construction	I. The Problem That Needed to Be Solved by the Invention II. Prosecution History/Prior Art That Fell Short III. Our Invention/Claim Language IV. Our Superior Construction Juxtaposed Against Theirs (Comparison-Contrast)

The classic topical structure is too predictable and is, therefore, not as persuasive. It does not accomplish what a story structure can accomplish, particularly by helping your judge gather the context of the claim interpretation and the significance of the disputed differences. The more persuasive story structure briefly helps the judge understand the context for the terms themselves, something your judge needs to be able to appreciate your interpretation.

(2) Make Motive One of Your Characters

Either in your brief or in oral argument, consider aloud the reality of the opposing side's motive to construe certain terms too narrowly or too broadly. Again, you may assume motive is obvious to the judge, but state it to be sure. Judges are human and react to a party's attempt to subvert fair play. Emphasize the unfairness of opposing counsel's misplaced motives.

An attack on the other side's motive is simpler when your claim interpretation uses less verbiage. For example:

> Your honor, take a look at the claim term as written. Now, take a look at the claim term as construed by the other side. Notice how much lengthier and more convoluted their interpretation is than is the claim term as written. Now, why would that be? Is their motive to add language in order to subtract from the patent's coverage?

Make certain you are not doing the same thing on your side of the fence. It is your job to defend your position that your claim interpretation stays true to the intended meaning of the patent language. In fact, a powerful argument is one that appeals to the judge's protective instinct for the jury. If you can make a legitimate argument that the wrong claim construction for a given term (theirs) could confuse the jury at trial, you are at the point of breaking a potential tie in claim term interpretation (assuming you can make a case for the fact that your construction clarifies rather than confuses).

(3) Define the Consequence of Ruling on Claim Terms

When in the thick of arguing claim terms, many *Markman* hearings seem to lose the "forest for the trees" amidst the morass of terms or, in this case, losing the "patent for the claim terms." Establishing the context of the claim term at hand is key to teaching your judge, yet far too many *Markman* arguments drop the context and focus on the patent after the introduction. For example, argue the consequence of erroneously construing the claim term according to the other side's construction. What will such an error do to the meaning of the patent? Contemplate this aloud for your judge.

Be careful. Many judges do not react well to argument based on whether one interpretation of the claims over another will result in a finding of infringement or not. However, it is sometimes important to point out why the opposing party is arguing so vociferously. You might note:

> Their interpretation makes no sense in light of the plain language of the claim. However, it is the only way they can avoid a finding that they [infringe/do not infringe].

Making a point like this adds real significance to the judge's decision-making process in the *Markman* hearing.

(4) Comparison-Contrast: Try (and Fail) to Use the Other Side's Construction for a Claim Term

One of the most helpful persuasion tools you can use is to verbally make a "good faith" effort to use the other side's claim construction. In this attempt, you inherently emphasize the logical disconnect between the true claim term's meaning and opposing counsel's misplaced interpretation. Then follow that failure with the reasoning behind your more logical claim construction. This commonsense approach helps "operationalize" the claim terms in a more concrete manner. If you do this well, this method may well break any tie in the judge's mind between opposing claim interpretations. For example:

> Let's assume the [other side's] interpretation of this claim is correct. If it is, that means the term would also apply to "x." Yet "x" is opposite the intended meaning of the claim. Therefore, the [other side's] interpretation cannot be right.

(5) Use an Effective Internal Construction by Claim Term

To effectively teach (and, therefore, persuade) your judge, you should do everything possible to ensure that your internal argumentation is *not* a memory test for him. In other words, it is far better to organize your internal structure by claim term so that it is unnecessary for the judge to repeatedly return to the claim chart to try to recollect each side's claim construction. The following table delineates two approaches to an internal structure. We would argue that the first approach taxes the judge's memory, thereby weighing down your persuasion opportunity. The second approach stands a far better chance of keeping the judge's focus on your interpretation.

Structuring Your Internal Argument by Claim Term

Poor Approach	Improved Approach
I. We say . . . II. We are right because . . . III. They say . . . IV. They are wrong because . . .	I. We say . . . II. They say . . . III. We are right because . . . IV. They are wrong because . . .

This simple rearrangement of points improves the odds that the judge will stay with you as you make your argument. The persuasive importance of this approach also acknowledges the fact that, psychologically, the judge must go through a two-part process to reach a conclusion. She must accept one claim interpretation and reject another.

(6) Visually Apply the Legal Standard by Claim Term

Remember the sage advice of the federal judges we cited earlier in this chapter. They argued that a well-written brief tells the judge the standard and what to do with that standard. The same is true in oral argument. In addition, your oral argument should look different from your written brief. The following chart is one we have recommended with success in prior *Markman* hearings. We recommend using it as your recap when making a claim-by-claim argument. Assume you are the plaintiff.

Claim Term "X"

	Plaintiff Meets	Defendant Meets
1. Does it cite authority?	YES	NO
2. Does it avoid vagueness?	YES	NO
3. Does it add definition?	YES	NO

For each question, explain how your claim interpretation meets the key criteria and how theirs fails. Importantly, if/when they do meet one of the criteria, admit that fact and put a "YES" in their column for that criterion as well.

In addition to this table, consider where you can include demonstratives to make your point. We have surveyed federal judges in the past to ask about their preference for demonstratives in cases before them. They generally criticize trial counsel for using too few demonstratives rather than for using the right amount or too many.

Federal Judges' Perception of Demonstrative Exhibits

Compared to what you see in your courtroom, attorneys need to use demonstratives:	
More:	59%
The Same Amount:	38%
Less:	3%

Source: Persuasion Strategies, Holland & Hart LLP, Persuasion Strategies Federal Judge Survey (2008) (N=105)

Effective demonstratives do not need to be complex or expensive to be persuasive. Simple blow-ups can make a critical point, as can affordable 360-degree views of technology. In certain cases, animations are key to demonstrating innovations that cannot be viewed with the naked eye or whose component parts are internal rather than readily visible from an exterior viewpoint.

(7) Enumerate, Enumerate, Enumerate

Remember those law school days when your professor said something like, "There are three reasons why you should argue burden of proof in closing argument"? What did you do? You picked up your pen to make note of (or typed into your keyboard) the three reasons. We learned early on that enumeration was a sure sign that the teaching point would be on the exam. Had your professor said, "There are several reasons . . . ," you would not likely have mentally held on as long, since the number was uncertain. When you know the number is clear, you (and listeners like you) tend to hang in there while the speaker makes her point. Do the same in the *Markman* hearing and you will either keep the judge from speaking up or you will stand a greater chance of being able to complete your point post-interruption in a more mnemonic manner.

(8) Draw Your Conclusion Up Front

Given the number of sub-arguments present in any *Markman* hearing, keep your judge on track by drawing the conclusion up front. For example:

> Patentee's claim construction cannot stand because it contradicts its claim interpretation given the reexamination history. Let's look at what the patentee said during the reexamination process.

III. Conclusion

In the world of increasingly sophisticated technology, complex patents, and high demands on judicial time and attention, it is critical to consider your best approach to *Markman* hearings. Even with litigants increasingly turning to the Patent Trial and Appeal Board where judges and panels have more technical experience, the district court judge remains an audience that litigants must work to understand and persuade.

CHAPTER 3

Oral Advocacy Before the Patent Trial and Appeal Board

"I would say oral argument persuaded me to change my mind in a close case perhaps 20 to 25% of the time."[1]

—Administrative Patent Judge Brian Murphy

The most important part of your oral argument in *inter partes* reviews (IPRs) before the Patent Trial and Appeal Board (PTAB) rests in your ability to read the needs of the panel. It is that simple and it is that complicated. Persuasion before the panel of administrative patent judges (APJs) looks much different than persuasion before federal district court judges in patent trials. Some evidence points to the fact that this difference is *not* necessarily based on greater experience of the APJ compared with that of the federal district court judge.[2]

In fact, three key differences point to the need to think about persuasion differently than when you—the oral advocate—appear before a district court judge.

1. Email Interview with Administrative Patent Judge Brian Murphy (Sept. 2019).

2. Gene Quinn, *PTAB Judges Shockingly Inexperienced Compared to District Court Judges*, IPWatchdog (Mar. 6, 2018), https://ipwatchdog.com/2018/03/06/ptab-judges-shockingly-inexperienced/id=94438/. The author compared the background of 174 APJs with 178 district court judges in 2018 and found:

> There were *zero federal district court judges appointed with 10 years or less experience, while 46.55% of PTAB judges were appointed with 10 years or less experience.* Those familiar with the industry will well know that at many major law firms 10 years is the tipping point between partner and associate. Thus, this would mean that *46.55% of PTAB judges were appointed while they were still at best senior associates.* Worse, 4.60% of PTAB judges were appointed with 3 or fewer years of experience, which means those *4.60% of PTAB judges were appointed at a time when they were only at a junior associate level.*

Id.

Difference one. When the PTAB assigns a panel of three APJs to hear oral argument, it endeavors to match the APJ's technical experience with the technology of the patent under review (such as mechanical or chemical). District court judges do not pervasively have this kind of technical expertise and they certainly are not matched to the case subject matter.

Difference two. The process of the IPR dictates a key difference where the sole focus of the proceeding is that the petitioner has the burden of persuasion to prove unpatentability by a preponderance of the evidence.[3]

Difference three. The fact that the panel comprises three APJs rather than one federal district court judge can also affect the dynamic. Retired APJ James T. Moore served at the PTAB from 2001 to 2022 and noted in an interview while still there:

> The cases are interesting, and the work is fascinating, in part because you are sitting down with two colleagues who are incredibly intelligent. As a panel, you are looking at issues of law and technology, you are privileged to debate them, you are authorized to come to a conclusion, and required to report that decision to the public in a skillful, professional way. It's the practice of law at its finest. We really enjoy it.[4]

This chapter draws heavily from the authors' interviews with the target of your persuasive efforts—APJs, both sitting and retired. We also rely on combined wisdom from PTAB litigators and our knowledge of judicial persuasion. Little before now has been written about verbal persuasion before the PTAB. This should not be construed as meaning oral advocacy is de minimus in IPRs. To the contrary, after serving as a lead APJ, Brian Murphy[5] noted:

> The vast majority of PTAB judges, myself included, think oral argument is important and makes a difference in their decisions. There are always different points of view, and although the judges will have conferenced a case before the argument and have an idea of how they likely will decide it, the judges will keep an open mind and give counsel a meaningful opportunity to persuade them of a different point of view. Even if the oral argument does not change the judges' minds, the argument often clarifies the issues/evidence and helps the judges solidify the reasoning and evidence they will use in the decision.
>
> Sometimes, of course, the law and evidence is reasonably clear and the judges will have reached a firm decision going into the hearing. In such cases, judges will question counsel with the goal of having counsel

3. 35 U.S.C. § 316(e).

4. Gene Quinn, *Exclusive: Chief Judge James Smith and Vice-Chief James Moore*, IPWATCHDOG (Jan. 1, 2013), https://ipwatchdog.com/2013/01/01/exclusive-chief-judge-james-smith-and-vice-chief-james-moore/id=32132/.

5. At the time of this writing Brian Murphy is once again an APJ. His comments to us were made while he was in private practice.

acknowledge key points that weigh for and against counsel's position. Such acknowledgements may be cited in the final written decision.[6]

This chapter is organized in the following manner:

I. Making Effective Oral Argument Before the PTAB
II. Threading Them Throughout Oral Arguments
III. Handling Questions and Answers Effectively
IV. Hitting Your Rebuttal Points with (Some) Advance Preparation
V. Creating IPR-Friendly PowerPoints
VI. Considering Your Remote Judge in a Hybrid Panel of In-Person APJs and Online APJs

I. Making Effective Oral Argument Before the PTAB

A. Where Do You Begin?

It has already begun before you appear to make your oral argument before the PTAB. And what is "it?" Across the board, our interviews with APJs confirmed a common theme that "the decision has been *mostly* made" about the outcome of your matter among the three panel members. Judge One knows he or she will write the opinion. Judges Two and Three will weigh in and may act as contrarians or as supportive voices. Now in private practice at Perkins Coie LLP, Nathan Kelley most recently served as solicitor and deputy general counsel for intellectual property law for the U.S. Patent and Trademark Office (USPTO) and also served as the USPTO's chief APJ. He has contributed key insights to this chapter. But his history in a different role when clerking for Circuit Judge Randall Rader informed this quote:

> Even though an advocate may not be able to change the outcome, Judge Rader taught me that often the best use of the argument is to affect how the opinion is written, and to spin outcome spun as much as possible. At the PTAB, they are trying to decide if they need to address an issue and what is the quickest way to get to the end result. They think about the hardest part of their case.[7]

Given that reality, starting your oral argument before the PTAB is vastly different than starting oral argument before a district court judge. Think of the beginning of your oral argument as the middle of a sharply pointed, time-limited conversation with a highly informed audience.

1. Start With Where Not *to Begin*

Determining your best start demands first a determination of where *not* to begin. Consider these seven "do not's."

---

6. Email Interview with APJ Brian Murphy, *supra* note 1.
7. Telephone Interview with Retired Chief APJ Nathan E. Kelley (Feb. 2023).

1. *Do not* start with a recitation of the case facts that form the background of the case. This is a common mistake worth not making. Assume your panel has "a high degree of familiarity with the parties' arguments and evidence."[8]
2. *Do not* start by talking about things the panel does *not* have to decide.[9]
3. *Do not* make arguments about the process that led you to the PTAB.[10]
4. *Do not* start with a "silver bullet" (which typically encapsulates your entire argument as a story wrapped in theme).
5. *Do not* start with an inoculation of your case weaknesses. This approach sometimes works well in district court but does not feel persuasive to APJs.
6. *Do not* start with your client's "wish list" of arguments when you believe those arguments are inadvisable for your case.
7. *Do not* start by citing past PTAB panel cases. Panels are not required to follow PTAB cases in making their determinations.[11]

These differences underscore one "persuasion departure" from district court arguments. One APJ we spoke to offered an example of an ineffective start when patent-owner counsel started her oral argument by talking about how great the claimed invention was and how she had been able to use the invention herself. This approach may be well-suited for district court, but our interviews revealed that APJs do not value this use of speaking time.

2. Winnow Down Your Winners

Assume you are allotted 15 minutes for your main argument. (You may be allotted more but the teaching point here is one of proportion.) Now, begin with an assumption that you only have five minutes to present your best points. Whether you think in terms of "five" or "15," consider the universe of your most winning arguments. Then, revisit the list and rank order those arguments from strongest to weakest. This is where the difficult part begins. Make the tough choice of deletion and do not look back. It might be tempting to put your weaker arguments in your back pocket "just in case" and to bring along a fat PowerPoint slide deck "just in case." Holding onto "runner up" arguments only clutters your outline (and therefore your brain). Fully commit to your three best arguments and *let go of the rest*. There is a reason those arguments fall below your top three. From a practical standpoint, the odds are high that you may not even get to your top three if your panel actively questions counsel and cuts to the chase.

---

8. Email Interview with Retired Lead APJ Brian Murphy, *supra* note 1.
9. Video Interview with Retired Lead APJ Jessica Kaiser (Feb. 2024).
10. PTAB, USPTO, Guide to the Administration of Oral Hearings Before the Patent Trial and Appeal Board (2019), https://www.uspto.gov/sites/default/files/documents/PTAB%20Hearings%20Guide.pdf.
11. Video Interview with PTAB Practitioner Lori Gordon (Mar. 2024). Gordon has participated in more than 250 PTAB trials.

3. Can You Ignore Your Case Weaknesses During Oral Argument?

The prior section might seem to suggest that you can ignore weaknesses during an opening argument, but the strategy around your case weaknesses is more nuanced than that. The USPTO's official website offers this insight about preparing for oral argument before the PTAB: "Do not avoid the difficult issues. The APJs will be most interested in the weakest parts of your case, because those are the points on which the outcome of the case may turn."[12]

In light of that, how do you time your weaknesses? Practitioner Lori Gordon has more than 250 PTAB trials under her belt. As she notes: "You know where you're likely going to lose. You cannot approach [oral argument] by responding to every single argument."[13]

Rather than devote time in your oral argument to your case weaknesses, those we interviewed recommended that you prepare to handle weaknesses as they arise in questions from the panel. Know your response and make it in a pointed way. We offer a word-efficient structure later in this chapter.

4. So, What Does *Your First Minute Look Like?*

We have talked enough about where *not* to start. The APJs we interviewed universally urged that you get to the substance of your argument as quickly as possible. Still, several of them acknowledged that you may need to first set some context for your first winning point. Retired APJ Jessica Kaiser made this recommendation: "Present whatever is necessary to give context to the arguments that are key in the case. Is there something you want to highlight about the specification or about a particular claim limitation or claim construction dispute? Explain you are doing this to provide context to your argument."[14]

APJ Brian Murphy agrees and extends his recommendation into the first five to ten minutes of your oral argument:

> [U]se the opening five to ten minutes to frame the dispositive issues and state the reasons/evidence for why their client should win. PTAB judges, particularly "APJ One" who is assigned to prepare and draft the decision, don't need much background introduction and advocates can presume a high degree of familiarity with the parties' arguments and evidence.[15]

Your first minute may also be your most strategic opportunity to ferret out *the panel's priorities* for your oral argument:

> For a PTAB argument, I have seen people go in and linearly push through their materials. It's often better to briefly roadmap everything in a minute about what you will argue. [This will] put your cards out and then it will prompt a question [often about an issue you listed further down in your preview]. Do it to get to what the judges care about.[16]

12. PTAB, *supra* note 10.
13. Video Interview with PTAB Practitioner Lori Gordon, *supra* note 11.
14. Video Interview with Retired Lead APJ Jessica Kaiser, *supra* note 9.
15. Email Interview with Retired Lead APJ Brian Murphy, *supra* note 1.
16. Telephone Interview with Retired Chief APJ Nathan E. Kelley, *supra* note 7.

5. Can You Raise New Arguments at the Oral Hearing?

Typically, you cannot raise new arguments at this phase of your case. The panel may allow an exception if something unexpected happened that no one had the opportunity to address earlier. In a webinar moderated by Lead Judge Georgianna Braden, the panel of APJs recommended that the advocate explain the situation to the panel *beforehand*, even if that explanation comes only a day or two before the hearing. If the panel agrees to let you raise a new argument, most judges will ask for additional briefing.

6. How Do You Keep Your Arguments Concise and Powerful?

For a specific argumentative point, we recommend something we have observed the strongest oral advocates use. This approach is a decidedly Western approach called "applications first" persuasion.[17] When making a discrete argument, Western cultures like the United States generally focus on "bottom lining" your point up front, followed by your logic. Other cultures value an approach called "principles first" where they provide the logic first before drawing the conclusion. (This "principles first" approach can feel akin to first establishing your foundation before hitting your conclusion. This may explain why so many attorneys are prone to use this approach, even though our experience and the advice of APJs is to reverse the order of argument to follow a more "applications first" organization.)

When we work with oral advocates, we teach a simple argument-by-argument approach called the "what/why/where" structure that goes in this order:

What is the issue?

Why does it matter—or—why is it significant?

Where does it leave the case/the decision?

Your "applications first" use of the "what/why/where" might look something like this:

What. A person of ordinary skill in the art (POSITA) would have been "market motivated" to combine the teachings from these two pieces of prior art.

Why. Doing so to arrive at the claimed combination would have improved safety and efficacy in a fast-moving field where the market demanded innovation around these kinds of features.

Where. Those teachings and motivation demonstrate the obviousness of the challenged claims.

APJ Brian Murphy says this kind of completeness during argument is important because judges look for a detailed technical explanation and supporting references to establish why a POSITA would or would not have taken certain technical steps to reach an invention.

---

17. Erin Meyer, The Culture Map: Breaking Through the Invisible Boundaries of Global Business (2014).

At first glance, you may think, "Of course. Makes sense." But ask yourself: Do you consistently make the "why" *explicit* in your argumentation? Many fact finders miss an argument's point because the advocate failed to do so. You may feel the argument's significance is self-evident, but you have also thought about your argument more than anyone. "Self-evident" does not always translate to "fact finder-evident." In fact, others in the PTAB have identified a gap in oral advocates' completeness of argumentation. The panelist APJs speaking at the 2021 "Inside PTAB" webinar commented that extensive fact coverage is less important than explaining *why the facts matter*. Relatedly, they said (when referring to written briefs, which we suggest applies equally to oral argument): "The most powerful thing you have on your side is the word 'because.' Use 'because' liberally throughout your papers."[18]

The word "because" links your "what" to your "why." Adding the "where" is ideal but is not always practical when your panel seems impatient and ready to move to the next issue or, as practitioner Lori Gordon puts it, if the questions are technical: "It depends on the question. Many questions are technical questions so the 'where' doesn't even matter. The reason they are asking the question is because the other side may have been telling them a different thing." She further notes the importance of building the "where" somewhere into your argument:

> The "where?" concept is important for your entire presentation because the Board always wants to simplify their writing, so they will want to know if they argue in one direction (i.e., agree with patent owner), what will happen next (i.e., if I find in favor of patentee, is the case over?).[19]

7. How Might You "Refresh" Attentiveness with Your Panel?

Any oral argument can suffer from gaps in audience attentiveness. It is the authors' experience that two key factors exacerbate those gaps: (1) being too vague or redundant in noting the relevance of your point, and (2) having too little variety in your persuasive techniques. Later in this chapter, we offer guidance on making a crisp argument to deal with the first factor. Here, we address the second "low variety" issue by capitalizing on advice provided by three sitting APJs in 2021.

In the "Inside PTAB" webinar panel presented by then-sitting APJs White, Kaiser, and Kauffman, the panel observed that splitting your argument among team members can be effective. Having a new person at the podium partway through your oral argument can refresh a panel's interest in content. In a tongue-in-cheek but highly apt comment, Lead Judge Stacey White noted that she has observed a dynamic in oral argument she calls the "post-it army." Paraphrasing her comment:

---

18. Summary provided by practitioner Kaitlin Dryden who attended the PTAB's August 26, 2021, "Inside PTAB" webinar. Lead Judge Georgianna Braden presented an overview of the Board and led a panel discussion on effective written and oral advocacy. Panel members included Lead Judge Stacey White, Lead Judge Jessica Kaiser, and Lead Judge Phil Kauffman.

19. Video Interview with PTAB Practitioner Lori Gordon, *supra* note 11.

> The post-it army is comprised of the people who have done the work in the back, have written the brief, and when questions come up, they are furiously scribbling things on post-it notes and passing them [to the lead advocate]. Don't be afraid to give those people a moment at the podium. It's good to hear from people who really know the case and know the facts. It doesn't always matter that they don't have the polish someone has who has been doing this their whole life. This is how they get that polish, getting them a chance to get up here, answer questions, build the confidence, in an arena where they know the facts. Sometimes the most powerful advocate you have is the most junior one on your team who knows why you should win.[20]

The panelists also recommended that you be ready to refer the panel to parts of the record that support your argument or answer a question. If needed, they suggested that it is appropriate to tell the panel your team member is looking for a reference and continue your presentation while they look.[21]

8. How Do You Organize Your Argument for "Pivots"?

You probably have spent at least a conscientious amount (if not an extraordinary amount) of time organizing your argument outline in a way that flows logically and persuasively. Your transitions from one point to the next are magic. And then the APJ tells you she is most interested in hearing first about something embedded deep in your outline. "You can be surprised about what the judges think is the main show. That is the main thing about flexibility and pivoting. You may think you know what the main issue is, but then you may end up winning on a different issue."[22]

Practitioner Lori Gordon offers this wisdom: "I structure my oral argument in modular concepts. I practice so it's easy to jump around depending on where the questions come."[23]

Former APJ Jessica Kaiser observed the price practitioners paid when they could not flex their argument structure to focus on the panel's priorities:

> The hardest thing is when people come in and their number one priority is to say what they want to say about their demonstratives. If you interrupt them with a question, when they're done, they go back to where they were in discussing their demonstratives instead of following up on what they just learned the judge is most concerned about.

---

20. Summary provided by practitioner Kaitlin Dryden who attended the PTAB's August 26, 2021, "Inside PTAB" webinar. Lead Judge Georgianna Braden presented an overview of the Board and led a panel discussion on effective written and oral advocacy. Panel members included Lead Judge Stacey White, Lead Judge Jessica Kaiser, and Lead Judge Phil Kauffman.

21. Summary provided by practitioner Kaitlin Dryden who attended the PTAB's August 26, 2021, "Inside PTAB" webinar.

22. Video Interview with Retired Lead APJ Jessica Kaiser, *supra* note 9.

23. Video Interview with PTAB Practitioner Lori Gordon, *supra* note 11.

> You have to be ready to bend to the interests of the panel but also be ready for a cold panel. You have to be prepared to march through your slides and give your speech, but you also have to be prepared to talk about the issues the judges identify through their questions.[24]

Being able to pivot and reorganize your argument on the fly is a definite skill. But there is a less stressful way to pivot that abandons the *vertical* outline approach of a typical Word document. We call this *horizontal* organization. Picture a side-by-side organization of your argument on index cards. The advantage to this old-fashioned concept of index cards is that it allows you to "reshuffle" your discrete arguments on the fly. Today, electronic alternatives exist if you choose to use this horizontal approach on your laptop. One software program is NoteDex and it can be found at https://www.notedexapp.com/. The app looks like this:

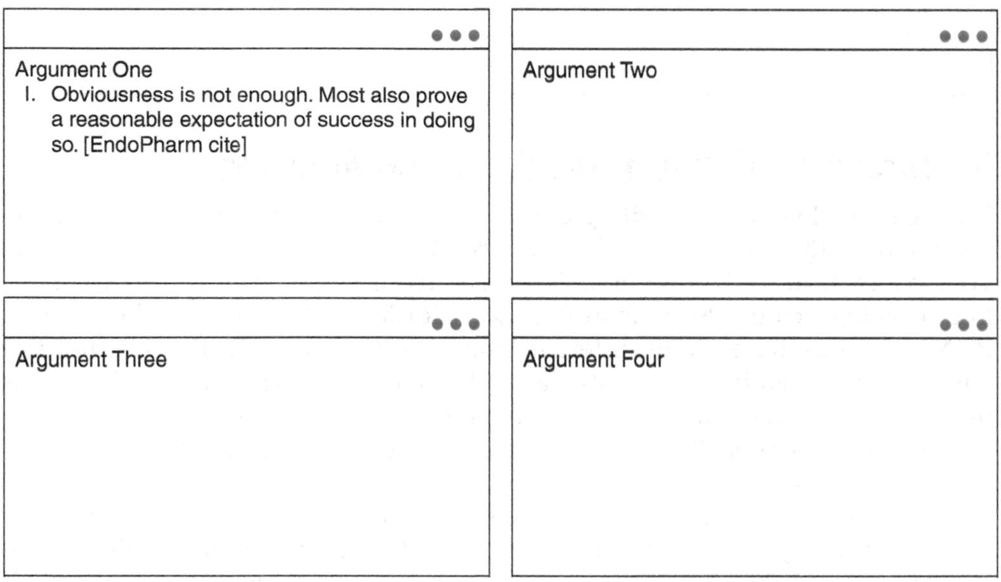

If you prefer to stick with a word processing program like Microsoft Word, you can create index cards there as well. In Word, go to:

Mailings > Labels > Options > Index Cards

24. Video Interview with Retired Lead APJ Jessica Kaiser, *supra* note 9.

Argument One

I. Obviousness is not enough. Must also prove a reasonable expectation of success in doing so. [EndoPharm cite]

Argument Two

Argument Three

Argument Four

II. Threading Theme Throughout Oral Argument

We are in the business of writing persuasive themes. Rule Number One is making them fit the audience (and, more specifically, the "tougher audience" on your panel or jury). Being quotable is still advisable, but you cannot cross the line to being "cute." As practitioner Lori Gordon aptly notes: "[Themes in a PTAB hearing] are entirely different than in a district court. People miss this and their presentation style falls flat and is met with eye rolls. . . . The APJs don't care about the quippy themes that litigators often come in with."[25]

This is *not* a good theme: "There are three reasons we should be here and one reason we shouldn't."

This is *not* a good theme: "They are half right, but it's the wrong half."

Former APJ Jessica Kaiser describes a good thematic option: "A theme that can work is about the burden (e.g., 'This is why the petitioner did not meet their burden in the case.') It's not like a trial theme; it is more vanilla. You can have themes but not in the way you have in [district court] litigation."[26]

Concurring, former APJ Nathan Kelley noted:

> If you have to think hard about the theme in advance, you probably shouldn't have one. I think people go the wrong way when they talk about how good or how important a patent is or how bad the patent is. It won't get you anywhere. That annoys the judges. It's almost insulting. You're not going to trick them. They want to get to the issue and the prior art.[27]

25. Video Interview with PTAB Practitioner Lori Gordon, *supra* note 11.
26. Video Interview with Retired Lead APJ Jessica Kaiser, *supra* note 9.
27. Telephone Interview with Retired Chief APJ Nathan E. Kelley, *supra* note 7.

This *is* a good theme: "The protracted struggle to come up with this invention underscores that the claims were not obvious."

III. Handling Questions and Answers Effectively

Given the importance of the question-and-answer aspect of a PTAB hearing, this section of the chapter may be the most important. Exceptional preparation for handling any kind of question is key. We spend so much time preparing witnesses to handle questions in deposition, arbitration, and trial. Counsel would be well-advised to hone their skills at answering questions as well.

A. Follow the Path of the Panel's Questions

As former APJ Nathan Kelley bottom-lines it: "When more than one judge is asking the same questions, that is the *only* thing you should talk about until the panel appears satisfied that you've answered their questions."[28]

Two-time APJ Brian Murphy noted that he prepares for hearings by putting together a list of questions to ask of petitioner's counsel and of patent owner's counsel. He described the question-and-answer segment as "the most important opportunity for persuasive argument."

He advises:

> Answer the judges' questions—directly, clearly, and with specific reasons and supporting evidence from the record. This can be a golden opportunity to clear up any confusion in the record, such as conflicting interpretations of the law or disclosures in a patent or prior art reference. It is also an opportunity for an advocate to give the judge confidence in his or her position, particularly in a "close call" case.[29]

B. Understand the Depth Endemic to PTAB Questioning

The depth of most questions posed in PTAB hearings can often surprise those who are new to this forum. Brian Murphy explains why APJs can get more granular:

> PTAB judges have electronic access to a bookmarked pdf of the most important evidence in a case, which they will refer to during a hearing—e.g. the patent and prosecution history, key prior art references, expert declarations, and deposition testimony. Therefore, PTAB judges will get very granular with their questions and will even quote from documents, declarations, and deposition testimony and expect counsel to be very familiar with the evidence in order to answer the questions.
>
> Most judges try to obtain clarity by asking very specific questions of counsel and often citing/quoting specific documentary language in

28. *Id.*
29. Email Interview with Retired Lead APJ Brian Murphy, *supra* note 1.

the question. For example, "Counsel, at column 4 lines 5–10, the patent describes the compound as including a 'heterocyclic group' at position 7 of the molecule. Why does/doesn't Example 3 of the prior art reference disclose such a heterocyclic group at the same position?" Or "Counsel, at page 53 lines 5–15 of your expert's deposition transcript he/she testified as follows: [quote]. Counsel for Patent Owner argues this testimony is an admission that the prior art does not disclose a heterocyclic group at position 7 of the molecule. What is your response to that argument?"[30]

C. Return to the "What/Why" Structure to Provide "Next Level" Answers

A well-framed answer is your opportunity to address the panel's question while furthering your persuasive point. The "what/why" structure works well for this circumstance.

Assume an APJ asks you a hypothetical question to test your position in the case:

> **Question:** *Counsel, assume we rule in your favor on this issue. Won't we set a precedent for other cases if we construe this particular claim language as broadly as you suggest?*
>
> **Answer:** *[What] No, we don't believe you will undertake that risk.*
>
> *[Why] In fact, construing this claim language as we suggest will align with what has come before, so you will actually be affirming prior constructions.*

Former APJ Nathan Kelley underscores this approach:

> A great answer is one where you immediately answer the question and then explain a problem with the premise of the question with something the asker didn't think about. You might agree with their hypothetical but explain the errors in their logic. Sometimes the panel is asking a hypothetical because they are worried that if they rule your way, other cases will go your way as well.[31]

D. Avoid Nonresponsive Habits That Will Annoy Your Panel

Of course, the last thing you would aim to do is to handle a question in a manner that actually puts off your panel. When we queried the APJs, it seemed that their most common pet peeves flowed from unintentional gaffes spoken by oral advocates. Those gaffes included

30. *Id.*
31. Telephone Interview with Retired Chief APJ Nathan E. Kelley, *supra* note 7.

	What the APJs Say They Want Instead
"I'm going to get to that question later."	Answer the question *now.* I posed it now for a reason.
"I'm going to get to that question later." (And then counsel ignores the question.)	"You would be surprised how often this happens."[32]
"My partner will address that question later."	Have your partner address the question *now.*[33]
"That's a great question."	APJs see this sentence as a classic stall tactic. Instead, pause and address the question directly.
"Let me surmise the intent of your question. . ."	You have a right to a clear question. If you have to guess at the judge's meaning, ask for clarification. Never guess aloud.
Press forward with a "close enough" response. (Do not.)	"Don't be afraid to say, 'I need to look at the record. May I come back to that?' If it's a new issue, ask to submit new briefing. There is a fear of having to answer in a definitive way, but if you need more information to be accurate, do not just throw a bad answer in."[34]

And, ultimately, do not be concerned about the questions they do not ask: "If I'm not asking questions, it's probably something I already understand and I'm not trying to test my thinking."[35]

IV. Hitting Your Rebuttal Points with (Some) Advance Preparation

A number of PTAB practitioners are quick to say that rebuttal is the hardest point of oral argument. For those who rely on scripts or detailed outlines, the impromptu feeling of rebuttal can be a stressor. Still, there are ways to loosely prepare for rebuttal in advance, as long as you have the wisdom to abandon your favorite talking points if they have been rendered redundant or unnecessary by the events in the hearing that precede your time on your "rebuttal feet." Seasoned practitioners caution strongly against returning to points the panel has clearly resolved. Do not reiterate your argument. It will hurt your credibility with the panel.

You will receive the other side's slides one week before the hearing so that content may give you advance notice of crisp points to prepare for rebuttal. Again, consider preparing with the "horizonal structure" described earlier in this chapter.

When you stand to make your points, *enumerate*. This seemingly minor technique helps you hold the floor: "Keep rebuttal short and have a defined point

32. Video Interview with Retired Lead APJ Jessica Kaiser, *supra* note 9.

33. Summary provided by practitioner Kaitlin Dryden who attended the PTAB's August 26, 2021, "Inside PTAB" webinar. Lead Judge Georgianna Braden presented an overview of the Board and led a panel discussion on effective written and oral advocacy. Panel members included Lead Judge Stacey White, Lead Judge Jessica Kaiser, and Lead Judge Phil Kauffman.

34. Video Interview with PTAB Practitioner Lori Gordon, *supra* note 11.

35. Video Interview with Retired Lead APJ Jessica Kaiser, *supra* note 9.

that is fresh. Say, 'I have three points on rebuttal and here's what they are.' Be succinct, answer any questions, and be done."[36]

V. Creating IPR-Friendly PowerPoints

A. The "Don'ts"

As we have done in other parts of this chapter, we start with what APJs (and we) recommend *against* doing.

1. *Do not* create an exhaustive deck simply because you want to have slides "just in case" the panel asks you a question that a slide might help. Make the hard choice to severely narrow your slides. Several APJs we interviewed groaned that they encountered counsel who came prepared with more than 100 slides. Their sheer volume can create pressure on you to "shop them" to find the key slide you really do need.
2. *Do not* create text-heavy slides, or as one APJ noted, "include so much text that they make your eyes bleed." The more text you have, the more likely you are to read to your panel (which is insulting) or, when you deviate from/add to the text, to have your text-heavy slide compete with your verbal point. In fact, neuroscience research finds that "bullet point" slides can *decrease* the viewer's learning because the viewer is likely reading ahead of you and is (unsuccessfully) dividing his or her attention between you and your slide.[37]
3. *Do not* create slides that have numerous points on them. One slide should convey one key point.

B. The Dos

While your panel will not decide your case based on your PowerPoint, a number of APJs noted that they find visual pictures helpful on slides. For example:

> I am very much a visual learner and like when counsel use a few well-prepared demonstratives to highlight key evidence, e.g., color-coded claim language compared to prior art disclosures, expert deposition admissions/inconsistencies compared with their declaration testimony or claim language; distilling complicated process sequences, systems, or products into a well-ordered easy to understand format—this is particularly helpful when addressing complicated electro/mechanical systems and chemical/biological processes.[38]

So, if you can make a persuasive point using a visual, *do* create PowerPoint slides that are their most effective:

---

36. *Id.*
37. *Id.*
38. Email Interview with Retired Lead APJ Brian Murphy, *supra* note 1.

1. *Do* consider slides that focus on "contrast" and "comparison" points. In fact, among the APJs we interviewed for this chapter, this visual focus was the one they most frequently identified as useful for their evaluation. For example, if you show claim language, consider showing how the claim language would have to (fictitiously) read for the other side to be correct. You can highlight this language in a different font color to point out its absurdity. You might also compare figures from the claimed invention next to the prior art.
2. *Do* use the "B" key on your keyboard to avoid keeping "expired slides" on the screen. Practitioners frequently keep a slide up after it has run its course simply because they do not know a simple mechanism exists to make your screen go black. When in "presentation mode" in your PowerPoint show, hit the "B" key and your screen will go dark. When you are ready, hit the "B" key again to wake your screen back up.
3. *Do* make use of "action buttons" in PowerPoint if you have an introductory slide that previews your key points. Assume, for example, that you list three key points. If your panel wants you to fast forward to point three, you can link the point three language on your introductory slide to the specific slide later in your deck that illustrates point three. When in PowerPoint, go to:

   Insert > Links > Actions

   The dropdown menu there will offer you a number of options to go to a specific slide in your deck. This simple step enables you to flex within your deck's order rather than having to scroll through slides to address an APJ's question.
4. *Do* follow the rules for identifying demonstratives as described on the PTAB website:

   > Demonstrative exhibits used at the oral hearing are aids and not evidence, and should be clearly marked as such. For example, each slide of a demonstrative exhibit must be marked with the words "DEMONSTRATIVE EXHIBIT—NOT EVIDENCE" in the footer. Demonstrative exhibits cannot be used to advance arguments or introduce evidence not previously presented in the record. See *Dell Inc. v. Acceleron, LLC*, 884 F.3d 1364, 1369 (Fed. Cir. 2018) (noting that the "Board was obligated to dismiss [the petitioner's] untimely argument . . . raised for the first time during oral argument").[39]

VI. Considering Your Remote Judge in a Hybrid Panel of In-Person APJs and Online APJs

Among your three judges, you may encounter a hearing where one or more of the judges appears remotely. Consider your remote judges when making oral argument. As of the publication of this book edition, two things are true about remote judges.

39. PTAB, *supra* note 10.

First, the remote judge appears by monitor next to his or her peer judges. You will be able to see and interact with that judge as if that person is in the room. Give that judge equal attention to those physically present.

Second, PTAB hearing rooms do not have internet access capabilities, meaning your slide deck will need to be played locally from your laptop. It also means the remote viewer will not see demonstratives on their screen while you display them via a projector in the hearing room. Be prepared to cite to a document the remote viewer can reference.

VII. Conclusion

We conclude where we began. Even if you believe the panel's decision is largely made, you know oral argument can make a difference in 20%–25% of cases. You will undoubtedly put 100% effort into making a strong presentation. With deep gratitude to the former judges and current practitioners who generously contributed to this chapter, we hope you consider our collective advice in preparing for your next "on your feet" appearance before the PTAB.

CHAPTER 4

Your Unique Niche with Juries

"Every person in there said, 'What the hell do we know about patent law?' But I said, this is the nature of the jury system, and they don't want experts to be deciding. We read through it and tried to parse out, what does this mean?"

—Patent juror who found infringement

"You may think the technical merits of your case are the heart of winning and losing. In fact, having your fact witnesses tell a compelling narrative that includes the technical facts is the key to winning. It's about communicating through lay folks. I tell my team to tell me the strengths and weaknesses of the case and then to tell me separately your narrative. It doesn't matter what I think of my case. What matters is what eight people in the box think, what the judge thinks, and what the court of appeals thinks from the written record. We often forget, at the end of the day, we are communicators."

—William Lee, patent litigation partner, Wilmer Hale[1]

The door closes, and a group of people who knew nothing of one another before trial begin to stare at a list of strange and complicated questions they must answer before they can resume their daily lives. They think about the mountain of evidence they just finished seeing and hearing and they try to figure out where to start. Across countless mock deliberations, we have observed the substantive conversation beginning like this:

1. Video Interview with William Lee, Patent Litigation Partner, Wilmer Hale (2021).

Camera Anywhere Co. v. BigPhone Corp.[2]

Juror	Statement	Commentary
Juror Elena	"I definitely feel like BigPhone took advantage of CAC. They could have designed this thing ten times over with their billions of dollars, but chose this instead?"	Jurors care deeply about the parties' behavior and use fairness as an important measuring stick for a variety of dimensions by which they measure the parties' actions. In this chapter we talk more about what helps form jurors' opinions about patent disputes and how it influences their perceptions and decisions in patent trials.
Juror Dante	"The first thing we need to do is determine the meaning of a patent. What does it mean to have a patent in this situation?"	Even by the point of deliberations, many jurors still have misconceptions about what a patent does and does not cover, and what gives a patent value. In Chapter 7, we offer strategies for presenting your most persuasive "validity or invalidity" case.
Juror Sam	"Well, we know a patent exists because a patent was awarded. What else is there to know?"	A strong majority of jurors give great deference to the U.S. Patent and Trademark Office. In Chapter 5, we discuss who is more likely to show this deference and how you can address it in jury selection.
Juror Elena	"If the plaintiff has a patent, then where is the product? They have no product! It's just an idea floating in the wind. You can't patent that!"	Most jurors clamor to see the tangible value of a patent and are typically curious about how the patent might affect them personally. In Chapter 6, we discuss ways to appeal to jurors' own values in your opening statement.
Juror Dante	"Maybe, but infringing means taking what has already been invented. The infringing company took it and only changed some tiny thing. They basically copied it. But CAC made it first. This big company just took it and changed it a little so they could make a bunch of money."	The deliberations phase is not the time to first anticipate jurors' street definitions and interpretations of the key issues in your case, including their interpretations of what is or is not infringement under your case facts. See Chapter 2 for ways to persuade during the *Markman* process, focus your case early, and develop persuasive themes with the court that can last through trial.
Juror Elena	"Well, I think it's just that the first patent—CAC's patent—didn't work. There was no product, so BigPhone Corp. waited awhile and went and changed it a little bit so they could make the same basic product, but make something that worked."	Most jurors assume profit motive and aggressive competition are part of the corporate landscape. In a case involving a corporation either as the accused infringer or a non-practicing entity (NPE) as a patent holder, jurors' biases can be magnified. In this chapter, we discuss perceptions of corporate litigants in patent disputes.

2. See Appendix A for a description of the case.

Juror Dante		
	"CAC patented a method for making this thing and described how to make the product. There are lots of ways to skin a cat, but this company infringed because they made the product just like they outlined in the patent. That is clear. You can't do that, no matter who you are."	For plaintiffs and defendants, the invention story is one of the most unique and critical parts of a persuasive position in a patent infringement dispute. In Chapter 6, we discuss ways to present your infringement/noninfringement case.
Juror Elena		
	"Come on! They were probably working on this exact same idea the entire time CAC was. You're assuming that everyone else was stupid and CAC was the only one who could have come up with this idea. That's not what happens in real life. Everyone is trying to make the same new widgets, and the corporation figured out how to make it work where he could not."	A patented product's utility is often a key consideration for determining the value (and validity) of the patent itself. As consumers, jurors appreciate the party that produces the best (and cheapest) product *as long as* that party also played fair along the way. While your case does not hinge on commercialization of the invention, it is something the jury often considers.
Juror Sam		
	"Yeah, but it's still CAC's idea. Maybe they tweaked it a little bit, but it's not their idea and it never was. They needed CAC's idea to make their product. I think they infringed. I think they owe him everything they made on that thing."	At the end of the day, jurors' emotional reactions to the case facts are powerful motivators. Parties' behavior matters, and jurors' motivations are often filtered through their perceptions of the parties' conduct as much or more than the legal standards of infringement. Chapter 8 provides strategies for enhancing or defending money damages.

The next stage of deliberations also follows a common trajectory that is always more heavily focused on behavior than it is on claim language. We do not use the term "always" lightly. Jurors typically dive into the claimed invention, scrutinizing the individual or team who claims to have invented it, as well as everything that happened in the process of taking a novel idea (or not), developing it into something patentable, securing a patent, and (frequently) trying to make a product. In cases that focus on individual inventors or corporate but personalized invention stories, jurors conjure the idea of the "American Dream," and often focus on the individuals with whom they have far more in common (e.g., an inventor or team of inventors) than they have with a faceless corporation. When the patentee is a non-practicing entity (NPE), jurors consider how the invention came about, how and why the current patent owner pursued the patent, and what that conduct says about it as a litigant.

Jurors rely on their own experiences, share stories of the things that have happened to them, and talk about how those experiences influence their views of the case. Then they typically talk about the defendant's conduct in the case, often in the biased context of the evils of today's corporate America. Jurors weigh their inherent anti-corporate bias against the values of innovation and technological advancement born from the research and development wings of America's corporate giants. When the patentee is a corporate entity or NPE, jurors rely on their collective experiences as the context under which they decide a case.

On which side do the scales of justice typically fall? Do they favor the inventor or the corporation that delivers the products jurors want on the shelves of their local retail stores? Do they favor the NPE that bought a patent portfolio or the manufacturing company accused of infringing hard-earned patents? To what extent does the historic folklore of American inventions and world-changing patents become entangled in jurors' and judges' views of today's patent lawsuits?

> *"[The plaintiff] went in his garage and started this whole thing up by himself. He did everything by the book like he was supposed to. [The accused infringer] didn't do that. And if [the accused infringer] wanted to do that, they have to come up with a whole new system that's not the same as what he had."*
>
> —Patent mock juror

Even in the more common disputes between two corporations, operating or nonoperating, there is always a bigger company—a company with more power and resources that often translates to more responsibility. Even in cases involving two large international corporations, jurors tend to see the difference between a monopolistic motive and those of the perceived underdog.

> *"We have this big company [patentee]. Yes, you guys capitalized on something that should have been obvious . . . but now to try and keep the little guy down so we can't get that?"*
>
> —Patent mock juror

We study federal judges[3] and potential patent jurors across the United States, exploring what they think about the issues and arguments in patent lawsuits, and their answers might surprise you. Three-fourths of potential jurors (75%) believe an issued patent is often or almost always innovative and unique, and 74% also believe it is difficult to obtain a patent for an invention today.[4]

Potential jurors and judges have overwhelmingly positive views of patents; 98% of district court judges[5] and more than 90% of potential jurors[6] support the practice of protecting inventions with patents. At the same time, potential jurors

---

3. Data is cited from research the authors helped conduct when with Persuasion Strategies, a service of Holland & Hart LLP. Persuasion Strategies, Holland & Hart LLP, Persuasion Strategies Federal Judge Survey (2008). Persuasion Strategies surveyed a total of 105 federal court judges and federal magistrate judges in April 2008. The survey assessed opinions of attorneys, attorney performance, corporations, litigation, and the patent system. Of the 105 respondents, 52% were appointed by Republican presidents and 48% by Democratic presidents. Sixty-two percent reported presiding over 50 or more trials, 67% have served on the federal bench for 11 years or more, and 97% have presided over an intellectual property lawsuit.

4. Persuasion Strategies/K&B Research, National Juror Survey (2011). Data is cited from research the authors helped conduct when with their prior group, Persuasion Strategies, a service of Holland & Hart LLP.

5. Persuasion Strategies, *supra* note 3.

6. Persuasion Strategies/K&B Research, *supra* note 4. This data is consistent with hundreds of mock jurors in various studies conducted across patent litigation venues in 2023 and 2024.

support competitive (read inexpensive) alternatives in the consumer market, and nearly one in three (31%) say the patent process somewhat or strongly hurts competition. Jurors' views of patents are complicated by their inherent trust that patents protect innovation and their desire to directly experience the benefits of a competitive consumer market.

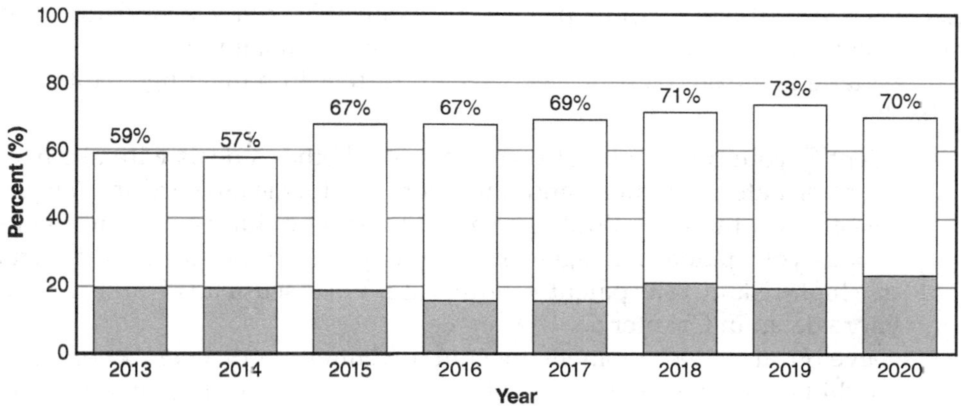

Source: PERSUASION STRATEGIES, BIGJURY 2013–2020 (N=2,881)

These and other data inform the overarching question: How do juries (and district court judges) decide patent cases? What can attorneys do to more effectively persuade fact finders?

I. The Jury: Your Patently Unique Fact Finder

Our pretrial jury research and mock jury data also show us that jurors react uniquely to patent disputes, particularly when a corporation is involved, as is almost always the case these days. They are challenged by the factual and technical complexity and they can struggle to keep up with the evidence they are told should inform their decisions.

> *"Just trying to get a general understanding of what [patents] are can be a challenge. I hope I get a murder trial the next time [I'm a juror]."*
>
> —Patent juror

> *"[This case] is about a small guy getting run over by big companies, because he tried to come up with an idea, he tried to run with it, but these big companies, knowing what they are doing, kind of ran over him."*
>
> —Patent mock juror

These statements are common when we interview patent jurors and mock jurors who hear detailed presentations from litigants, both massive corporations and unknown, smaller entities or individual inventors. They focus on the challenging complexity of being patent jurors and their natural focus on the things they feel they understand and are qualified to evaluate: people's behavior. So, how does that translate to today's large-scale corporate patent litigations? What about disputes involving NPEs?

The jury research, survey data, and the human stories that illuminate these questions may surprise you. Based on years of public and our private research, our direct experience observing and interviewing potential and actual patent jurors, and our work with trial counsel on how best to persuade jurors in complex cases, we shed light on how patent infringement juries make decisions and how trial counsel can more effectively persuade individual jurors.

Consider a few examples that we develop further in remaining chapters of this book:

- Identify your opponent's strongest case—whether it deals with infringement or patent validity—and aim your case themes toward the *tougher audience* on the jury. While it may surprise you, jurors who are high-risk in your patent infringement case may not be the same jurors who are high-risk in your patent validity case. We discuss this "juror flip" in more detail in Chapter 5.
- Develop an "aha" moment in your invention story even where you might believe none exists. We offer a few alternatives to patent holders and accused infringers for helping jurors see their competing invention stories as compelling and persuasive narratives of the time, toil, and trial and error that went into an idea or invention.
- Make jurors' trust in and respect for the U.S. Patent and Trademark Office (USPTO) an advantage at trial regardless of whether you are an accused infringer or a patent holder.
- Teach jurors about patent *invalidity* by first making abundantly clear how a patent applicant should behave when applying for a patent and how the USPTO behaves when issuing a valid patent. Teaching how a patent *should be* issued will help jurors more easily understand the concept posed in a positive way. Second, it allows you to subtly present the patent holder's options had she gone through the patent process in a legitimate manner.

These and other strategic recommendations flow directly from what we know about patent jurors. One thing we know with certainty is that jurors' views of patent lawsuits are heavily influenced by their views and evaluation of the patent system.

II. Juror Perceptions of the American Patent

"If a budding Edison feared that the rewards of his inventive efforts would be reaped by copyists—copyists who did not even bear the costs of original research—he might abandon the laboratory for other pursuits."[7]

—A.L. Durham, law professor

---

7. *See* Alan L. Durham, Patent Law Essentials: A Concise Guide 2 (2d ed. 2004).

Thankfully, jurors are persuaded by evidence, and strength of evidence is a substantial predictor of jury decision-making, but it is not the only thing that influences jury decision-making. Jurors' perceptions of extralegal factors such as the credibility of industry regulators, the public perception of the respective litigants, and jurors' perceived personal relevance to the parties' conduct are more important in patent trials than in other types of jury trials. That may sound like an extreme declaration. No doubt, jurors' perceptions of extralegal factors are important in other case types too. Jurors' feelings about their own employment experiences are central to employment termination disputes. Their perceptions of the polarizing tech industry are critical in any case involving claims against a technology company. Theft of trade secrets, personal injury, and medical malpractice cases are all significantly impacted by jurors' perceptions of factors not specifically introduced during trial—factors that will never be evidence. Litigators going to trial in any civil case must consider and address the relevant extralegal factors.

Yet, jurors' extralegal perceptions in patent trials carry greater weight than in other case types for one critical reason: Patent jurors simplify more than they do in other cases by using their extralegal perceptions to help make verdict decisions (in Chapter 5 on jury selection strategies, we address jurors' high-risk perceptions in greater detail). Those perceptions begin where patent disputes often begin—with the patent process itself.

A. Patent Jurors Still See Magic in the Patent Process

> *"I would really defer now to the patent office. If they have determined twice that it was a valid patent, they have a level of expertise far beyond what we have, and it's unfair to come back around to a layman and find that the patent office made a mistake."*
>
> —Patent mock juror

Observe a typical mock patent jury deliberation and you can expect to see how powerfully jurors' perceptions of patent disputes are linked to the history and tradition of American patents. Patents began as a core symbol of innovation. They began as protection for the value of individual ingenuity and the vessel by which individual innovation and discovery could benefit the public and encourage continued innovation. Examples of famous patented inventions demonstrate the value of patents past, and the way that value shaped public perceptions. Edison's lightbulb, Bell's telegraph, and numerous other patented inventions from airbags to iPhones literally changed the world. Partly because of personas like Edison, Einstein, and Steve Jobs, the jury-eligible American public still imagines the prototypical inventor as an individual laboring in a workshop or brainstorming late into the night to make real an idea that will indelibly alter the course of everyday life. It is every potential invention's meaningful intersection with the public—the fact that it can change our lives overnight—that substantially influences patent jurors and the lens through which they view patent trial issues. Jurors summon this view when they think about patents, as reflected in their overwhelming support for the practice of protecting inventions with patents, even as jurors acknowledge the fact that patents can create monopolies.

How do you feel about the practice of protecting inventions with patents?
94% Support

Source: PERSUASION STRATEGIES/K&B RESEARCH, NATIONAL JUROR SURVEY (2011) (N=900)

Jurors imagine a creative process that rivals Edison's or Einstein's. They give great deference to innovators and inventors, particularly individuals who embody the American archetype of hard work, ingenuity, and progress. And that enters into their views of the parties in patent litigation. What also remains unchanged is the fact that every patent case involves a patent in one way or another.

B. Patent Jurors Are Marked by History

If the rich history of American patents sets the stage for jurors' perceptions of patent trials, the patent explosion of the 1980s closes the curtain on Act II, at least for older jurors in today's venires. More on that in a moment.

Patent filings steadily increased from the 1980s into the 2000s, and the number of patent lawsuits filed in U.S. federal courts approximately doubled from 1997 to 2007.[8] District court filings hit a peak of more than 6,100 in 2013, remained steady around 4,000 from 2017 to 2021, and fell to 3,111 in 2023.[9] Economic changes, growth in technology (specifically information technology), and the dawn of widespread computer use greatly enhanced the speed and breadth of research productivity.[10] Businesses took advantage of the market, with the increasing value of intangible assets such as patents resulting in their growing attractiveness.[11] Businesses made and continue to actively patent technology as well as purchase and enforce patents. NPEs have become some of the biggest movers and shakers in the patent litigation sphere, with data showing NPEs are highly active in district court filings, including an NPE, WSOU Investments, LLC, filing the most district court cases from 2019 to 2021, and another NPE

8. *See* Joseph P. Cook, *On Understanding the Increase in U S. Patent Litigation*, 9 AM. L. & ECON. Rev. 48 (2007).

9. LEX MACHINA, PATENT LITIGATION REPORT 2022, 2024 (Lex Machina Data Team eds., 2022, 2024).

10. *Id.*; Adam Jaffe, *The U.S. Patent System in Transition: Policy Innovation and the Innovation Process*, 29 RSCH. POL'Y 531 (2000).

11. *See High-Tech Industry in the U.S. Economy: Hearing Before the Joint Economic Committee*, 106th Cong. (1999) (statement of Alan Greenspan, Chairman, Federal Reserve Board).

filing the second-most in that span, both responsible for significantly more filings than any other entity or litigant.

Today, NPEs function as a result of the abundance of enforceable patents and the business model to monetize them. Some argue that the patent boom was due primarily to the vast increase in research productivity that resulted from the explosion of computers creating faster and more complete information access.[12] This finding is supported by the relationship between research and development dollars spent and impending patent filings. Others believe there may be more to increases in patent litigation than the simple explanation that more patent grants mean more patent lawsuits.[13] Patentee successes at trial, and in recent years in Patent Trial and Appeal Board (PTAB) proceedings, encourage other patent holders to file lawsuits and aggressively defend PTAB actions. Trial outcomes positively influence litigation filings, with increased median damages awards correlating with an increase in patent lawsuit filings,[14] and the filing activity in some patent hotbed jurisdictions, such as the Western and Eastern Districts of Texas, Delaware, and the Central and Northern Districts of California, reflects the tendency of positive plaintiff trial verdicts to increase litigation filings.[15]

Regardless of the cause of the patent increase beginning in the 1980s—and you could believe in the contributions of a solid economy, an information-technology boom, a patent-friendly market, and patent-friendly courts, among other contributors—today's jurors live in a world directly influenced by the fact that technology advances at an exponential rate, with each year proliferating more innovation than the prior year. Technological and medical innovations are commonplace. They are both expected and necessary for progress and the perception of progress in everyday life. This is now the rule, not the exception.

Consumer sophistication and access to technology influence how people consume and process information, including information and evidence at trial. This influence also affects how people view the novelty and value of new ideas and innovations. Juries today are different than they were just a few years ago, in part because the world has changed so quickly and because the composition of America has changed.

1. Generational Differences on Patent Juries

Perceptions of innovation and technology specifically depend heavily on a number of factors, not the least of which is a potential juror's generational position in society, where juror behavior and societal norms are moving as quickly as the technology that influences them. In 2016, Millennials (people born 1981

12. *See* Jaffe, *supra* note 10.
13. *See* Cook, *supra* note 8.
14. *See id.* at 70.
15. *See* PATSTATS: U.S. PATENT LITIGATION STATISTICS (Jeffrey Johnson ed.).

to 1996) became the largest generation in the labor force.[16] They were briefly the most educated generation in the work force, though Generation Z Americans (born after 1996) are quickly overtaking Millennials in that regard. Both Gen Z and Millennials are less likely to view America as one of the world's greatest countries, more likely to view other countries as greater than the United States, and more likely to have distinct views of democracy, the environment, and corporations, among many others.

Perhaps most important to views of innovation are the younger generations' tech tendencies. Critically even if unsurprisingly, as of January 2022, Gen Z and Millennials are far more likely than Baby Boomers (born 1946–1964) to own a smartphone (96% compared to 61%) and to use social media (84% compared to 45%). Roughly half of Gen Z adults say they are constantly online compared to just 8% of Baby Boomers and about 25% of Gen X.[17] These gaps are likely to increase with time. The differences in how jurors born in different generations process information and evaluate innovation will remain highly relevant to how jurors perceive patents and patent litigation. Our private mock trial research bears this out. The way jurors use technology and process information influences how they view and value patented technology on trial and must influence how you address and persuade them in the courtroom.

Younger Jurors' Changing Views of Innovation and Innovative Rights

	18–34 years old	35–54 years old	55+ years old
It is common for corporations to use patented ideas without permission.	86%	82%	71%
Combining two existing concepts counts as innovation.	60%	53%	45%
The USPTO often/almost always makes mistakes when issuing patents.	37%	35%	25%

Source: Persuasion Strategies National Survey Data (Data from 2016–2019, Analyzed in 2019)

C. Patent Jurors' Trust in the USPTO

1. The Authority to Promote Innovation

> *"If they can prove to me that it was innovation to meet the market and stop a monopoly, I would favor [the accused infringer]."*
>
> —Patent mock juror

16. *See* Michelle Faverio, *Share of Those 65 and Older Who Are Tech Users Has Grown in the Past Decade*, Pew Rsch. Ctr. (Jan. 13, 2022), https://www.pewresearch.org/fact-tank/2022/01/13/share-of-those-65-and-older-who-are-tech-users-has-grown-in-the-past-decade/.

17. *See id.*

While we observe generational perceptual differences that might be expected to translate to changing perceptions of patents and the USPTO, most jurors continue to put great faith in the work of the USPTO and its examiners, who jurors consistently believe are thorough and hardworking. This faith is predicated upon the firm expectation that examiners engage in a thorough review process for every patent application—and, at a minimum, jurors believe the examiner's process is more thorough and complete than jurors' investigation of the patent at issue. The perceived magic of the patent process contributes to jurors' trust as well, in part because jurors are happy to believe the USPTO is entrusted with the authority to endorse innovative ideas and give them wings. Jurors generally believe the USPTO is fulfilling that mission, and few are interested in questioning that belief by pursuing data about its successes and failures or information that is not at their fingertips. What may be changing is where younger jurors simply discount the value of innovation more broadly because technological innovation in particular has been so fast, furious, and common in their lifetime it can carry less weight than it does with older jurors.

2. The Power to Promote Competition in the Marketplace

> *"A patent by its very nature is affected with a public interest. As recognized by the Constitution, it is a special privilege designed to serve the public purpose of promoting the 'Progress of Science and Useful Arts.' At the same time, a patent is an exception to the general rule against monopolies and to the right to access to a free and open market."*[18]
>
> —Supreme Court Justice Frank Murphy

A strong majority of jurors (though proportionally fewer in the younger generations) believe patents help drive innovation, production, and opportunity for consumers to get access to the latest technology. Patents give innovators a reason to innovate by protecting the fruits of their labor in the market. And make no mistake: jurors consider how the invention and the patent-in-suit relate to their everyday lives. A product that makes their lives easier is something in which they can find value, and that value allows jurors to more easily place confidence in the USPTO's decision to grant the patent. Perhaps most importantly, jurors are motivated to support a system that protects a fair process and prevents or addresses unfair competition at the core of infringement. When most jurors think of patent infringement, they translate to their own sense of fair competition and fair behavior in part because they feel more qualified to evaluate behavior than infringement, and in part because a sense of fairness is an arguably hardwired human value.

18. *See* Precision Instrument Mfg. Co. v. Automotive Maint. Mach. Co., 324 U.S. 806, 816 (1945).

3. Shifting Infallibility (Depending in Part on Your Venue and Jury Panel)

> *"I think [the patent examination process] is very long and I think [patent examiners] take their time and they do investigate the patent—I really do."*
>
> —Patent mock juror

Jurors openly communicate their perceptions that the USPTO is a credible authority, but these views are also changing with time and with the age of jurors.

It is easy to mislead the USPTO during the patent approval process

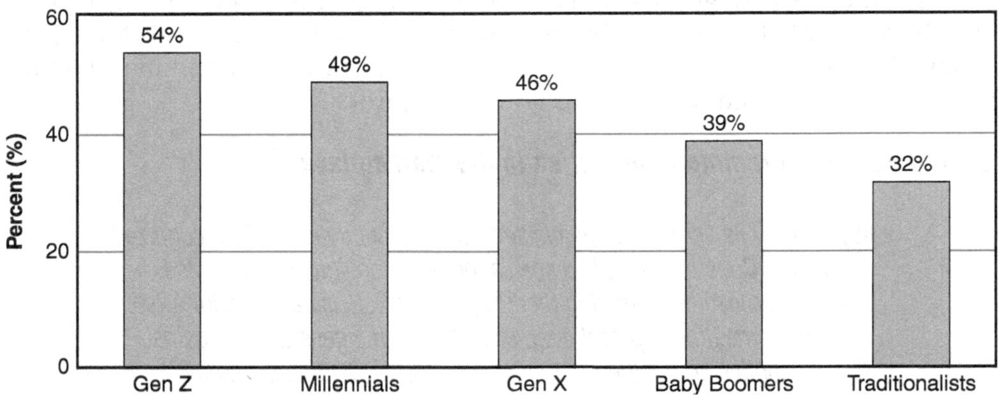

Source: Persuasion Strategies Big Jury, 2016–2019 (N=1,631)

Much of the shift can be explained by generational changes ("Traditionalists" were born between 1922 and 1945). We began this research at Persuasion Strategies and continue to observe patent jurors in our roles at Perkins Coie. Some historical and political context is also relevant. Beginning in 2008, there was an increase in media coverage and commentary about the USPTO, including more widespread awareness of the large number of pending patents. President Obama's administration coincided with change in the USPTO, including new initiatives to reform, and the appointment of a new director, David Kappos. The America Invents Act brought additional attention to the patent system and its evolution. Further changes to the patent system and the rise of PTAB proceedings are less familiar to average Americans, who are much more influenced by their own experiences and interactions with innovation, the corporatization of innovation and patent rights, and ultimately the shifting view that innovation is common, swiftly evolving, short-lived, and therefore less valuable than it once was.

Still, the typical American juror is focused on the same factors that dominate his or her patent trial decision-making, starting with the perceived value of the claimed innovation, the likelihood it will influence them in their lives, and, to a lesser degree, the authority of the USPTO to examine and appropriately award innovation with patent protection. The presumption that the USPTO's work is complete and correct dominates juror decisions.

> *"They wouldn't be in the patent office unless they were very good lawyers, top of their class."*
>
> —Patent mock juror

D. Juror Perceptions of the Federal Judicial Center Patent Video

> *"The defendant was saying they do this research. They showed a film that shows that they go through a research process and then it goes to the [Food and Drug Administration] and all that. . . ."*
>
> —Patent mock juror

In 2002, the Federal Judicial Center (FJC) released an 18-minute video tutorial designed to orient prospective jurors to the patent system and its basic elements. The video combines narration, dramatization, and imagery to demonstrate what a patent is, to walk prospective patent jurors though the patent application and examination process, and to discuss patent invalidity, the jury's role in the case, and the different burdens of proof that apply at trial. The video was updated in 2013 to reflect changes in patent law and included a more current set of imagery and concepts that better reflect the reality of patent lawsuits.[19] The individual courts have discretion in deciding whether or not to present the video to prospective jurors prior to their service. Our data indicates some judges routinely incorporate the video into their juror orientations, while others do not.

Reactions to the video have been varied. Parties remain concerned the video influences opinions of the patent process, the USPTO, and issues of patent validity. We have done our own analysis of the video, joining attorneys, legal analysts, and trial consulting colleagues who have evaluated the video content and its effects on mock jurors and potential jurors. Some have labeled it pro-patentee in typical patent infringement lawsuits because inspiring imagery of patents and innovative inventions primes jurors to favor the typical patent-holding plaintiff. One study by Tsongas Litigation Consulting found support for the conclusion the video is pro-patentee, increasing potential jurors' perceptions that obtaining a patent is difficult and the USPTO correctly grants patents.[20] A

19. U.S. Courts, *The Patent Process: An Overview for Jurors*, YouTube (Nov. 22, 2013), https://www.youtube.com/watch?v=ax7QHQTbKQE.

20. Alexis Knutson & Jeffrey Jarman, *How Federal Patent Tutorial Video Influences Jurors*, Tsongas: Advantage Blog (Aug. 6, 2020), https://www.tsongas.com/post/how-federal-patent-tutorial-video-influences-jurors.

third measure in the study showed an increase in jurors' confidence for determining patent validity, highlighting the influence the video has to empower jurors to favor an accused infringer's invalidity claims.

We have also repeatedly shown the FJC video to mock jurors in our mock jury research. Mock jurors' responses to the FJC video favor the patent holder in a few ways, but also favor a patent defendant in a few even more powerful ways.

First, the video generally confirms jurors' already pro-USPTO and pro-patent beliefs about the patent process. Those beliefs include the following:

1. Jurors believe the patent process is relatively complex.
2. Jurors believe completing the patent process requires great time and effort.
3. Jurors believe the USPTO plays a substantial role in examining patents.

> *"I know they said over and over that people make mistakes, but I think if it took just short of three years in front of that patent officer and he had that [prior art] and he still issued the patent, I think he did enough of his due diligence that the patent is valid."*
>
> —Patent mock juror (after seeing the FJC video)

The FJC video's imagery and themes communicate the challenge that jurors believe typifies the patent application process and also represent inventors' innovative thought processes made concrete. At the same time, however, the difficulty of achieving a patent emphasizes the challenges facing the USPTO, and the video helps some jurors see the patent process as more likely to lead to mistakes and human error.

Here are the primary ways the video favors accused infringers:

1. The potential for human error when evaluating a patent application is higher than expected and is influential.
2. An invalidity defense is a justified and typical response to infringement claims.
3. The USPTO suffers from the same or similar limitations that hamper the effectiveness of other government agencies.
4. Jurors are empowered to make the determination of a challenged patent's validity or invalidity.

In one multiday study, we observed a net 17% increase in the number of mock jurors who said they believe juries definitely have the power to find a patent invalid after watching the video compared to before watching the video. There were also net increases in the perceptions that it is easy to mislead the patent office, that the USPTO often makes mistakes in granting patents, and that only new and original products count as innovation.

Although our research data to date supports the conclusion that the FJC video bolsters some perceptions of patentees but also favors defendants claiming patent invalidity, the question is worth testing in your venue. In some venues, patent jurors begin the case with their powerful perceptions of the patent process and the USPTO reinforced by the judge and the court in which they will hear your case. Will your judge show the FJC video? Do you want him or her to do so? These questions are worth asking.

III. Juror Perceptions of Patent Litigants

> *"Judges have difficulty understanding modern technology and jurors have even greater difficulty, yet patent plaintiffs tend to request trial by jury because they believe that jurors tend to favor patentees, believing that they must be worthy inventors defending the fruits of their invention against copycats."*[21]
>
> —Judge Richard Posner

A. The Power of the Individual Litigant

The statistics are clear. Compared to corporations, individual litigants are significantly more likely to win patent jury trials.[22] Jurors identify more readily with individual plaintiffs. We repeatedly find it is difficult for jurors to find against someone with whom they identify. Notwithstanding jurors' predisposition to favor individuals over corporations and mid-sized organizations across most litigation types, jurors almost automatically integrate their extremely positive perceptions of individual inventors with individual plaintiffs who can tell a reasonable invention story. When asked to describe their impressions of individual inventors in patent suits, mock jurors consistently use positive terms such as inventor, hardworking, honorable, dedicated, knowledgeable, and smart. Jurors glamorize individual litigants by combining known characteristics about the individual with the imagined characteristics derived from their expectations of the American inventor. Despite the clear power of the individual litigant, and the individual patent-holding inventor in particular, individuals do not always prevail in litigation against corporations. And clearly, today's patent litigation landscape is dominated by practicing entities and NPEs much more than individual inventors.

B. The Importance of Initiating the Action

Do jurors care about the type of party that initiated the lawsuit? Does being a plaintiff provide an advantage over being a defendant? According to some statistics, individuals acquire about 15% of patents issued each year and initiate

---

21. Richard A. Posner, *Why There Are Too Many Patents in America*, ATLANTIC (July 12, 2012), http://www.theatlantic.com/business/archive/2012/07/why-there-are-too-many-patents-in-america/259725/.

22. Kimberly A. Moore, *Populism and Patents*, 82 N.Y.U. L. REV. 1 (2007).

12% or less of patent lawsuits, and individual patentees are involved in just 7% of actual patent trials.[23] On the other hand, corporations or assignees own approximately 85% of patents and initiate as many as 88% of lawsuits.[24] For jurors, the value of initiating the lawsuit lies in one party's ability to position itself as the harmed party instead of defending against claims that it caused harm. Make no mistake, jurors appreciate the difference.

While there are certainly cases in which a defendant can make a strong claim that it has suffered harm, jurors consider which party initiated the lawsuit in order to determine which party may be "fighting to protect its rights"—a phrase that many mock jurors have used to describe patent plaintiffs whether they are corporations or individuals. Statistics also demonstrate the small but clear advantage to being a plaintiff, with both individual and corporate plaintiffs enjoying slightly greater proportions of trial wins regardless of the type of defendant (individual or corporate) they are suing.[25]

Lex Machina's *Patent Litigation Report 2022* identifies the most common trial finding from 2019 to 2021 as a finding for plaintiffs of *no* invalidity (34% of all findings), followed closely by a finding of infringement (30% of all findings).[26]

C. The Advantage of Patent Holding: Inventors and Patent Assignees

Getting a patent for invention today is difficult

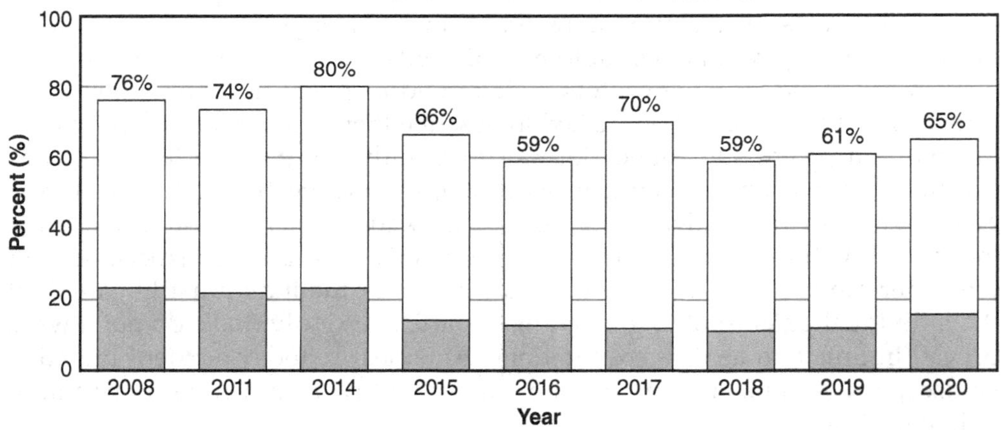

Source: Persuasion Strategies Big Jury, 2008–2020 (N=3,634)

Patentees hold a considerable advantage in statistics on how patent infringement lawsuits are resolved. For some historical context, Law Professor and Chief Judge at the U.S. Court of Appeals for the Federal Circuit Kimberly Moore found that from 1990 to 2003, patentees enjoyed a 52% win rate in bench trials and a 65% win rate in jury trials regardless of the type of defendant. That win rate increased

23. *Id.*
24. *Id.*
25. *Id.*
26. *See* Lex Machina, *supra* note 9.

to 78% when the individual patentee faced a corporate defendant.[27] In the same study, Judge Moore concluded that patentees are significantly more likely to win when three conditions are present: (1) patentee is the plaintiff; (2) patentee is an individual; and (3) the accused infringer is foreign.

More recent statistics show an even greater advantage for patentees in jury trials and bench trials. From 2006 through 2011, patent holders won about 76% of jury trials and 59% of bench trials going to verdict, with a median damages award of about $8.7 million in jury verdicts.[28]

From 2013 to 2017, a growing proportion of trials were heard by juries (77%) and patent holder win rates remained high at approximately 74%, compared to 52% with judges in that same time period.[29] One thing is clear: juries are more likely than federal judges to find in favor of patentees and that trend has been consistent for a few decades.

Jurors clearly favor the story of the individual inventor, but how do jurors' perceptions change when the invention is developed by a group of inventors? Yet again, Judge Moore's analysis is helpful:

> The lower the number of inventors, the more likely the patentee is to win with a jury. Juries like the image of the solitary inventor toiling away at a problem. The idea of teams of people working together on a solution is not as appealing. Even when a corporation owns the patent, the patentee is more likely to win if a solo inventor rather than a team invented the technology at issue.[30]

The patentee advantage is clear and powerful when the patent holder is an individual, but the advantage is substantial for other patentees as well. In PwC's *2018 Patent Litigation Study*, the win rates in jury trials from 1998–2017 for practicing entities (76%) and NPEs (72%) were nearly indistinguishable. [31]Some jurors also clearly believe that assignees have and deserve the same rights to an acquired patent as an original patentee. But they also expect the assignee to live up to the responsibilities that come with ownership.

> *"Just because you didn't start something doesn't mean you're not equally responsible if you climb on board."*
>
> —Patent mock juror

This juror sentiment applies directly to the rising number of assignees and entities that do not develop or, in many instances, do not practice patents involved in patent disputes.

---

27. Moore, *supra* note 22.

28. PwC, 2012 Patent Litigation Study (2012), https://patentlyo.com/media/docs/2013/03/2012-patent-litigation-study.pdf.

29. Landan Ansell et al., PwC, 2018 Patent Litigation Study (2018), https://ipwatchdog.com/wp-content/uploads/2018/09/2018-pwc-patent-litigation-study.pdf.

30. *See* Moore, *supra* note 22, at 46.

31. PwC, 2018 Patent Litigation Study (2018), https://www.ipwatchdog.com/wp-content/uploads/2018/09/2018-pwc-patent-litigation-study.pdf.

D. The Influence of NPEs

"Something I discovered the first time I came [to Congress] is that I am a troll, that a troll is someone who does not build and sell a product. That term has been replaced by a new phrase—NPE. I am not sure if that is a step up or down but I think that I am one of those too."[32]

—Dean Kamen, entrepreneur and inventor

There has been widespread discussion in the patent litigation community regarding the impressions and influence of NPEs (sometimes called patent "trolls")—patent-owning entities that neither invent nor "practice" the technology of their patents. Attorneys have spoken, authors have written, even judges have acted in response to NPEs. Patent filings data from 2019 to 2021 shows two NPEs[33] are by far the most active litigants, filing two to 3.5 more suits than any other party in the top ten.[34] NPEs mean business.

On average, all litigated patents contain more claims, cite more prior art, are cited more often in future patents, and result in more continuation applications. According to John Allison and colleagues, "The most-litigated patents have more than 50% more claims," and "cite nearly three times as many U.S. and foreign patents" and "nearly ten times as many nonpatent prior art references as other litigated patents."[35] NPEs bring a substantially greater number of defendants into litigation, a factor tracked by various analytics. For instance, data shows a peak of patent defendants in 2011–2012 just prior to the America Invents Act and a general decline in total defendants until 2018, when defendants in NPE-initiated patent litigation started a gentle increase that extended into 2021.[34] Overall, data shows a disproportionate and steady input of defendants brought by NPE-initiated lawsuits and a significant impact on patent litigation trends more broadly. Some analysis revealed an uptick in NPE activity during the COVID-19 pandemic and a shift toward litigation financing has helped maintain high risk for defendants into 2021 and 2022.[36]

"The most pronounced changes in the long-term litigation trends have been almost entirely driven by the behavior of NPE plaintiffs."

—RPX Insight

---

32. *Quoted in* Hayden W. Gregory, *Trawling for Trolls*, LANDSLIDE, July/Aug. 2009, at 1. Dean Kamen's comments came during his April 30, 2009, testimony to Congress on patent reform.

33. IP Edge LLC and WSOU Investments, LLC.

34. *See* LEX MACHINA, *supra* note 9.

35. John R. Allison et al., *Extreme Value or Trolls on Top? The Characteristics of the Most-Litigated Patents*, 158. U. PA. L. REV. 1 (2009).

36. *See What 15 Years of US Patent Litigation Data Reveal About the IP Market*, RPX EMPOWER (Jan. 25, 2021), https://insight.rpxcorp.com/news/65081-what-15-years-of-us-patent-litigation-data-reveal-about-the-ip-market.

So, what do jurors think about NPEs? Jurors are not nearly as concerned with a non-practicing status as are many patent litigators. In our *current* experience, whether a patent holder is a practicing entity or NPE is not what drives most jurors' decision-making.

While NPEs' influence on the patent system has been debated by the Patent Bar, and has shifted and become more nuanced with time, most jurors lack the context to understand what role, if any, NPEs play in the patent system, or even if their existence is anything but normal. Data from patent trials between 1995 and 2011 shows that patent-holding NPEs and practicing entities have a similar success rate at trial—both winning about two-thirds of trials.[37] Time spent trying to make jurors understand the context of an NPE may well be time wasted. However, an NPE's impact on juror perceptions is certainly worth testing in a mock trial. If a litigant's status as an NPE is truly important for the jury to contemplate, make sure the fact that the NPE does not practice the patent(s) is relevant to the jury's task and is not simply an unrelated (and presumed negative) fact you want jurors to consider as a reason to find in your favor. Jurors can appreciate the contrast:

> *"Clearly, [the accused infringer] is doing something beneficial for society, and not just buying up patents so that they can sue their competitors who are actually creating items that work."*
>
> —Patent mock juror

Regardless, as counsel for an NPE, there is still great utility in helping jurors understand the value of the protected innovation. This can and often should mean focusing on the inventor and the invention story to help motivate jurors to see excitement and innovation as something to protect more generally and, in the instant, aligning jurors with the NPE's role in trial. In many instances, the value of protecting innovation more generally is more salient to jurors than whether the patent holder is currently practicing or not. Helping jurors see the value of the patent, and thus the logic in taking an active step to enforce it, is logic jurors can support.

NPEs should also be mindful of the dominant narratives that can matter most to jurors, those dominant themes that overshadow practicing status. As discussed in other parts of this book, the question of, "Who was first?" is often a powerful question that guides jurors' perceptions, and NPEs can certainly leverage a narrative that focuses on the "untouchables" of primacy, quality, benefits, and overall value as dominant values that drive stories jurors will enforce in deliberations regardless of whether the patent holder is an NPE or not.

As counsel opposing an NPE, you might introduce the fact that the NPE does not develop its own patents, nor does it conduct its own research, by highlighting exactly how a practicing entity would have researched and developed a patentable idea. To be clear, this contrast alone does not make the distinction

37. *See* PwC, *supra* note 28.

relevant to jurors. They need to know how a practicing entity's research and development contributes to the trial story (and, by contrast, how it affects the NPE's trial story and the decisions that accompany it). For instance, if the practicing entity/accused infringer is able to show jurors how its ongoing research and ingenuity leads to recurring value and innovation in the form of new ideas and products that benefit consumers and society, *and* are related to the product- or patent-in-suit, the relevance is obvious and the distinction between a practicing entity and NPE becomes concrete. Jurors can believe the differences when they see them with their eyes—comparisons of the related product lines or "brother" and "sister" innovations that may stem from the initial innovation but are the product of hard work, resources, and additional research that comes with being a practicing business that develops and sells products.

E. Corporations and Their Offspring

> *"[Big companies] need to know they can't get away with it. They get away with it too often, any chance they get, and I'm sure they'll try it again."*
>
> —Patent mock juror

The overwhelming majority (85%) of patent disputes in past patent trials involved corporations suing other corporations. Of the remaining suits, 11% involved an individual suing a corporation, leaving just under 5% of all patent cases involving an individual as the defendant.[38] Analysis of "high-tech" patent cases in district court from 2000 through 2008 shows that 76% of all suits were brought by public or private corporations (not including NPEs).[39] Corporate litigants are the norm, and the data proves that corporate defendants face some substantial challenges.

Corporate defendants face an immediate burden given many jurors' perception that an easy case exists against them—accused infringers are thieves with resources and profit motive. Many jurors see them as faceless corporations that employ research and development teams the size of small cities. And when they cannot solve the problem themselves, jurors often conclude, they buy the solutions and innovations they did not create and have no right to own.

So, what happens when jurors apply anti-corporate bias and pro-patentee bias to the same corporate plaintiff in a patent dispute? Corporate patent owners win 50% of jury trials against an individual.[40] So, for a corporate patentee plaintiff, the punch-power of patentee bias weighs against typical anti-corporate bias to create substantially greater balance than when an individual patent-holding

38. *See* Moore, *supra* note 22.

39. Colleen Chien, *Of Trolls, Davids, Goliaths, and Kings: Narratives and Evidence in the Litigation of High-Tech Patents*, 87 N.C. L. Rev. 1571 (2009). "High-tech" patents were defined as those involving hardware, software, or financial patents as classified by the USPTO and coded by the Intellectual Property Litigation Clearinghouse.

40. *See* Moore, *supra* note 22.

inventor sues a corporation for infringement. It is important to recognize that the advantages of juror perceptions are by no means exclusive to individuals. Corporate patent owners benefit greatly by taking advantage of some of the basic case narrative characteristics that give patentees a head start. For example:

1. Tell a compelling invention and development story that focuses on human protagonists.
2. Demonstrate the dollars and dedication invested to secure the patent through the highly credible USPTO.
3. Demonstrate the individual and collective dedication to innovation and increased public access to cutting-edge advancements.
4. Embrace the profit motive behind being a competitive and innovative force in the relevant market in combination with the benefits it bestows on the consumer.

If plaintiff's counsel cannot or chooses not to openly apply negative labels to patent defendants, a handful of metaphors encourages jurors to apply a variety of negative labels. With just a little help from counsel, jurors frequently describe patent defendants as "opportunists" if not pirates, thieves, or parasites. However, as patent-as-a-business-strategy and predatory lawsuits have evolved and become more common, jurors are more likely to perceive a corporate litigant as going beyond its right to protect its property, and instead preying unfairly on its competition—a fine line to walk with a jury.

Corporate defendants must respond to these juror perceptions by demonstrating the good-faith work they performed to achieve success. Ideally, corporate defendants can tell the story of their own idea development and discuss relevant patents other than the patent-in-suit to help jurors perceive them as innovators working to provide new ideas and products to the marketplace. See Chapter 6 for more detailed recommendations focusing specifically on trial strategies for infringement claims.

IV. Patent Juries' Unique Challenges

A. Patents Inherently Involve Technical and Difficult Concepts

> *"To be sure, patent litigation almost inevitably involves science or technical arts. So if you are allergic to chemical equations, frightened by mechanical specifications, or feel that computer circuitry is the work of the devil, you may not want to don your pocket protector and venture into the world of patent litigation."*[41]
>
> —Thomas Selby, patent attorney

Many patent infringement trials involve the difficult combination of innovative technology and technical detail. Software and telecommunications were two of

41. Thomas Selby, *A Primer on Litigating Patent Infringement Claims*, 34 Litigation 15 (2007).

the most likely technology areas of the most frequently litigated patents from 2000 to 2007, with nearly 75% of the most litigated patents being software patents.[42] They are also two of the most prolific and evolving industries.

Two integral parts of a patent dispute—the patented invention and the patent itself—supply an overwhelming majority of the complexity and difficulty that jurors face in a typical patent trial. Consider the invention itself—a medical device, for instance. The device may have "membranes" and "filters" that interact with a tiny "pump." Devices often include novel technology unfamiliar to anyone outside the art. Jurors lack the basic framework for understanding the form, function, and interaction of the relevant pieces and need basic building blocks to develop an understanding from the bottom up. Jurors not only fail to grasp the specific parts that make up the claimed invention; they often fail to understand the way the parts work together to create a whole. You must give them the building blocks they need to understand your case.

To further add to jurors' intimidation, patents are complex documents requiring structural comprehension and jargon translation. It takes experience and expertise to interpret correctly and understand the entire document, at least in part because of patent law's dynamic terms and definitions, unique processes, and special persuasive challenges. To jurors, patents are a foreign country where an unfamiliar structure and unknown language are not only meaningless but serve as a source of confusion and frustration. Jurors hear that patents have specifications, embodiments, claim elements, references, and prior art. But they look at the patent and see little more than the USPTO's seal of approval and the paper upon which it is printed. Much of the rest sails over their heads at cloud level, in part because many fail to see the need to drop below the 36,000-foot level to answer the basic questions of infringement and invalidity. While you may address these questions weekly in your work life, most jurors live a lifetime without ever considering the same questions. Jurors would much rather focus on the *behavior* in the case—on the invention story and the people behind the story, and that is where their focus typically begins.

> *"I don't know anything about patents and I don't know anything about patent infringement. . . . I just felt like the Defendant was hiding stuff."*
>
> —Patent juror

The details of an invention are familiar and often elementary to the inventor steeped in its technology and art, as is the patent jargon to the attorney trained to interpret and deconstruct patents. Many times attorneys become so steeped in the claim language that they lose the ability to talk in simple terms about what it is and how it works. Inventors and attorneys have landed in their chosen professions for a reason and fare quite well on their own turf. But jurors do not get to choose where they sit for jury service. They do not get to choose the type of case they will hear. Considering the fact that the majority of Americans

---

42. *See* Allison et al., *supra* note 35.

have less than a college education and rarely have experience, let alone specialized training, in technical arts or advanced technology, the complexities of most patent lawsuits are a passively acknowledged but often underestimated obstacle.[43] Jurors have trouble comprehending many elements of the typical patent trial, with the technicalities of the patented invention and the patent itself being primary sources of the problem.

B. Patent Juries Do Their Job Well

We provide our strategic advice knowing you are reading this book with the goal of becoming more persuasive in front of judges and juries. In spite of the general findings that juries are more pro-patentee and tend to award higher damages than judges, the effects are not as extreme as you might think. So do not get the wrong idea about civil juries. They are competently fulfilling their civic duty and delivering justice. Despite criticism based on extreme examples of jury behavior and verdicts, our private research and experience give us great confidence in the American jury, specifically when a litigating attorney takes seriously his or her obligation to teach simply and effectively at trial.

Bench trials or trials before blue-ribbon panels comprising experts in the technology related to the patent-in-suit may result in improvement to today's patent jury system. As jury researcher Neil Vidmar points out regarding the jury system more broadly, however, we have "some reason to suspect that the combined judgments of jurors, enhanced through the deliberation process, may be as good or better than those that would be rendered by a randomly selected judge."[44] This is a true statement in complex cases where "jury verdicts are often defensible when examined against the evidence produced at trial."[45] Other recent conclusions are even more confident in jury performance, claiming, "Our verdict is strongly in favor of the American jury."[46] You will encounter outlying decision makers, but by and large, research and our own experience consistently suggest that the patent jury is doing its best with what you are able to put in front of them.

V. The Takeaway

A. The Future of Patent Trials

Beginning in the 1980s and lasting more than two decades, patent applications, patent grants, and patent lawsuit filings were consistently on the increase. Then, patent applications flattened and patent lawsuit filings decreased just

43. *See* Press Release, U.S. Census Bureau, Census Bureau Releases New Educational Attainment Data (Feb. 24, 2022).

44. *See* Neil Vidmar & Valerie P. Hans, American Juries: The Verdict 346 (2007).

45. *Id.*

46. *Id.*

before the full impact of the economic recession in 2008.[47] Companies tightened their belts to survive the recession, and budget cuts as large as 20% restricted activity, including patent lawsuit activity, with the major plunge in lawsuit filings occurring in the last five months of 2008.[48] But the downward trend was short-lived, with the number of issued patents increasing by 23% from 2009 to 2010 and another 5% from 2010 to 2011.[49] Total patent litigation then peaked in 2011–2012, cutting in half since that peak by 2019, then bumped again in 2020 and 2021, with patent lawsuit filings rising in both 2020 and 2021 but still well below the 2012 peak. District court filings continue to concentrate in a small number of venues, focused on the Texas jurisdictions in the Eastern and Western Districts as well as the District of Delaware, a perennial patent docket for many years.

What is next for patent litigants? Changes to practices in the Western District of Texas in July 2022 almost immediately led to reduced filings in that venue, with corresponding increases in the District of Delaware but also other venues, suggesting there may be some initiative to continue to share patent litigation among at least some number of district court jurisdictions.

B. Your Patent Persuasion Challenge

Simple, clear, and persuasive communication is paramount in patent litigation. Jurors need every bit of their attention engaged in patent trials. Most patent cases place exceptional demands on the civil justice system, including the attorneys, the court, parties involved, and certainly jurors. The costs of litigating a patent case are significant and increasing every day, with upwards of $5.5 million for a single party to take a $25 million patent infringement suit to trial in 2009.[50] The courts have felt the pressure too, with a greater proportion of cases going to jury trial—particularly in seven patent-laden jurisdictions where more than half of all patent cases are filed, including the well-known Western and Eastern Districts of Texas, District of Delaware, Central District of California, and Northern District of Illinois.[51] While the locations of these patent-rich dockets are likely to shift with time, it is clear that some districts will continue to absorb the court's burdens.

Litigators labor over massive amounts of data over months or even years of discovery and depositions, then face a trial docket that allows only a handful

---

47. See USPTO patent statistics from 1963 to 2009, summarized in Dennis Crouch, *Counting Defendants in Patent Litigation*, PATENTLY-O (Oct. 27, 2010), http://www.patentlyo.com/patent/2010/10/guest-post-counting-defendants-in-patent-litigation.html. Generally speaking, patent lawsuit filings began to decrease slightly in 2008 and continued to decrease slightly in 2009 and 2010. Patent grants are on the rise since 2008.

48. *See* Amanda Bronstad, *Patent Infringement Filings Take a Nosedive*, NAT'L L.J. (Jan. 19, 2009), https://www.law.com/nationallawjournal/almID/1202427537496/.

49. *See* PwC, *supra* note 28.

50. *See* AMERICAN INTELLECTUAL PROPERTY LAW ASSOCIATION, AIPLA 2009 REPORT OF THE ECONOMIC SURVEY (2009).

51. *See* PATSTATS: U.S. PATENT LITIGATION STATISTICS, *supra* note 15. This also includes the District of New Jersey and Southern District of New York.

of days to distill years of work into a palatable story. Making the case comprehensible is a challenge at many levels. But in the end, patent trials are about jurors, about how they make decisions based on the information provided and absorbed. Mock jurors in our private research consistently struggle with complexity and damages in patent cases and express sincere appreciation for the attorney who communicates clearly and makes certain that jurors can grasp the key issues upon which her side's argument depends. Communication is key to persuasion, and in no type of litigation is effective communication more elusive than in patent infringement litigation.

We know that juries can and do perform well when attorneys enable them to do so. We see them deliberate meaningfully in our private research, and academic research bears out their ability to comprehend complex issues as well. Scholars have considered jury performance in complex civil cases, including patent cases, and while jury performance is not perfect, reforms such as note-taking and pre-instruction facilitate comprehension and legal accuracy in more complicated scenarios.[52] Even in lieu of these reforms, you can provide jurors the guidance they need to do their job: clear comprehension of the tiebreaker issues through simple and persuasive advocacy. This book gives you concrete pointers on more effectively persuading your jury and other fact finders.

---

52. *See* Kenneth S. Bordens & Irwin A. Horowitz, *Mass Tort Civil Litigation: The Impact of Procedural Changes on Jury Decisions*, 73 JUDICATURE 22 (1989).

CHAPTER 5

Jury Selection

"The most important criteria for a juror in a patent case is that he or she be interested in the case."[1]

—Hon. Roderick R. McKelvie (ret.)

Adequate oral voir dire time is a rare luxury in most federal trial court venues, especially when it is the attorneys' turn to address prospective jurors. As the typical patent case continues to increase in information complexity, you need to unearth high-risk jurors with less voir dire time—or, in many instances, without any attorney-conducted oral voir dire at all. A competing duality of high-risk juror characteristics in typical patent cases involving both infringement and patent invalidity claims only further complicates your jury selection efforts. A risky juror for a plaintiff's patent infringement claim may possess the precise profile characteristics the same plaintiff's attorney finds desirable for her validity case. This duality is yet another reason patent jurors and patent litigation are unique, and another reason to thoughtfully invest in a jury selection strategy that includes developing a case-specific, high-risk juror profile and carefully crafting a jury selection strategy to wisely use your preciously narrow time.

As is the case with many time-sensitive tasks, doing an effective job with less information typically requires more effort and focus in preparation. Unfortunately, jury selection is often one of the last things litigators prepare before trial. It is an overwhelming challenge to identify the right criteria for deselecting high-risk jurors, to develop the most efficient and effective gathering of information, including what oral voir dire questions to ask (and submit to the judge), and to have a plan for what to do with prospective jurors' voir dire responses. A systematic approach provides structure and confidence in jury selection—a map for repeating what works and refining what has not worked in the past.

1. Personal Communication with Hon. Roderick McKelvie (2011).

Four Steps to Effective Patent Jury Selection

I. Identify Your Opponent's Stronger Case
II. Develop a High-Risk Juror Profile
III. Make the Most of Judge-Conducted Oral Voir Dire and Supplemental Juror Questionnaires
IV. Deliver an Effective Three-Part Oral Voir Dire

Though it may seem counterintuitive, begin with a thorough evaluation of your opponent's strongest claim in the case. Different types of jurors will be more high-risk depending on whether the focus of the case is more squarely on claims of validity/invalidity or on infringement/noninfringement. It is critical to identify your opponent's strongest appeals, and which juror characteristics are most salient and influential to *their* case, and therefore most salient and influential to your case. Then, develop a complete profile of the juror characteristics that translate into a predisposition or outright bias against your case. Use this profile to develop case-specific, high-risk criteria to help you identify the potential jurors who begin the case with an unfavorable view of your case or client. While it may be tempting to begin with a profile of the juror who is best for your case, the reality remains that voir dire gives you less control over keeping that ideal juror. Rather, it is a process of eliminating the few jurors who are most high-risk for your case. It is critical to develop a high-risk juror profile that specifically feeds your ability to make the difficult choices in jury selection. Use the profile to identify the information you need to gather in oral voir dire and with a supplemental juror questionnaire (whenever possible).

Create two sets of tailored oral voir dire questions. First, develop a set to submit for judge-conducted voir dire, and second, create a set to deliver in your oral voir dire time (assuming you are allowed to question the panel). Ideally, questions from the court and counsel should work in tandem with a supplemental juror questionnaire so that each of the three sources provides independent and valuable information. Evaluate the intelligence you are able to gather according to your high-risk criteria and make informed cause challenges and peremptory strikes. It sounds so easy on paper. Let us look at a more specific method for getting there.

I. Identify Your Opponent's Stronger Case

You have undoubtedly considered the juror characteristics that can translate into bias in patent trials, but perhaps without fully considering the dynamics that make patent jurors unique. Think for a moment about your most recent jury selection in a patent case. Think specifically about the juror who worried you most just before you exercised your peremptory strikes. They are most likely different from the juror who would cause the greatest concern for counsel trying a run-of-the-mill commercial litigation case for the same client—especially if you represent an accused infringer and your strongest facts are for patent invalidity. The complex tensions of a typical patent infringement defense (noninfringement) and an assertion of patent invalidity trigger a key complexity in evaluating high-risk jurors for parties in patent trials. The reality is that a juror who is likely to be biased in favor of patent infringement may also be the same juror who will most favor arguments for patent invalidity. Understanding this tension and how your opponent's stronger case relates to the most influential juror characteristics determines key aspects of your jury selection strategy.

To cite a specific example, a sophisticated and fiscally conservative juror who is willing to listen to and evaluate the details of an accused infringer's noninfringement defense, including the independent invention story, is not necessarily the same juror you can persuade with an assertion of patent invalidity. How can you discover which bias is most powerful and most important in a given case? How should you weigh the balance of risky factors and contrasting claims to make the best choice for your client in jury selection? How can you identify your opponent's strongest claims in order to make the best jury selection decisions? It starts with understanding the predominant factors that interrelate to influence how individual jurors perceive typical issues in a patent infringement dispute.

A. Understand the Risky Juror Tension

An outspoken juror in the *Camera Anywhere Co. v. BigPhone Corp.* case (see brief description of the example dispute in Appendix A) vehemently argues in favor of the patent-in-suit's validity, saying, "A patented nine-lens camera does something new and non-obvious, something never done before that warrants protection!" His speech persuades a few fellow jurors and helps steer a free-thinking jury to a verdict decision that the patent is valid. In his next breath, the same juror articulates a clear and persuasive reason the defendant has not infringed the same mobile phone camera patent: "The defendant company made something totally different." As a patentee plaintiff, you love this juror for your validity case, but he disarms and destroys your infringement case in a single stroke. Without him, the same jury may find the patent *invalid*. Should you strike him in jury selection? How could you when you are confident he will support your patent?

Many experienced litigators and trial consultants fail to recognize the importance of the risky juror tension in patent trials. Jurors likely to be open to your position in one part of your case may be extremely risky for another part. The need to address two different and opposing biases within the same individual juror is pervasive, and often more complicated, in patent trials than it is in other types of litigation. As counsel for an accused infringer, understand that noninfringement jurors do not necessarily have the same profile as invalidity jurors—those willing to believe a patent is invalid. As a patentee plaintiff, the patent infringement profile can contrast with the patent validity profile. You must anticipate in advance whether patent infringement or patent validity will be the most disputed claim in the case. So, what can you do to protect your client in jury selection?

First, consider six salient elements contributing to the tension in juror predispositions applied to a typical patent case.

Six Key Elements of Patent Juror Tension

1. Behavioral Orientation
2. Views of the Role of Government
3. Views of Competition in Business
4. Perceptions of the U.S. Patent and Trademark Office
5. Decision-Making Orientation
6. Dominant Perceptual Filter

1. Behavioral Orientation

> *"It would be based on my personal morals, and I would not want my corporation to be rude ever . . . my integrity would be the paramount decision-maker."*
>
> —Patent mock juror who favored the accused infringer

Every juror, no matter their background or capability, is qualified to evaluate human *behavior*. In complex fact scenarios *nothing* matters more to jurors than finding a way to cut through the difficulty and evaluate what they feel really happened—what did the people in the story *do*? Who was dishonest or manipulative? Was someone naïve or unaware? Who acted like a credible professional? Who behaved more like a child, or worse, a villain? This filter of evaluating the parties' *behavior* through the actions of the individual people is a dominant way for patent jurors to feel good about their evaluation of the case even when they cannot or do not understand or engage directly with the technical or factual evidence. It is our experience that if you cannot win the "behavior case" in patent litigation, you cannot win.

Analysis of a few mock jury studies conducted in 2023 illustrates this point, particularly when looking at mock jurors' self-reported level of tech savvy (aka perceived technical skill) and their overall leanings in mock trial studies. This summary demonstrates that "very tech savvy" jurors leaned in favor of the patentee 27% of the time in contrast with "not very tech savvy" jurors who leaned in favor of the patentee 52% of the time.

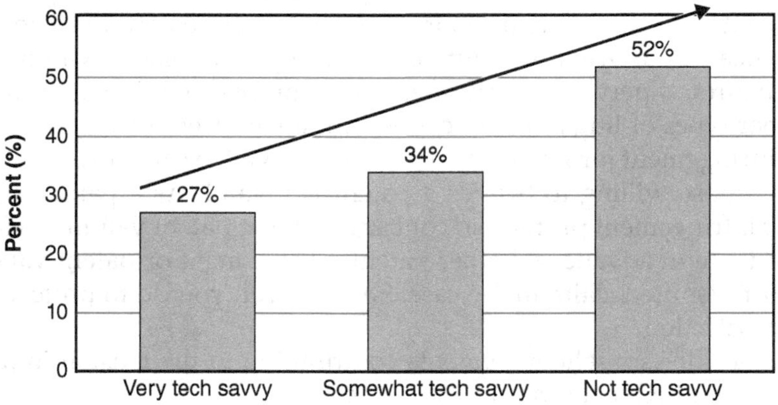

Source: 2023 Mock Jury Research Studies (N=101) in the Eastern District of Texas, Northern District of California, and District of Delaware

We see this trend across cases, mock and actual, where jurors with greater technical acumen and an ability to evaluate the detailed evidence tend to rely less on the parties' *behavior* and tend to favor accused infringers at a higher rate. At the same time, jurors oriented less toward the technical and more toward evaluating the human behavior at the core of the events tend to side more frequently with patentee plaintiffs' infringement claims. When it comes to evaluating patent validity, those same jurors oriented more toward human behavior will value evidence of human choices that may affect patent holders' credibility, including:

- Did the patent holder withhold relevant prior art from the U.S. Patent and Trademark Office (USPTO) during patent prosecution?
- Did the patent holder fairly identify the most relevant and not just the most helpful types of prior art?
- Did the patent holder reveal a clear and compelling story of innovation?
- Does the patent holder occupy a novel or innovative space in the industry?

Examples of the Tension in High-Risk Patent Jurors

	Pro-Noninfringement Juror	Pro-Invalidity Juror
Behavioral Orientation	Behavior in context Technical data matters more	Behavior as primary Technical data matters less

2. Views of the Role of Government

Jurors' views of the government factor into their case views. The jury-eligible public is divided in its beliefs about how active our federal government should be in our lives and solving the nation's problems. According to a 2021 Gallup poll, 43% of Americans surveyed felt the government should do more to solve the nation's problems while 52% said the government is trying to do too many things.[2] These views track historical views going back to the year 2000, with the exception of 2020 when a majority favored the government doing more to solve problems—a direct response to the COVID-19 pandemic. Not surprisingly, views of the role of government are correlated with a variety of potential juror characteristics, including political ideology, political party, and more.

For instance, in the Gallup survey, 78% of Democrats said the federal government should be doing more to solve the nation's problems, while just 15% of Republicans said the same. Fully 54% of surveyed Americans said the federal government had too much power in 2021 while only 9% said the government had too little power. Again, considering political party as it pertains to the federal government's regulation of American business, 72% of Republicans said the government is regulating business too much while just 11% of Democrats said the same.[3] Interestingly, a 2024 Pew Research Center survey showed white Americans reported less trust in government to do what is right than other

2. Jeffrey M. Jones, *Americans Revert to Favoring Reduced Government Role*, GALLUP (Oct. 14, 2021), https://news.gallup.com/poll/355838/americans-revert-favoring-reduced-government-role.aspx.
3. *Id.*

ethnic groups. In that survey, just 19% of whites, 27% of people who identify as Black, and 36% and 30% of Asian and Hispanic respondents said they trust the government to do what is right "just about always" or "most of the time."[4]

In a typical patent case with infringement claims and invalidity defenses, potential jurors' views of government—should it be active and large or small and laissez-faire—frequently play a significant role in how jurors view the case issues. In our private jury research, mock jurors' preferences regarding the role of the government influence perceptions of the patent process, while trust in the federal government often translates to trust in the patent process and in the patent examiners, who play an important role in issuing patents. On the other hand, mock jurors who favor a more limited government may approve of an accused infringer's approach to developing a product that works (and helps the consumer) in spite of "rules" laid down by a federal agency in which individual jurors have diminished trust and to which they feel little loyalty.

Potential jurors who favor smaller government are more likely to be politically and fiscally conservative, pro-corporate, pro-capitalist, pro-competition in business, and members of the Republican party.[5] These characteristics, and their counterparts in those who favor big government, are key to how jurors view the salient issues in a patent trial, where perceptions of competition and corporate involvement in business often predominate.

Examples of the Tension in High-Risk Patent Jurors

	Pro-Noninfringement Juror	Pro-Invalidity Juror
Views of the Role of Government	Small	Big
	Hands-off	Active
	Conservative views	Trust liberal views

3. *Views of Competition in Business*

> *"A lot of it is the way they're managing their company. They're not aggressive enough and there is competition out there going after their business. If we have to, we'll bring you to court instead of working on [our] own research and development and bringing [our] own product up to par. I think they probably could have stayed in the game better."*
>
> —Patent mock juror who favored accused infringer

Jury-eligible Americans have a range of tolerances for fair and just competition in the business world. According to years of national research we conducted as trial consultants, about two-thirds of potential jurors believe patents somewhat help or strongly help competition. While some jurors are comfortable with extremely aggressive competition in which individuals and businesses assert

4. *Public Trust in Government: 1958–2024*, Pew Rsch. Ctr. (June 24, 2024), https://www.pewresearch.org/politics/2024/06/24/public-trust-in-government-1958-2024/.

5. *See* Jones, *supra* note 2.

the freedom to pursue what is best for the consumer, other jurors are far more comfortable with business competition that is regulated to maintain balance and fairness among industry competitors. The role of the patent is bound up in these views. For some, the patent embodies aggressive competition in a positive way that biases them toward the patentee. To them, the patent is the finish line in a race for the newest and best technological innovation—with "firstness" being a common shortcut jurors use to help determine who is most deserving of protection. For others, the patent process represents a threat to open competition by restricting what competitors can legally do to aggressively compete in the marketplace, making those jurors more likely to support the accused infringer.

Also integrated into jurors' views of business competition is the effect competition has on American consumers. Some jurors balance the benefits of big business with its positive consequences for consumers (e.g., cheaper prices, greater product availability, etc.), while others believe the consumer's ability to have unfettered options and a market that encourages low prices should always win out. Identifying potential jurors' views of business and how they relate to the dominant facts in your case is another important part of understanding how juror attitudes will affect decision-making.

Examples of the Tension in High-Risk Patent Jurors

	Pro-Noninfringement Juror	Pro-Invalidity Juror
Views of Competition in Business	Competition is beneficial Should be aggressive	Competition is necessary Should be fair

4. Perceptions of the U.S. Patent and Trademark Office

The jury-eligible public's perceptions of federal government have waxed and waned over time, with recent confidence in the federal government reaching an all-time low and remaining low in 2024, with just 22% of Americans—and 11% of Republicans—saying they trust the government to do what is right most of the time or just about always.[6] Based on our national research and various survey data, potential jurors consistently rate the USPTO favorably—particularly in relation to other federal agencies. Potential jurors consistently rate the USPTO highest among federal government agencies.[7]

Jurors struggle most with the decision to invalidate a patent they believe the USPTO thoroughly investigated, evaluated, tested, and eventually issued. Jurors openly question their own right to call the most highly rated agency's decisions into question.

"Part of the blame lies with the patent office. I mean, they say that they read and research all of these, but how many do they get every year? Five million?"

—Patent mock juror who favored the accused infringer

6. *Public Trust in Government: 1958–2024*, *supra* note 4.

7. See Chapter 1 for a graphic depiction of Persuasion Strategies National Juror Survey results showing potential juror ratings of federal government agencies.

Fellow litigation consultants Ellen Brickman and Julie Blackman have described their experience that mock jurors in patent cases "[focus] on the fact that the patent is a government-issued document, and have even suggested that such a document cannot be invalidated by ordinary citizens."[8] Identifying jurors who are more likely to feel and voice powerful deference to the USPTO is a key to understanding how jurors will view your arguments. At the same time, knowing which jurors are least likely to blindly accept the USPTO's stamp of approval is equally critical to anticipating how jurors will react to patentees' validity arguments.

Examples of the Tension in High-Risk Patent Jurors

	Pro-Noninfringement Juror	Pro-Invalidity Juror
Perceptions of the USPTO	Trust in government agencies Authoritarian	Distrust of government agencies Skeptical

5. Decision-Making Orientation

Jurors approach their role as verdict decision maker in two primary ways. They are either predominantly evidence-driven or predominantly verdict-driven.[9] Evidence-driven jurors are motivated to evaluate the strength and meaning of evidence and tend to make a decision only after vetting and discussing the case issues and corresponding evidence during deliberations.

a. Typical Evidence-Driven Decision-Making Process

In our exemplar mobile phone camera technology lawsuit (see brief description of the *Camera Anywhere Co. v. BigPhone Corp.* dispute in Appendix A), the plaintiff Camera Anywhere Co. purchased a patent for a nine-lens microcamera for use in mobile phones and contends that BigPhone Corp. is infringing that patent by manufacturing and selling an infringing product. In such a case, evidence-driven jurors strive to compare and contrast specific evidence showing infringement of the microcamera patent, evaluate evidence of similar or comparable elements in the allegedly infringing product, and are more likely to "dig in" to the details required to prove a technical or document-intensive defense. Only after this evaluation of evidence would their attention turn to the infringement verdict questions that must be resolved (and voted upon) to determine how the perceptions of evidence comport with an ultimate verdict decision.

We often see evidence-driven mock jurors focus other jurors on the testimony ("But remember what the inventor said on the stand"), documents ("Look at Exhibit F"), and associated arguments first, then apply their collective view of the story to the questions required for a verdict.

8. Ellen Brickman & Julie Blackman, *Intellectual Property Cases: Ten Lessons from Pre-Trial Research,* 24 Jury Expert 1 (2012), https://thejuryexpert.com/wp-content/uploads/01Brickman.pdf.

9. Reid Hastie et al., Inside the Jury (1983).

b. Typical Verdict-Driven Decision-Making Process

Verdict-driven jurors have a different decision-making orientation. A verdict-driven jury will poll early and often, favoring the most efficient decision-making process over a comprehensive hearing and discussion of the evidence. They typically identify and understand the ultimate questions that must be answered before determining a path to reach a verdict decision and before thoroughly considering the evidence.

Vocal jurors recharacterize verdict questions to comport with the more basic questions they believe need to be answered, changing a question of substantial equivalence to, "Was it pretty much the same?" or changing a more general infringement question to, "Did they copy his idea?" If the verdict-driven juror perceives immediate agreement on six of nine verdict questions, he or she may see no reason to discuss any evidence related to those six verdict issues and typically moves on to discuss only the evidence viewed as related to claims or questions as yet unresolved.

While a jury often contains both evidence-driven and verdict-driven jurors, a single preference will undoubtedly prevail. In many instances, an individual jury leader (foreperson or vocal juror) will persuade others to adopt the decision-making approach that most supports his or her verdict preference or, at a minimum, his or her decision-making orientation. If a persuasive jury leader views the evidence as strongly in favor of her preferred decision, she may push for a more evidence-focused approach to the group's decision-making process.

Examples of the Tension in High-Risk Patent Jurors

	Pro-Noninfringement Juror	Pro-Invalidity Juror
Decision-Making Orientation	Evidence-driven or Verdict-driven	Evidence-driven

6. Dominant Perceptual Filter

In our experience, mock jurors who perceive trial evidence through a logical filter typically evaluate persuasive appeals based on a rational test—what makes sense—both in understanding how individuals and parties responded to events as they occurred and in how the jury should make a decision about the facts. Often evidence-driven in their decision-making, logic-oriented jurors are typically willing to "dig in" to the details of both sides' positions and to think critically about the reasons evidence favors one side or the other. They are usually more methodical in their approach and comprehensive in their deliberation of the issues. They tend to be the voice of reason if other jurors are headed down a decision path not supported by a rational interpretation of the evidence.

Alternatively, mock jurors who perceive trial evidence through a values filter tend to weight the fairness of the outcome over a rational balancing of the evidence on either side. Values-driven jurors are more likely to argue from a "gut feeling" they get from the evidence, arguments, litigants, and presenting attorneys. Individual juror decision-making is often swift and can be more resistant to change, since the basis of a given juror's decision is less about critical thinking and rational analysis than it is about an overall feeling of what outcome is just. It can be difficult to change a gut feeling with rational argument.

Summary of the Tension in High-Risk Patent Jurors

	Pro-Noninfringement Juror	Pro-Invalidity Juror
Behavioral Orientation	Behavior in context Technical data matters more	Behavior as primary Technical data matters less
Views of the Role of Government	Small Hands-off Conservative views	Liberal views
Views of Competition in Business	Competition is beneficial Should be aggressive	Competition is necessary Should be fair
Perceptions of the USPTO	Trust in government agencies Authoritarian	Distrust of government agencies Skeptical
Decision-Making Orientation	Evidence-driven or Verdict-driven	Evidence-driven
Dominant Perceptual Filter	Logic or values	Logic

B. The High-Risk Juror Profile Prioritizes Risk

It takes a systematic approach to consistently identify high-risk jurors and remove them from the panel. The duality previously described does not simplify the matter. You need to know what you are looking for and how it interacts with the strongest and weakest parts of your case and ask the right questions to discover the most useful information from each and every juror in the venire. That kind of systematic approach begins with a high-risk juror profile.

Every high-risk juror profile should focus first on prospective jurors' relevant attitudes and beliefs that might predispose them against your client. Why attitudes and beliefs first? Many trial attorneys' favorite question for litigation consultants goes something like this: "Do you think men or women will be best for us in this case?" It is well established that simple demographics are generally poor predictors of individual juror verdicts.[10] Fortunately, the strength of the evidence and other relevant factors can be strong predictors.[11] The way jurors interpret evidence is influenced to some extent by their demographics, somewhat more by their life experiences, and most significantly by their attitudes and beliefs. As the iceberg graphic at the end of this section depicts,

---

10. *See, e.g.*, Katherine V. Vinson et al., *Predictors of Verdict and Punitive Damages in High-Stakes Civil Litigation*, 26 Behav. Sci. & L. 167 (2008).

11. *See, e.g.*, Steve M. Wood et al., *The Influence of Jurors' Perceptions of Attorneys and Their Performance on Verdict*, 23 Jury Expert 23 (2011), https://thejuryexpert.com/wp-content/uploads/Woodetal.TJEJan2011Vol23Num1.pdf.

attitudes—case-specific and case-relevant attitudes in particular—are the most powerful and often the most underappreciated predictors of juror bias.

While demographics are a part of the analysis, attitudes are more powerful criteria for identifying jurors who pose the highest risk. We want to utilize every piece of available information, including demographics and the data that comes with them. The high-risk juror profile, however, focuses more on the attitudes and beliefs likely to levy the most influence on decisions.

Take a typical commercial litigation dispute as an example. Both sides are likely to focus on opposing aspects of the same juror characteristics or opposite sides of the same coin. For instance, in a contract dispute with an individual employee plaintiff and a large corporate employer defendant, both sides should be interested in juror attitudes about the importance of having and relying upon signed agreements. A juror's attitudes and beliefs about this important dimension may be enough to warrant a strike by either party. A juror who believes signed contracts are set in stone and supersede all oral or implied agreements could be risky for the plaintiff. A juror who believes signed contracts are meant to be amended by oral agreements and party behavior could be risky for the defendant. Two sides of the same coin.

The complexity of patent infringement claims (especially when combined with claims of patent invalidity) is only made increasingly complicated when cross-patent claims exist and accused infringers are asserting their own patents while attempting to invalidate their opponent's. Testing the case-specific issues is a critical step to developing a clear high-risk juror profile—the next step in making sure your approach to jury selection is thorough and complete.

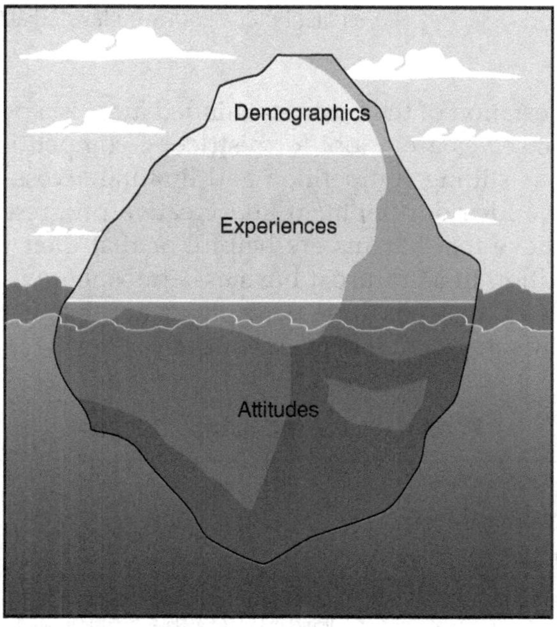

Credit: Nick Bouck

II. Develop a High-Risk Juror Profile

A. High-Risk Jurors for Patentee Plaintiffs

1. *Typical Thought Processes for High-Risk Jurors*

a. Business Is Business

"Competition! You've got to have competition in this world."

—Patent mock juror who favored accused infringer

Some jurors openly admit sympathy for a patentee plaintiff accusing another party of infringement—not for its losses and honorable attempt to protect its patent, but for assuming that business would be fair. This subset of jurors sees business as business, and not a place for the faint of heart. They are much less willing to view the patentee plaintiff's case through a lens of fair conduct and fair outcomes, focusing instead on the reality that a minority of businesses succeed, and those that do must be focused on what keeps them afloat rather than what keeps them from being perceived as unfair.

(1) Patents Stifle Competition

"I think that it keeps people down when you say 'no one else can have this idea' because you are going to run out of ideas."

—Patent mock juror who favored accused infringer

One specific manifestation of the business-minded juror is a perception that patents in and of themselves are a tool for restricting competition. A minority of jurors see patents as stifling competition and limiting access to the wide-open world of innovative idea development and creative progress. Persuading this set of jurors to believe that patents are helpful or that their predisposition for aggressive competition in a cutthroat business atmosphere is somehow off the mark is often difficult. Instead, these perceptions and biases translate into risk for patentee plaintiffs in patent infringement trials.

Perceptions of the Patent Process

The Patent Process:	
Helps Competition:	67%
Hurts Competition:	33%

Source: 2023 Mock Jury Research Studies (N=101) in the Eastern District of Texas, Northern District of California, and District of Delaware. Note: this data is highly consistent with years of national surveys showing about two-thirds of the jury-eligible population perceives patents as helpful to competition and about one-third perceives them as hurtful.

(2) Progress Means Building on Prior Innovation

The role of prior art and prior ideas is critical in patent infringement disputes. Most jurors will not have heard a term like "prior art" before sitting on a patent case. Yet they can understand it in simple but accurate terms. Jurors recognize prior art as what has been done before, but at least a subset of jurors will appreciate an accused infringer's ability to build upon what has been done and meet market needs in providing something that still qualifies as "new" in jurors' minds.

> *"I think that it would be way more advanced if there were not all these patents restricting people from getting creative and building on ideas."*
>
> —Patent mock juror who favored accused infringer

For obvious reasons, patentee plaintiffs should be wary of potential jurors who admit to a belief that progress almost always requires building on prior innovation as opposed to completely novel ideas. While it certainly depends on the facts of the case, this subset of potential jurors is typically more likely to give accused infringers the benefit of the doubt, particularly when they can demonstrate market need or improved consumer benefits from an accused invention that builds upon prior art such as the plaintiff's patent.

b. The Government (and the USPTO, More Specifically) Is a Poor Watchdog

> *"They are part of the government, aren't they? They make mistakes."*
>
> —Patent mock juror who favored accused infringer

While a majority of potential jurors have favorable opinions of the USPTO, approximately one in five potential jurors will approach a case with skepticism toward government regulators, with 10% reporting unfavorable attitudes toward the USPTO.[12] These jurors are far more likely to be persuaded by the accused infringer's argument that the patent is not valid for a variety of reasons, including the belief that the government agency responsible for issuing the patent is overworked, understaffed, inefficient, ineffective, and bureaucratic. Patentee plaintiffs must identify in jury selection those potential jurors most likely to accept the accused infringer's arguments on invalidity and to repeat the arguments in deliberations.

2. Sample High-Risk Juror Profile for Patentee Plaintiff

The characteristics listed in this section delineate the attributes of jurors who are likely to prove risky for the patentee plaintiff. The topic areas appear in order of importance. Within each topic area, attitudes far outweigh life experiences and demographic characteristics in identifying pro-defense jurors. While no single

---

12. Persuasion Strategies/K&B Research, National Juror Survey (2011).

characteristic may warrant a strike, a pattern of numerous risky characteristics within a given person indicates an especially dangerous juror for the patentee.

a. Innovation Cynic

A subset of jurors will harbor cynicism toward the value and proliferation of "small" innovations and take a skeptical view of a claimed invention. This group of jurors should be a small proportion but based on higher education or technical experience can also masquerade as good jurors but for their measured feelings about innovation. These characteristics include:

- Believes only the most extreme innovations should be granted patents
- Feels there are few new ideas that deserve a patent
- Trivializes innovation and invention (e.g., endorses the ideas that "Most tech workers are capable of a meaningful invention," or "There are no more great innovations in technology")
- Believes innovation and invention are ubiquitous
- Has been or knows someone who has been an inventor but never applied for a patent
- Has never worked for a company that holds patents or has only worked for companies where innovation is a daily experience
- Sees inventions as "a dime a dozen"
- Holds an unfavorable opinion of patents

b. Patent Process Skeptic

Some jurors find the patent process and the USPTO less credible than do others. These jurors will make winning a patentee's case (infringement and patent validity) especially difficult. However, a small minority of jurors will hold these views, which should make it easier to identify your highest-risk strikes in voir dire. These characteristics include:

- Believes the USPTO can be fairly easily misled
- Believes patent examiners are often mistaken
- Believes it is easy to get a patent these days
- Believes most inventors overestimate the value of their ideas
- Trusts common sense over the USPTO's rulings
- Views patent examination as a bureaucratic/administrative process rather than as an evaluative/testing process
- Knows patent examiners do not practice the invention themselves when reviewing the patent application[13]
- Is or knows someone well who is an inventor but has not applied for patent protection
- Has patent/trademark law expertise
- Is more educated

13. Many patent jurors erroneously believe that patent examiners dissect the invention and test it in a laboratory setting before issuing a patent. This misunderstanding works to your benefit in this case.

- Is a Democrat or more politically liberal
- Has an egalitarian personality

c. Free Market Absolutist

Some jurors find the concept of a patent, or the prospect of literal and functional enforcement of a patent, to be overly restrictive to fair competition and innovation. These jurors will be motivated to respect the accused infringer's invalidity case and less likely to support the patentee's infringement case. These characteristics include:

- Strongly believes the patent process hurts competition
- Believes the market should define what consumers can get rather than a patent holder determining what is available to consumers
- Believes claims of copying stem from typical fair market competition
- Feels it is unfair if a company's actions reduce the number of competing companies selling the same product(s)
- Feels it is unfair for a company's actions to limit consumer choices
- Believes too many rules exist to protect players in the marketplace
- Believes patent protection should be shorter than the 17- or 20-year standard to allow for new competition on the same invention sooner
- Believes the patent holder should be required to liberally award licensing rights to competitors
- Believes companies should look for cutting-edge ways to compete versus asserting patent rights in court
- Strongly believes competing products (as well as "knockoffs") benefit the consumer by lowering costs
- Supports the development of technology that builds on prior inventions
- Supports collaboration and development over invention and innovation
- Works for a company that has been harmed by a patent
- Is strongly pro-capitalism
- Is fiscally conservative

d. Distinction-Finder

The juror who tends to look for and find distinctions is more likely to perceive differences in the accused products that equate to noninfringement. While these jurors are also more likely to see distinctions between the plaintiff's patents and prior art, jurors more likely to dig into distinctions and look for differences tend to be higher risk for patent plaintiffs. These characteristics include:

- Expresses an interest in finding differences and attending to details
- Describes self as a "detail oriented" thinker but tends toward menial work
- Prides self on being "analytical" or "thorough"
- Believes they are more subject matter savvy than they actually are (i.e., "tech overconfidence")
- Has a moderate need for cognition and detail when making decisions
- Has had occupation or work-life with moderate analytical requirements

- Has had occupation or work-life with role of spotting differences or details (e.g., quality control, compliance, etc.)
- Possesses a moderate level of understanding/sophistication
- Exhibits high-communication in voir dire in combination with other high-risk traits

Preferences for Generic Products and Perceptions That a Patent Infringement Case Against a Corporation Almost Always Has Merit

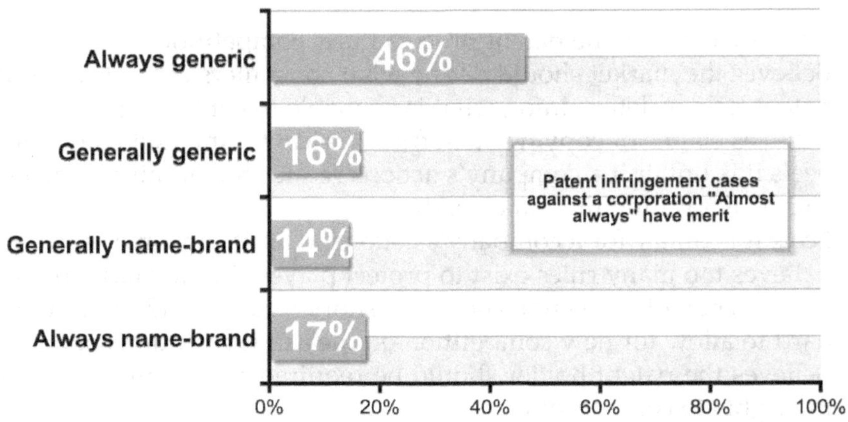

Source: Persuasion Strategies/K&B Research, National Juror Survey (2011) (N=400)

e. Accused Infringer Sympathizer

Jurors who identify more readily with the accused infringer will be more receptive to its arguments and more resistant to the patentee plaintiff's arguments. These characteristics include:

- Believes alleged infringement is more likely to stem from competition in the marketplace than illegal copying
- Has been accused of stealing or copying an idea in the past
- Has worked to develop or market new products in the past and finds the patent process to be unnecessary/cumbersome
- Focuses on law over ethics
- Feels there are too many lawsuits these days
- Has considerable business sophistication
- Has been accused of taking advantage of others in a business dealing
- Has been or someone close to juror has been taken advantage of in a business deal
- Has been or someone close to juror has been a prior defendant
- Has a negative opinion of the defendant and/or the defendant industry
- Is familiar with the plaintiff patentee and formed a negative opinion
- Is "status inconsistent" (combination of low education level and high-status occupation)
- Has experience, education, or training in the hard sciences (engineer, mathematician, physical scientist)

- Has been or is close to someone who has been sued for money damages
- Has experienced financial or property damage loss and took responsibility for the loss without blaming others
- Has had a claim (insurance, worker's comp, etc.) denied and was never adequately compensated

f. Damages Mitigator

Certain jurors are more conservative in awarding damages, even if they favor the plaintiff. These characteristics include:

- Believes there are too many frivolous lawsuits today
- Feels damage awards are far too high
- Has experienced economic losses and dealt with them without blaming others (or receiving compensation)
- Feels punitive damages are rarely, if ever, justified
- Strongly believes that plaintiffs inflate damages (e.g., can cite examples)

B. High-Risk Jurors for Accused Infringers

1. Typical Thought Processes for High-Risk Jurors

Just as high-risk jurors for patentee plaintiffs show consistent markers that help counsel identify and strike them in jury selection, so do high-risk jurors for accused infringers.

a. The Supremacy of Innovation

The most dangerous high-risk jurors for accused infringers place an extremely high priority on the freedom to create and develop unique and inventive ideas that change the world. One of the most admired and supremely appreciated aspects of that inventiveness is the inventor.

(1) Invention as King

A compilation of mock jury research shows that 95% of mock jurors who have invention experience found a patentee plaintiff credible just prior to jury deliberations, while just 60% of jurors who lacked invention experience reported the same perceptions of patentee plaintiffs.[14] The data illustrates the power behind jurors' perceptions of inventors. In today's landscape, individual inventors and classic invention stories may not be as common or as easy to tell as they once were, but jurors still place great faith and confidence in the inventor of an idea or product that comes under scrutiny.

(2) Primacy as Prince

Jurors look for shortcuts to a thorough analysis, not because they are lazy or unmotivated (although, of course, some of them are less motivated than you might want), but because of the human tendency to seek the path of least

---

14. Based on analysis of proprietary mock jury research data conducted in patent cases around the country. The difference noted is statistically significant, $p<.01$.

resistance. One common and influential shortcut is to evaluate which party was "first"—first to have an idea, first to take steps to develop an idea, first to apply for a patent, first to sell in the open market. All of these and many other "firsts" give jurors a simple and easy reason to lean in favor of one party over another. Jurors' tendency to place great weight in evidence on who was first typically poses a disadvantage to accused infringers, making high-risk for accused infringers those jurors with a strong presumption that primacy is critical.

(3) The USPTO as Parliament

> *"[The accused infringer's] lawyers really want us to believe that the patent office didn't do their homework. But I believe, and I think I know, that they do do their homework."*
>
> —Patent mock juror who favored patentee plaintiff

Jurors who are high-risk for the accused infringer also include those with great deference for the USPTO. A belief in the infallibility of the agency's decisions generally equates to the belief that the patent is valid and should not be challenged. The same jurors who believe in the infallibility of the agency are often financially conservative and thus pose higher risk for the patentee plaintiff on damages. This is a simple illustration of the tension in high-risk juror characteristics in patent cases. Our private mock trial research also finds that less education correlates with stronger belief that no party should have a right to challenge a granted patent. The same less-educated jurors may pose an even greater challenge for an accused infringer's noninfringement case, primarily because the defense often involves complex evidence and contextualized arguments that require attention to detail and significant comprehension of evidence and arguments.

Once a patent is granted, no one should be allowed to argue that the patent is invalid

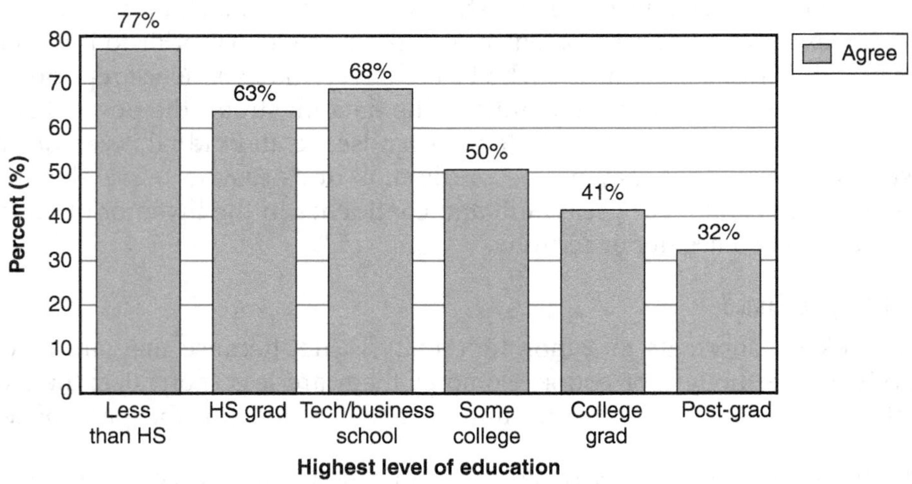

Source: Persuasion Strategies National Juror Survey (2006) (N=500)

Consistent with others' findings,[15] conclusions supported by the previous data often confirm juror education as an important characteristic to consider when the accused infringer asserts patent invalidity claims in a typical noninfringement/patent invalidity defense. In our experience, low education—when considered alone and outside of other factors—is typically a high-risk characteristic for accused infringers in both the noninfringement and patent invalidity case.

> *"We have found that jurors who are well educated often have the cognitive training and are willing to engage in the complex information processing that is necessary to challenge the validity of a patent."[16]*
>
> —James Stiff, Ph.D., litigation consultant

When considering an accused infringer's case for invalidating the patent, political views can also be a critical factor to explore when screening jurors. It is more than a statistic, but something we see exposed in mock jury research.

It is easy to mislead the patent office during the patent approval process

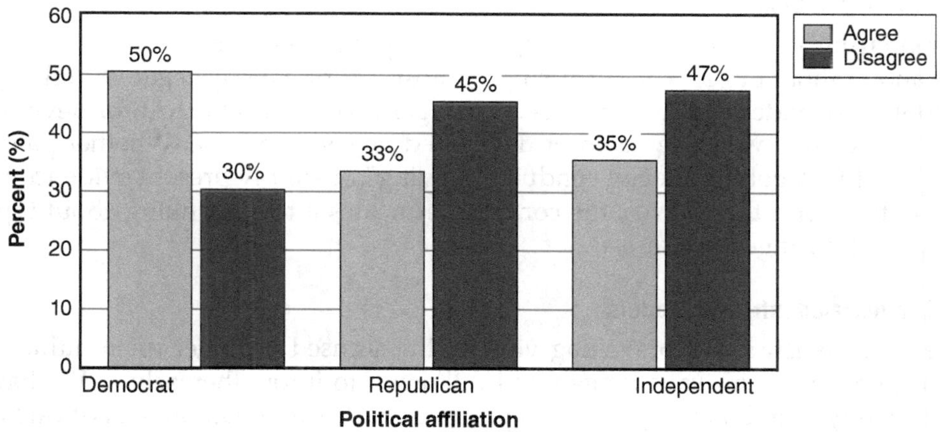

Source: Persuasion Strategies National Juror Survey (2006) (N=500)

The data illuminating the link between some demographic characteristics and relevant attitudes also illuminates the high-risk juror tension. Corporations constitute the overwhelming majority of accused infringers, and patent plaintiffs are more likely to demand a jury trial when the accused infringer is a corporation.[17] Given this reality, less-educated jurors are more likely to be high-risk for accused infringers (in terms of both winning a noninfringement case and

15. James B. Stiff, *Combating the Presumption of Validity in Patent Lawsuits*, Trial Analysts (2006).

16. *See id.*

17. Kimberly A. Moore, *Jury Demands: Who's Asking?*, 17 Berkeley Tech. L.J. 847 (2002).

asserting an invalidity case), yet higher-educated jurors (presumably "better" for accused infringers) are also more likely to lean toward or be members of the Democratic party[18]—and to hold anti-corporate attitudes that work against accused infringer corporations.[19]

b. Case-Specific Evaluations Are Critical

Case-specific evaluations are critical to identifying the issues upon which your case hinges, particularly for an effective defense of an accused infringer. The facts of the case matter greatly, and learning how mock jurors will react to those specific facts and related arguments is key to developing and testing a high-risk juror profile.

Some juror thought processes seem to transcend most fact patterns and correlate with high-risk attitudes, perceptions, and outcomes for accused infringers.

c. Fairness Rules the Marketplace

Accused infringers must be cognizant of the most predominant high-risk thinking in typical infringement cases: fairness is the golden rule in evaluating the parties' conduct.

(1) Copying Is Unfair

Potential jurors learn at an early age that copying another's work is dishonest and dishonorable. Not surprisingly, most jurors have a negative reflexive response to evidence that an accused infringer chose to take credit for developing an idea that was originated or developed by someone else. Whether patentee plaintiffs label the alleged conduct "copying" or simply present evidence for jurors to label it themselves, the concept permeates jurors' thinking about typical patent infringement cases.

d. The Accused Infringer Matters

The characteristics and prevailing view of the accused infringer often influence juror perceptions in ways known and unknown to jurors themselves. We have consistently found that the perceived power of parties in litigation is a critical factor in how jurors assess responsibility and make determinations about the parties.

(1) The Bigger the Accused Infringer, the More Power They Wield

When the accused infringer is a sizable company with a perceived wealth of resources—financial or otherwise—jurors typically see that company as having greater power to effect change, and therefore greater ability to make better choices. In jurors' eyes, a company with "the world at its fingertips" should be able to conduct business responsibly and make the best available choices,

18. Frank Newport et al., *Democrats More Liberal, Less White Than in 2008*, GALLUP (Nov. 7, 2011), http://www.gallup.com/poll/150611/Democrats-Liberal-Less-White-2008.aspx.

19. For instance, Persuasion Strategies national survey research of 2,348 potential jurors from 2009 to 2011 shows that potential jurors who report Democratic leanings are statistically more likely to report anti-corporate attitudes.

including designing around the patents or independently developing its own ideas. The combination of power and resources with the great potential for informed and effective choices creates a burden that corporate accused infringers must meet. For instance, jurors take exception to an accused infringer that has a massive research and development budget and thousands of employees domestic and abroad, yet still chooses to infringe a known competitor's patented product. Jurors see this type of company as having the smarts and the money to develop its own ideas, and by choosing not to do so, it is using its power to make choices the jury will not likely appreciate.

(2) Knockoff Companies Often Start at a Disadvantage

Companies making knockoff products that are obviously based on others' inventive products and/or patents may also suffer juror bias. For the same reasons previously articulated, jurors can perceive knockoff companies as taking the easy (read unfair) route rather than doing the hard work on their own. In our private jury research we have seen the plaintiff persuade jurors with the simple story (and evidence) of copying that immediately puts the accused infringer at a significant disadvantage. This disadvantage is especially powerful when jurors perceive the accused infringer as basing its entire business on selling knockoff products that were created and developed by others instead of developing its own ideas. Demonstrating the accused infringer's value to the market and to jurors themselves is a critical part of addressing the bias resulting from jurors' belief that the defendant is taking a shortcut to profits through the work of competitors.

"If you couldn't duplicate things, whoever is on top would have a corner on the market and they would be multibillionaires. You can't do that. You have a monopoly and no competition."

—Patent mock juror who favored accused infringer

e. The Market Matters

Juror perceptions can be complicated, however, by the belief that knockoff companies are increasing consumer options and keeping name-brand prices low—a clear advantage to jurors (consumers). This is a critical aspect to explore in jury selection if one of the parties is a company making generic or "knockoff" products. A simple way to think of this key issue is to understand that what helps the consumer may help the accused infringer. Defendants must be careful to present this position delicately to the jury, which can often find at least one juror among its ranks to believe a defendant's rhetoric misses the heart of the matter.

"I favored [defendant] when I thought this was about free enterprise, but this isn't about free enterprise. It's about the stupid patent."

—Patent mock juror who favored patentee plaintiff

2. Sample High-Risk Juror Profile for Accused Infringer Defendant

The characteristics listed in this section delineate the attributes of jurors who are likely to prove risky for the defendant, accused infringer BigPhone Corp. The topic areas appear in order of importance. Within each topic area, attitudes far outweigh life experiences and demographic characteristics in identifying pro-defense jurors. While no single characteristic may warrant a strike, a pattern of numerous risky characteristics within a given person indicates an especially dangerous juror for accused infringer BigPhone Corp.

a. Big Picture Decision Maker/Detail Averse

Jurors whose natural inclination is to focus on the "big picture" or on knee-jerk decision-making are less likely to complete the more thorough analysis required to understand more complex defense explanations. These characteristics include:

- Has a low need for cognition (i.e., prefers less effortful tasks and thinking)
- Avoids complexity and difficult problems when possible
- Describes self as a "big picture" thinker rather than "detail oriented"
- Is a holistic rather than analytic thinker (speaks in broad conclusions rather than specific elements and reasons)
- Prioritizes intuition and "common sense" over specific analysis
- Dislikes mathematics and hard science
- Is uncomfortable using or unable to digest detailed documents
- Is a poor or distracted listener
- Has training, education, or experience in arts, menial work, or soft sciences (psychology, sociology, etc.)

b. Patent Process Supporter

Our national research of jury-eligible respondents finds that most hold the USPTO in higher regard than any other federal agency. Beyond that, a juror who more absolutely supports the USPTO is especially dangerous for an accused infringer in its invalidity case. These characteristics include:

- Believes the fact that a patent has been granted inherently makes it valid
- Feels intimidated about second-guessing the USPTO's decision to issue a patent
- Believes patent examiners are highly specialized, detailed individuals who are unlikely to commit errors in the course of their work
- Believes the majority of patents are invaluable
- Does not believe an innovation has to be dramatically different from prior innovations to be patent-worthy
- Believes patents spur innovation and help competition
- Is a less educated, deferential juror
- Is authoritarian (versus egalitarian)

c. Low Sense of Personal Responsibility

Jurors who focus on external factors in determining individual outcomes are more likely to scrutinize first what the patentee plaintiff did or could have done to better protect itself, and will be less likely to focus on the accused infringer's power and choices. These characteristics include:

- Has strong external locus of control: believes that outside factors (and not individuals themselves) bear the greatest amount of responsibility for successes or misfortunes
- Refers to external factors (she, they, it) rather than internal factors (I, me, my) when describing unfavorable outcomes
- Describes self as an idealist rather than a pragmatist
- Is or has been a transitional or unstable employee
- Is a low-level employee
- Has a victim mentality

d. Values Driven

Jurors who view commerce primarily through a values filter are more likely to believe the accused infringer's conduct was unfair and inconsistent with the spirit of fair business dealing. These characteristics include:

- Believes more in the phrase "business should be fair" than in "business is business"
- Believes that "a deal is a deal," come hell or high water
- Believes a more powerful party to a transaction has an obligation to look out for others' interests
- Believes ethics and fairness are more important than contracts or the law in evaluating conduct
- Has been or is close to someone who has been taken advantage of in a business dispute
- Has been or is close to someone who has been a party to a business deal that they feel was unfair
- Uses value-laden language: "It is not fair that . . . ," "It is not right that . . . ," "I feel that . . ."
- Describes self as "feeler" versus "thinker"
- Was a social science major in college
- Has been a social worker

e. Presumptively Pro-Plaintiff

Certain jurors are more oriented toward plaintiffs or those who position themselves as "fighting for justice." These characteristics include:

- Has little business sophistication
- Is "status inconsistent" (combination of low-status occupation and high education level)
- Has background in social services/social work
- Has been a plaintiff in a prior dispute
- Was a social sciences or fine arts major
- Describes self as politically liberal, libertarian, or anti-establishment
- Belongs to/supports a consumers' advocacy group
- Describes self as "feeler," not thinker

- Is a blue-collar employee
- Has held numerous short-term jobs over the years (post-secondary school)
- Is a welfare recipient
- Has been a worker's compensation claimant

f. Damages Aggravator

Certain jurors are more liberal in awarding damages. These characteristics include:

- Feels financial rewards are the best way to encourage responsible business behavior
- Feels that if a lawsuit made it to court, it must have some merit
- Feels lawsuits are often the only way to resolve a dispute with a company
- Feels punitive damages are the only way to get a company's attention and change its behavior
- Has current or past affiliation with a consumer protection organization
- Has little to no employment experience in the business sector
- Is less educated
- Earns a low income or lives in a low-income home
- Is younger

C. The Importance of Jury Leadership

Counsel should consider jury leadership in all types of cases, but particularly in patent cases. When the complexity of the evidence increases and jurors struggle to understand technology, testimony, and documents, the influential role of individual jurors also tends to increase. You must identify potential jury leaders in jury selection, and make educated predictions about how they are likely to perceive the case and affect others' views in jury deliberations.

Leaders are often easy to spot in jury selection, but patent jury leaders exhibit some specific characteristics that should be identified in jury selection.

1. Leadership Profile in Patent Lawsuit

a. Patent-Specific Leadership Traits

These traits include:

- Is familiar with the patent, trademark, or copyright application process
- Has worked to a limited or extensive degree with patents, trademarks, or copyrights in some professional or personal capacity
- Has training, education, or experience in the industry/industries related to the patent-in-suit
- Has worked around patents or patented technology
- Has invented something worthy of a patent
- Is employed in a highly analytical profession
- Is employed in a profession that relies on mathematics or science

b. Typical Leadership Traits

These traits include:

- Has had supervisory or management experience (decision-making authority over other individuals)
- Has served on a jury in the past
- Has teaching experience
- Has training, education, or experience in the law or legal system
- Possesses a bachelor's degree or higher
- Has military or police experience at the officer level (captain or higher)
- Is active in politics or nongovernmental organizations
- Has a problem-solving orientation
- Consistently gives whomever is speaking full eye contact
- Is inclined to take notes (e.g., brought their own pen and paper to court)
- Speaks louder than others
- Gestures while speaking
- Answers questions in full sentences
- Answers open-ended questions with more than one sentence

III. Make the Most of Judge-Conducted Oral Voir Dire and Supplemental Juror Questionnaires

You can learn a lot about your jury pool before you ever set foot in the courtroom. Asking the right questions in a supplemental juror questionnaire will help you more than your opponent and will establish some key criteria for assessing potential jurors and exercising strikes. The first step, however, is getting the court to administer a questionnaire.

A. Sample Motion for Supplemental Juror Questionnaire

U.S. DISTRICT COURT

Camera Anywhere Company, Plaintiff, v. BigPhone Corporation, Defendant.	MOTION FOR SUPPLEMENTAL JUROR QUESTIONNAIRE

The [Plaintiff/Defendant] respectfully moves [or Plaintiff and Defendant jointly move] this Court for its order directing:

1. That the written supplemental juror questionnaire attached to this Motion be submitted to prospective jurors in this case. The purpose of this questionnaire is fourfold:

a) to explore in a time-saving manner prospective jurors' experiences with and biases toward sensitive, case-relevant topics and other related attitudes and experiences, including sensitive issues pertinent to the nature of this case;

b) to ascertain jurors' knowledge of parties and witnesses in this case;

c) to collect other pertinent information that might contribute to a challenge for cause; and

d) to expedite the process of oral voir dire, given the fact that the written questions cover numerous life experiences that may pertain to the case.

In addition to providing background information quickly and easily, use of a pre-voir dire written questionnaire is also likely to elicit more accurate information from potential jurors. Providing written answers to a questionnaire is more confidential than providing an oral response to a question in an open and crowded courtroom, particularly for the sensitive nature of some of the topics and issues that must be explored in this case. Whereas the pressure of a courtroom situation might lead a potential juror to provide an inaccurate or incomplete response to a voir dire question, the questionnaire provides an opportunity for prospective jurors to think both about the questions and about their responses in a less pressured situation.

2. That the questionnaire be handled in the following way:

a) That the questionnaire be distributed to prospective jurors on [insert date that allows a week or more for completion and a week for the court to compile and make copies for both sides].

b) Once each juror has completed his/her questionnaire, jurors will return to the jury room while counsel and the Court review the completed versions for hardships and/or cause.

c) Those jurors who are candidates for excusal for either hardship or cause would then be called back into Court on Friday to resolve the question of their service in this case.

d) All remaining jurors will be dismissed until jury selection commences Monday morning, [insert date], when oral voir dire commences. This would allow sufficient time to have the questionnaire copied and reviewed by the attorneys before oral questioning begins.

e) If more challenges for cause arise based on a more detailed review of the questionnaires, counsel would raise those issues with the Court immediately before oral voir dire commences Monday morning.

3. That prospective jurors be questioned out of the hearing of the panel of other prospective jurors during oral voir dire if their

questionnaires indicate they wish to discuss any of their answers in private. Given the questions regarding their experience with personal medical issues, the sequestered questioning will cover their experience and knowledge and the possible effect such experience and knowledge may have on their ability to hear and decide this case in a fair and impartial manner.

4. That the information contained in the supplemental questionnaires concerning the prospective jurors' attitudes shall not be disclosed to any person other than the Court, the attorneys for the parties, their staff, and the parties themselves.

Date ____________________

By ____________________

B. Basic Juror Questionnaire Elements

See a sample of basic elements of a supplemental juror questionnaire in Appendix B.

C. Juror Questionnaire Elements for Patent Plaintiffs

See sample supplemental juror questionnaire questions for a patentee plaintiff at Appendix C.

D. Juror Questionnaire Elements for Accused Infringers

See sample supplemental juror questionnaire questions for an accused infringer at Appendix D.

IV. Deliver an Effective Three-Part Oral Voir Dire

Judges with patent-heavy dockets balance the need for thorough jury selection with a long list of competing demands. While practice standards vary greatly, the result is often limited time to conduct voir dire and a preference for the judge to conduct some or all of the oral voir dire. Effective voir dire begins with your submissions for judge-conducted questioning and ends with effective use of the time you have to follow up and ask questions of your own.

Note: Where relevant throughout the remainder of this chapter, we refer to the industry and/or product related to the patent-in-suit based on our exemplar fact pattern involving a mobile phone camera invention (see Appendix A for a brief summary description).

A. Judge-Conducted Oral Voir Dire

While some attorneys prefer a scorched-earth submission of dozens of proposed questions, our experience is that fewer questions can increase the likelihood of your proposed questions being asked. Submitting dozens of alternatives encourages judges to pick and choose the questions they like best or are most comfortable asking—or, at worst, to reject them all and ask the questions the judge prefers. While fewer questions does not eliminate judges' propensity to ignore prejudicial or obviously imbalanced questions, it does seem to grant the proposing party more control over the questions the court will ask, and includes the added benefit of being judicious and sensitive to the court's inherent time pressures. While the best number of proposed questions can vary by case complexity, we often recommend 15 to 25 proposed questions for judge-conducted voir dire, including the assumption that counsel will have some ability to follow up on jurors' responses.

You can create advantage through judge-conducted voir dire. While many attorneys believe the judge's questions must be neutral or innocuous ("or he won't ask them"), carefully crafted questions based on pretrial jury research can help your side more than it helps your opponent. Knowing what questions to ask—even if they seem innocuous—and how to ask them is key to identifying high-risk jurors and masking your best jurors in voir dire. Coordinating submissions for judge-conducted voir dire with questions on a supplemental juror questionnaire is also critical to a successful voir dire strategy.

1. Sample Judge-Conducted Oral Voir Dire Questions (General)

The sample questions in this section include a variety of approaches and are not intended to be used as an entire collection. It is more likely and more effective that you would use a selection of the included questions.

a. Judge-Conducted Voir Dire Submissions

Camera Anywhere Co. v. BigPhone Corp.

- Have you, any family member, or any friend been employed by a technology company or a business involved in the design, development, manufacture, or sale of mobile phone technology? If yes, please identify the individual, his/her relationship to you, the company, and the nature of the employment.
- Have you, any family member, or any friend been employed by a camera, lens, or microscope company or a business involved in the design, development, manufacture, or sale of camera technology? If yes, please identify the individual, his/her relationship to you, the company, and the nature of the employment.
- Have you ever worked at a job where you were involved in the development or marketing of new products? If so, please describe your involvement.
- Have you ever worked on a job where you negotiated agreements with other companies? If so, please describe your responsibilities.
- In connection with your current occupation:
  - Do you have any supervisory responsibilities?
  - If yes, please describe.
- How many of you have any training, education, or any experience in the following:

- Computers or microcomputers
- Software or software design
- Cameras or lens technology
- Accounting or economics
- Engineering (of any kind)
- Mathematics
- Technology design
- The law or the legal system
- For each area in which you have some experience, describe the nature of your experience.
- How much do you use your training or experience?

- How many of you have some experience with patents?
  - Please describe the nature of your experience.
  - Have you ever applied for a patent?
  - How many times have you applied for a patent?
  - What was the subject matter of your patent application(s)?
  - What was the outcome of your application(s)?
  - Has your patent been practiced?
  - Please describe your involvement in the patent application process.
- How many of you have some experience with patent law?
  - Please describe the nature of your experience.
- How many of you have some experience with patents in connection to your work?
  - Please describe your experience.
- How many of you have ever worked with patented technology?
  - Please describe your experience.
- How many of you have ever worked for a company that has patents?
  - What type of technology has your company patented?
  - Are you trained in the technology that your company has patented?
  - What has your experience been like working with patented technology?
  - How many patents did your company have?
  - Did you have a role in the patent applications?
  - What has your experience with patents been like?
  - How is your work affected by patents?
- How many of you have ever developed an invention related to your work?
  - Please describe the circumstances.
  - Who owned the invention, you or your employer or both?
- Regardless of whether it was work-related, has anyone here invented something or does anyone here know someone who has invented something?
  - Please describe the nature of the invention.
  - Was a patent applied for, and if so, what was the outcome of the application?
- Have you heard or read about any lawsuit involving the parties in this lawsuit? If yes, please explain.

- Have you ever had a bad experience in business? If so, what was it?
- This lawsuit involves a dispute over patents for a mobile phone camera. Do you have any knowledge about mobile phone technology, camera technology, or mobile phone camera technology? If so, please describe.
- Have you ever purchased, used, or owned a BigPhone product? If so, which products, and how often and for what purposes have you used them?
- Are you a member of any clubs or organizations, civic, religious, political, social, etc.? If yes, please list them.
- Do you have any health problems or other limitations (for example, bad back, poor eyesight, hearing difficulties) that would make it difficult for you to serve as a juror? If so, please describe.

2. Sample Judge-Conducted Oral Voir Dire Questions (for Plaintiff)

- Have you, any family member, or friend ever been employed by the U.S. Patent and Trademark Office or the U.S. Copyright Office? If yes, please identify the person and his/her relationship to you, as well as the person's employer.
- What is your opinion about protecting certain rights, such as copyrights, trademarks, and patents?
  - Are these protections important or not important to society?
- Do you feel patents should be awarded for only complicated or technical devices? If so, why do you feel that way?
- How many of you feel a lengthy protection for patent rights is fair? If not, why not?
- How many of you, for any reason, have an unfavorable opinion of the U.S. Patent and Trademark Office? If so, why do you feel this way?
- Do you believe too many rules exist to protect fair competition in this country?
- Do you have any concerns that the patent process hurts fair competition since it limits others from producing copies of the patented product?
- Specifically, do you have an opinion on the role of patents in promoting or preventing innovations? If so, what is that opinion?
- Some individuals may think there are too many rules to protect inventors of a product or process, and others might think there are too few. Do you hold either of those views? If yes, which view and why?
- Have you ever been accused of infringing a patent, or has anyone you know well been accused of the same behavior?
- How many of you feel the patent process hurts competition?
- How many of you feel it is unfair that an award of a patent means the patent owner has a legal monopoly on that invention for a number of years?
- How many of you think it is common for companies that hold patents to overstep their patent rights?
- What are your perceptions about how tough or easy it seems to be to get a patent these days?

- Have you ever been involved in a lawsuit? What was it about? Were you a plaintiff or a defendant?
- How many of you have any personal beliefs that would prevent you from awarding substantial monetary damages, possibly millions of dollars, if the evidence and the law supported such a verdict? Why do you feel this way?
- How many of you believe that changes should be made to our jury system to prevent large jury verdicts?

3. *Sample Judge-Conducted Oral Voir Dire Questions (for Defense)*

- What is your opinion of the U.S. Patent and Trademark Office or of the patent process?
- How many of you have some experience or familiarity with the U.S. Patent and Trademark Office?
  - What has your experience been like?
- How many of you, for any reason, have a favorable opinion of the U.S. Patent and Trademark Office? If so, why do you feel this way?
- How many of you have experience with product development?
  - What has your experience with product development been like?
  - How many of you have experience bringing a new product or item into the marketplace?
  - What has your experience bringing new items to the marketplace been like?
  - Were you compensated for bringing the item to market?
  - By whom were you compensated?
- How many of you hold an opinion of inventors that might make it hard for you to have a completely open mind as you listen to the evidence?
- How many of you feel that once a patent is granted, no one should be allowed to challenge that patent? Why do you feel that way?
- Do you work in an industry that is highly competitive? If so, please explain.
- Have you ever worked in a business that was unfairly accused of being a "bad guy" company? If so, please explain.
- Have you ever worked with a company or with someone accused of infringing a patent, copyright, or trademark? If so, please explain.

B. Three-Part Attorney-Conducted Oral Voir Dire[20]

Your opportunity to conduct attorney voir dire is the first and most important opportunity to develop rapport with potential jurors and begin the persuasion process. Different schools of thought emphasize as primary one of three goals in voir dire: (1) develop rapport; (2) develop themes; and (3) identify and strike high-risk jurors. The best voir dire accomplishes all three goals. One inherent criterion in accomplishing all three goals is reaching as many potential jurors

20. Karen Lisko introduced this method in PROVEN JURY ARGUMENTS AND EVIDENCE (2010).

as possible in your allotted time. This requires a voir dire approach that at once encourages (or requires) participation from the entire jury panel.

The following triple-layer structure combines group and individual questions to achieve two important goals. First, the group/individual combination ensures that you collect everyone's general response to an initial attitudinal question. Second, the group/individual combination allows the venire to feel engaged given the variety of approaches to questioning.

1. The Triple-Layer Oral Voir Dire Structure[21]

a. Layer One: The Warm-Up

The "warm-up" layer orients the venire to your topic and encourages them to begin thinking about the topic in general terms. This is the warm-up before the workout. It gets the juices flowing and primes jurors' general feelings so they are more likely to share their opinions. The purpose is not necessarily to collect vital information about the topic—just to introduce the issue and get jurors' minds focused on the topic before probing more deeply into it with specific questions. Usually one or two questions are enough to get jurors warmed up and open to questions that will follow as you narrow the focus and begin to address your case-specific goals.

Question Template: Layer One

Group Question

"Have you seen *[general topic area]* in the news lately?"

"What have you seen or heard about *[general topic area]* lately?"

Individual Question

"Mrs. Walters, how about you? Have you seen *[general topic area]* in the news recently?"

"Mr. Tate, how do you feel about *[general topic area]*?"

b. Layer Two: Questions to Create Clear Group Contrast

Layer Two takes advantage of the rapport you have developed and the priming you have achieved with your warm-up questions and divides the panel into two clear groups: a majority group that favors your position on the case-specific issue and a smaller, identifiable group with attitudes or beliefs opposed to your position. The questions you ask in this layer are critical, and careful language choices will help ensure you get the intended result. These second-layer questions should be framed to establish two distinct response choices that are different enough to allow jurors to identify which is closer to their view, but also reasonable enough that jurors will not reject them both out of hand. In choosing your question wording, keep in mind your primary goal of dividing the group

21. *See id.*

into a "safe majority" of jurors who you are confident will not be risky jurors and a "strikable minority" of high-risk jurors. This allows you to identify your strikes while not helping the other side identify theirs. To achieve this balance, you may need to use qualifying or polarizing language to make the response options work in your favor: "How many of you *strongly* believe . . ." or "Raise your hand if you would *rarely if ever* . . ." Here is a generic model demonstrating how this layer works in practice, assuming the questions are on behalf of a plaintiff.

> **Question Template: Layer Two**
>
> "When it comes to *[case-specific issue]*, some people tend to feel 'X,' while others generally feel 'Y.'"
>
> "By a show of hands, how many of you tend to feel 'X'?" *[Introduce anti-plaintiff option.]*
>
> "How many of you generally feel 'Y'?" *[Introduce pro-plaintiff option.]*

c. Layer Three: Individual Follow-Up That Invites Thematic Response

You probably noticed that the Layer Two model includes posing the response option that represents opposition to your side (or is anti-plaintiff in this example) first, and the positive or low-risk (pro-plaintiff) response option last. This allows you to seamlessly address follow-up questions to individuals who offer what you view as positive responses to your questions. While you have the same opportunity with jurors who offer the high-risk (anti-plaintiff) response, you do *not* want to follow up with jurors who expressed anti-plaintiff attitudes unless you intend to pursue and believe you can achieve having that individual juror removed for cause.

By choosing not to "pass the microphone" to high-risk jurors, you are preventing them from sharing their high-risk opinions and beliefs with the entire panel. While reasonable minds may differ on how damaging "poisoning the panel" may be, there is no need to use your jury panel as a data point for the debate. Assuming you cannot confidently pursue a cause challenge, identify those who offer high-risk responses in Layer Two, then spend just a little time encouraging a few of your "good" jurors to voice your themes. Do not be overly concerned about revealing these jurors as potential strikes for your opponent. Sure, it may expose one of their peremptory strikes a little sooner than would have otherwise occurred, but it will help normalize pro-plaintiff opinions and elicit your case themes before opposing counsel has even had a chance to stand up.

> **Question Template: Layer Three**
>
> "Ms. Patterson, I noticed that you indicated that you generally feel 'Y.' Can you tell us a little about that?"
>
> "Mr. Walker, how do you feel about what Ms. Patterson just said?"

C. Sample Oral Voir Dire Questions for Patent Plaintiffs

The following examples demonstrate the three-layer structure for a few topic areas relevant to a patentee plaintiff in a patent case.

1. Views of the Patent Process

Layer One: (Warm-Up Question)

- In today's business world, innovative ideas are critical to success. I'm curious about your opinions of how companies should protect their ideas from being copied or used by other companies. Raise your hand if you think companies should be able to protect their ideas.

Layer Three: (Thematic Follow-Up Questions)

- Mr. O, why is that important?
- Ms. D, why do you think it's important?

Layer Two: (Group Experience Questions, if not covered in judge voir dire)

- As you know, this case is about a patented invention. How many of you have had an idea that you believed was patentable?
- Have you ever applied for a patent?
- Have you ever applied for a patent that you did not receive?

Layer Two: (Group Bias Question)

- I'm curious about your perceptions of how easy or difficult it is to get a patent today. Some people might believe it's fairly easy to get a patent while others believe it's pretty difficult. How many of you believe it is fairly easy? [Note, but do not follow up.] How many of you believe it is fairly difficult to get a patent today?

Layer Three: (Thematic Follow-Up Question)

- Mr. K, what do you think the process is like?

Layer One: (Warm-Up Question)

- How many of you have experience with the federal government agency, the U.S. Patent and Trademark Office, or USPTO? What are your perceptions of the USPTO?

Layer Two: (Group Bias Question)

- I'm curious about your beliefs about the patent evaluation process. Some people believe that in the process of evaluating a patent application, the USPTO is often misled or mistaken in awarding a patent. Others believe the USPTO is rarely misled or mistaken. How many of you fall more in the first group, thinking the USPTO is often misled or mistaken in awarding patents? How many think the USPTO is rarely misled or mistaken?

Layer Three: (Thematic Follow-Up Questions)

- Mr. E, why do you think that is?
- What about you, Ms. B?

Layer Two: (Group Bias Question)

- Do any of you believe the USPTO does not do a thorough job in evaluating patent applications? [Note, but do not follow up.]

Layer Three: (Thematic Follow-Up Question)

- [Call on a juror who did not raise his hand who believes the USPTO is rarely mistaken.] Mr. H, how important is the patent process to make sure inventions are made available to consumers like you and me?

2. Views of Competition in the Marketplace

Layer One: (Warm-Up Question)

- Patents are a part of American history, but I have to ask how much different you think patents are today than they were 50 years ago.

Layer Two: (Group Bias Question)

- People have different views of how the patent process—the fact that an invention or idea is patented—affects competition in business. Some believe that the patent process severely hurts competition. Others believe the patent process helps competition. Which is closer to your view? How many believe the patent process severely hurts competition? How many of you believe the patent process helps competition?

Layer Three: (Thematic Follow-Up Questions)

- Mr. L, why do you feel that way?
- Ms. J, what is it about the patent process that helps competition?
- How do consumers like you and me benefit from the patent process?

Layer One: (Warm-Up Question)

- At its core, this case is about how a business goes about its business. So I need to ask you, what should a business do to be successful in the United States today?

Layer Two: (Group Bias Question)

- Some people think that "all's fair in business" today, and that a business should do everything in its power to increase profits. Others think that business should always be conducted fairly and within the law. How many of you fall more in the first camp, that "all's fair in business"? How many of you fall more in the second camp, that business should be conducted fairly and within the law?

Layer Three: (Thematic Follow-Up Questions)

- Mr. D, why do you feel that way?
- Ms. J, why is it important to you that business be conducted fairly?

Layer Two: (Group Bias Question)

- When it comes to competition in business more generally, how many of you feel that companies should never build new products and ideas based on a competitor's product or idea? [Note, but do not follow up.]

Layer Two: (Group Experience Questions to Identify Cause Challenge)

- Have you or has anyone you know well ever been accused of stealing someone else's business idea or invention?
- Without getting into any uncomfortable details, what were the circumstances? How was it resolved? Were you satisfied with the way it was resolved?

3. Product Preferences

Layer One: (Warm-Up Question)

- I want to talk to you about the kinds of products you like to buy. How many of you are familiar with the concept of a knockoff product or a "generic," as they are sometimes called?

Layer Two: (Group Bias Questions)

- People have different preferences when it comes to buying products. Some people like buying name-brand products, some people like buying less expensive knockoffs.
- How many of you prefer to buy generic or knockoff products? [Note, but do not follow up.] How many of you prefer to buy name-brand products when they are available?

Layer Three: (Thematic Follow-Up Questions)

- Mr. D, why do you prefer the name-brand products?
- Ms. G, how about you?

Layer Two: (Group Bias Questions)

- In a typical consumer situation, say when you are shopping for something like a cell phone, there are benefits from buying a name brand and possibly benefits from buying a knockoff. How many of you think the benefits from buying a knockoff are greater than the benefits of buying a name brand? [Note, but do not follow up.]
- How many of you think the benefits from buying a name-brand product are greater?

Layer Three: (Thematic Follow-Up Question)

- Mr. O, why is that?

4. Anti-Litigation Attitudes

Layer One: (Warm-Up Questions)

- Now, as you know, in this case I represent the plaintiff, or the party bringing the lawsuit, Mid-Sized Patentee Co. My client is going to ask you to award money damages in this case. The defendant, Accused Infringer Corp., is alleged to have infringed my client's patent.
- Mr. D, what are your thoughts about companies that sue for money damages in a dispute with a large corporation?

Layer Two: (Group Bias Questions)

- I want to give you two options and ask which one reflects more of what you feel. Some people believe lawsuits do very little good when they are between two businesses. Others think there are many cases where lawsuits are important—for instance, when someone has been accused of copying an idea.
- By a show of hands, how many of you believe lawsuits do very little good?
- Now, how many of you believe there are many cases where lawsuits are important?

Layer Three: (Thematic Follow-Up Question)

- Ms. E, why are lawsuits important in cases like this?

Layer Two: (Group Bias Questions to Identify Cause Challenge)

- Is there anyone here who is opposed to civil lawsuits no matter what the circumstances?
- Ms. F, you raised your hand. In what way would your feelings about civil lawsuits affect your ability to give my client a fair chance in this case?

Layer Two: (Group Bias Questions to Identify Cause Challenge)

- Is there anyone here who, based on anything we have talked about specific to this case, would have a hard time giving my client a fair hearing?
- Ms. F, you raised your hand. In what way would your feelings about this case affect your ability to give my clients a fair chance in this case?

Layer Two: (Group Experience Questions to Identify Cause Challenge)

- By a quick show of hands, is there anyone here who believes they had reason to sue in the past but decided against bringing the lawsuit?
- As a result of that experience, how many of you feel you would have a difficult time giving my client a fair chance in this case?

D. Sample Oral Voir Dire Questions for Accused Infringers

The following examples demonstrate the three-layer structure for a few topic areas relevant to an accused infringer in a patent case.

1. Views of Patent Protection

Layer One: (Warm-Up Questions)

- As you've heard by now, this case involves a dispute over patent rights. I'm curious to know about your own experience with ideas that could possibly have been patented. How many of you are familiar with intellectual property protections like patents?
- How many of you have ever believed you or someone you know well had a patentable idea?
- If I may ask, what was the idea?
- How far did you go into the process of looking into a patent?
- [Presuming the juror stopped short of application:] What made you stop?

Layer Two: (Group Experience Question)

- How many of you have known or know someone well who has had to enforce intellectual property rights—such as a patent—personally or in business? [Note, but do not follow up.]

Layer Two: (Group Bias Question)

- I'm curious about your views of patents and the limits of using patents in business. How many of you believe there are circumstances in which a company might get a patent for the wrong reasons?

Layer Three: (Thematic Follow-Up Questions)

- Mr. G, tell me why you feel that way.
- Why would that be a misuse of a patent?

Layer Two: (Group Bias Questions)

- I need to ask which of the following is closer to your opinion. First, some people believe that companies should have extremely broad freedom to protect their intellectual property with patents even when it harms competitors. Others believe that companies should protect intellectual property that has value, but should not protect intellectual property just to harm competitors.
- How many of you fall more in the first camp: companies should have extremely broad freedom to protect their intellectual property even if it causes harm to competitors?
- How many of you fall more in the second camp: companies should protect intellectual property that has value, but should not do so just to harm competitors?

Layer Three: (Thematic Follow-Up Questions)

- Mr. G, why do you feel that way?
- What is your opinion on the role of patents in promoting or preventing innovations?

Layer Two: (Group Bias Question)

- Some people may think that a patent gives a person or a company too much power and may even create a monopoly. Others think such protection is only fair. Which of those is closer to your view?

Layer Two: (Group Experience Questions)

- How many of you work in a field that depends, at least in part, on the existence of patents, trademarks, or copyrights for its financial success?
- How many of you feel that you or someone you work for has had an original idea or invention stolen or copied?

Layer Two: (Group Bias Questions)

- You will learn that my client (among others) has been accused of copying the plaintiff's product. We will present evidence that no such thing occurred. I would like to know if any of you feel that the fact that you have personally experienced the theft of an original idea would make it difficult for you to assess this case impartially.
- Mr. X, how did you feel about that?
- Without getting into any uncomfortable details, how was that issue resolved? Were you satisfied with the resolution?
- [Follow up only if you want to pursue a cause challenge.]
- How long have you felt that way?
- Are your feelings likely to change in the next day?
- Knowing you've had that experience, how might that influence your evaluation of this case?
- Can you see how your feelings/experience might be concerning to my client in this case? Would you be a good juror for another case?

2. *Perceptions of the USPTO's Infallibility*

Layer One: (Warm-Up Questions)

- Without having to think of a specific example, how many of you believe you have ever reached the wrong conclusion about something—even though it was in your area of expertise?
- How do you think that happened?
- [In the event you get less than full agreement:] How many of you believe you have never reached the wrong conclusion in your area of expertise due to incomplete information?

Layer Two: (Group Bias Questions)

- Now let's talk about your perceptions of the U.S. Patent and Trademark Office. Some people might have the perception that patent examiners are so thorough in their review of patent applications as to make it very difficult for them to make a mistake/be misled. Others believe it possible that the patent office can be vulnerable to mistakes/being misled with the information provided by applicants. Again, if you were to put yourself in one camp or the other:

- How many of you believe it would be very difficult for patent examiners to make a mistake/be misled in their review of patent applications?
- How many of you believe it would not be difficult for patent examiners to make a mistake/be misled in their review of patent applications?

Layer One: (Warm-Up Question)

- In this case, we will need to prove to you that a patent that the patent office has already issued should be found after the fact not to be valid [because it was obvious to an ordinary user of that product all along; because it did not describe how to make and use the invention, etc.].

Layer Two: (Group Bias Questions)

- Some people feel comfortable with the fact that a jury has a right to second-guess the patent office after it has issued a patent. Others may feel that a jury should not have the right to second-guess the patent office.
- How many of you feel comfortable with the fact that a jury has the right to judge the patent office's judgment?
- How many of you do not feel comfortable with the fact that a jury has the right to judge the patent office's decision?
- In what way might that make it difficult for you to sit on this jury?
- In this case, there is a question about whether a patent is valid or not. How many of you would have even a little difficulty with finding that a patent that has been issued by the U.S. Patent and Trademark Office is not valid? [Note, but do not follow up.]
- Layer Three: (Thematic Follow-Up Question)
- [Call on someone who did not raise their hand:] Mr. H, why might you be able to evaluate whether the patent was valid or invalid?

3. Views of Competition in Business

Layer One: (Warm-Up Question)

- I'm curious about your opinions of what companies should and should not do when competing in business with other companies. Who here loves to see companies compete aggressively in business? [Note, but do not follow up. Any response to this question is high-risk.]

Layer Two: (Group Bias Questions)

- When it comes to competition in business more generally, how many of you feel that companies should never build new products and ideas based on a competitor's product or idea? [Note, but do not follow up.]
- Let me ask your opinions on a slightly different question. On one hand, some people believe that the most important thing about conducting business is that it be fair—they say competition is great, but "fairness first." Some people tend to believe that "business is business," and it should be aggressive and competitive regardless of whether or not it's always fair. Knowing that you may fall somewhere in between the two views, which do you feel more closely mirrors your opinion?

- How many of you feel strongly that business should be fair? [Note as higher risk, but do not follow up.]
- And how many of you are closer to the second view: Business is business and it can't always be fair?

Layer Three: (Thematic Follow-Up Questions)

- Ms. J, why do you say that?
- Mr. K, you also raised your hand. What is it about business that makes aggressive competition important?
- Who usually benefits from aggressive competition between businesses that sell a product like cell phones?
- Mr. L, you think that it is possible to focus on being a profitable company while also being fair, is that correct?[22]

4. Views of Values in Business

Layer One: (Warm-Up Question)

- As you know, if you end up on this jury you are going to have to resolve a dispute that couldn't get resolved any other way. Who here has had the experience at work, or in their personal life, or on a previous jury of resolving a dispute between two sophisticated parties?

Layer Two: (Group Bias Questions)

- People may have different approaches to looking at a dispute like this. Some would say that you have to look at the big picture and what is fair overall. Others would say that you are best off sticking to what the law says.
- How many of you would be closer to that first group: you have to look at the big picture and what is fair overall? [Note, but do not follow up.]
- And how many of you are closer to the second group: you are best off sticking to what the law says?

Layer Three: (Thematic Follow-Up Questions)

- Mr. G, why do you say that?
- Ms. H, would you add anything to that?

5. Familiarity with Phone Cameras/Technology

Layer One: (Warm-Up Question)

- Finally, I'm going to switch gears and ask you a few brief questions about camera phone technology. How many of you have some familiarity with the patented product at issue in this case—a mobile phone camera?

---

22. This is to prevent jurors from thinking that you do not expect competition in business.

Layer Two: (Group Experience Questions)

- How many of you own a phone with a camera?
- When did you first start using a mobile phone with a camera?
- In your mind, how much do mobile phone cameras today differ from what they used to be?
- Do you perceive the phones as continuing to change and evolve? How so?
- Do you think each new small change in this technology is meaningful, or are only some such innovations meaningful? Why?

6. Plaintiff Sympathizer/Damages Augmenter

Layer One: (Warm-Up Question, pursue for cause)

- Lawsuits seem to be in the news a lot. [Choose an otherwise pro-plaintiff juror.[23]] Mr. S, what is your opinion about the number of lawsuits in this country? Why do you believe there are so many lawsuits?

Layer Two: (Group Experience Questions)

- How many of you have ever filed a lawsuit or know someone well who has?
- How many of you have ever claimed workers' compensation?
- Based on what you know, how many of you believe today's laws make it too difficult for people to recover money from companies in lawsuits?

Layer Two: (Group Bias Questions)

- Does anyone believe that, whether an amount has been specifically proven or not, a large-dollar verdict is simply a good way to send a message? [Note, but do not follow up.]
- On the other hand, who believes that damage amounts should be limited to the amounts specifically proven to be caused by a party clearly at fault?

Layer Three: (Thematic Follow-Up Question)

- Mr. V, why is that important?

Layer Two: (Group Bias Questions)

- How many of you believe that if a case against a company has made it to court, then the company probably did something wrong? [Pursue for cause strike.]
- How many of you would likely vote against a company no matter what the evidence? [Pursue for cause strike.]

---

23. Nearly all jurors will say there are too many lawsuits. If you choose one of plaintiff's likely favorites, you may trick them into striking one of their own. Or at least, by choosing a pro-plaintiff juror, you prevent them from using the question to single out one of yours.

CHAPTER 6

Patent Infringement

"The idea of a jury trial is that it is incumbent on each side to make a strong case and the jury has to decide. But everybody in there was fairly confused as to what was going on with the patents. We read through it and tried to parse out, what does this mean? What does this mean?"

—Patent juror who found infringement

I. Patent Infringement and the Jury

Jurors struggle mightily with the law of infringement, yet it becomes greatly accessible to them when they reframe "patent infringement litigation" as "idea theft" litigation. Throughout this chapter, you will find repeated evidence of jurors' reframing from the erudite to the practical in handling questions of patent infringement. When you get inside jurors' minds, persuading them to your position—even with tough technology—becomes much easier.

Trial consultants Laurie Kuslansky and Daniel Wolfe put it this way:

> Based on juror prejudices (e.g., that inventors are special geniuses who deserve protection at all costs, and that the [U.S. Patent and Trademark Office (USPTO)] doesn't make mistakes), it is even more likely that jurors will mold information that is inconsistent to their views to fit those views, rather than change them. Attempting to change jurors' minds is like swimming upstream: There is little hope for progress. It is more productive to incorporate their preconceptions into trial strategy. Consequently, it may be useful to become familiar with commonly-held juror beliefs, folk myths, and specific perceptions in patent cases.

No matter which side you represent in a given patent matter, certain universal truths exist when it comes to patent infringement and the jury, irrespective of venue and patent subject matter. The next section summarizes many of those truths that affect all parties to an infringement action.

A. Behavior Predominates

> *"Although patent infringement requires proof that every element of a patent claim is found in the accused product, it is often the propriety of each party's conduct that is the most critical element in determining victory in a patent case."*
>
> —Jane Michaels, Holland & Hart LLP[1]

There exists no verdict form language in the infringement section that asks, "Did the plaintiff/defendant behave in a decent manner?" Yet there might as well be. In every patent case on which we have consulted, jurors have spent a substantial amount of time in their deliberations (mock or actual) discussing the parties' behavior, all while cognizant of the fact that the infringement questions on the verdict form ask about specific claims in the patent at issue.

Whether you call it "behavior" (as we do), conduct, non-technical evidence, or something else, the way human beings behave during the events at issue, and what motivates those human beings, are key factors in how jurors decide infringement claims. Our experience is not isolated. Other trial consultants have witnessed the same phenomenon. In the words of colleague Tom O'Toole: "Any attorney who thinks jurors are going to decide a patent case on the technical details should consider another area of law."[2] And according to trial consultant George Speckart:

> [I]nvalidity and infringement questions are not generally decided on substantive technical issues so much as they are decided on conduct issues. In this context, the term "conduct" is a very broad concept that consists of factors such as the initial notice of infringement and various aspects of communication between the parties; the prosecution history of the file; characteristics and behavior of the inventor; licensing negotiations and agreements; royalties paid to others; and the marketing and sales information associated with the related or accused products.[3]

We, like many of our colleagues, also continue to observe the important role of counsel's behavior in the courtroom as at least an additional relevant layer for how jurors perceive and evaluate the parties' actions during the events at issue. Arrogant trial lawyers force jurors to work harder to find a corporate defendant was not arrogant. Disorganized trial lawyers ask jurors to distinguish between a patent owner's claim that it identified and provided all the relevant prior art from the perception that its lawyer cannot find his notes for a cross-examination. There is no one way to try any case but jurors know and care about a consistency between what lawyers do and what they ask jurors to believe.

---

1. Personal Communication with Jane Michaels, Senior Counsel, Holland & Hart LLP (2013).
2. Personal Communication with Thomas O'Toole, Ph.D., Litigation Consultant (2022).
3. George Speckart, *Navigating the Road to a Jury Verdict*, 50 For Def. 10 (2008).

B. The Patented Technology's Effect on Jurors' Lives

> *"Patents are not simple and they do not lend themselves to easy digestion unless you are in the business."*
>
> —Patent juror who found infringement

In our research, we have had the fascinating experience of watching thousands of mock jurors deliberate. We have also interviewed hundreds of actual jurors after trials. Experience with both types of fact finders reminds us that art imitates life in the overlap between reasoning in mock deliberations and reasoning in actual deliberations. Some theories exist that jurors spend upwards of one-third of their time in deliberations talking about *themselves* and their experiences as a filter for the case. That percentage may well vary from case to case but we certainly observe some degree of that self-filtering in every mock exercise we conduct. Whether or not jurors have direct experience with the patented technology, they often find a way to interpret the potential effects of the patented technology on their own daily lives, if only as a way to try to simplify and understand the technical details.

C. The "Magic" Matters

In preparation for a recent patent litigation trial, we assisted in the preparation of expert witnesses whose role was to explain the technical side of the invention on behalf of a patent-owner plaintiff. The technology was complex, unfamiliar, and difficult. At first, one of the experts was, too. After some discussion about how to simplify and make the explanations accessible to jurors, we landed on a concept that works both for expert witnesses who may be wedded to overly technical detail, and jurors who want and need to understand how the technology works. The guiding principle that helps is that patentees must strike a balance between making the technology simple enough to understand but unfamiliar enough to feel magical and inventive. The question of whether or not a claimed invention is magical matters a great deal for both patentees and accused infringers who want to help jurors see there is no magic in the claimed invention. Advocates must understand and develop their case-specific ways of incorporating the magic (patentees) or demystifying it (accused infringers).

D. The Need for a Compelling Infringement Story

As the first researchers to write well on story in the courtroom in the 1980s, authors W. Lance Bennett and Martha Feldman made a profound case for combining narrative with evidence.[4] Today, the clear benefits of framing as much evidence into a story as possible are well known. However, a number of clients

---

4. W. Lance Bennett & Martha S. Feldman, Reconstructing Reality in the Courtroom: Justice and Judgment in American Culture (1981).

have said to us over the years, "We have no 'aha moment' story to tell. What do we do then?" Fair question. The truth is that you are still on the hook to find story where you can, whether it be as infringement plaintiff or defendant. Consider these alternatives when no clear "aha moment" story exists.

Alternatives to an "Aha" Moment of Invention

The Slow (but Still Meaningful) "Aaaahaaaa" Story	When the "aha" moment is a collection of a multitude of moments, be candid with jurors about that fact. For *patent-holding plaintiffs*: Jurors will be looking for one unless or until you can educate them about the fact that so many inventions occur over a long period of starts and stops. Where lab notebooks (or other documentary evidence) memorialize those periods, create a demonstrative that shows the multitude of notations or bring in physical evidence of failed attempts at the ultimate invention. For *accused infringers*: The absence of an "aha" story may be good support for your point that no true innovation occurred here.
The Story of Problems to Be Solved	Sometimes jurors can better relate to the problems the invented device or process solved than the invention itself, especially when that invention is complex. Personalize the problem(s) to individuals in the industry who were most adversely affected by the lack of the invention. For instance, in our mobile phone camera example, personalize the struggles that customers were having with prior mobile phone camera performance or the problem of marketing a mobile phone without a camera-related innovation. For *patent-holding plaintiffs*: As infringement plaintiff, if your invention simply solved or eradicated that problem, your story sets jurors up to appreciate that the innovation was significant (and nonobvious). For *accused infringers*: If the problem had either been solved long before the plaintiff came along (via prior art) or if your product or process solves the problem better than the plaintiff's claimed invention does, you are on your way to establishing noninfringement and/or invalidity.
The Surrogate "Aha" Story	Absent anything interesting in either of the first two alternatives, consider hitching your innovation to something better known. For *patent-holding plaintiffs*: If you are the patentee and you want to have people understand the "behind the scenes" effort that went into the ultimate invention, consider the fact that it took Swiss engineer George de Mestral eight years to develop Velcro® after encountering cockleburs on his dog and his clothing after walking through fields. Even after his first U.S. patent for his hook-and-loop device issued in 1952, it still took time before the invention was appreciated. It was only after the National Aeronautics and Space Administration (NASA) started using the product that it achieved widespread recognition. As plaintiff, if any or all of the elements of that story parallel your infringement story, pair them with something like this household product. For *accused infringers*: If you can contrast the plaintiff's claimed invention story with the story of something like Velcro®, that would prove helpful as well.

E. Presumption of the USPTO's Credibility and Enforcement Authority

As noted in previous chapters, the USPTO has enjoyed the top favorability slot for governmental agencies among jury-eligible respondents for as long as we have been collecting or observing national data on jurors' views of numerous federal agencies.[5] Therefore, the more *both parties* can endorse the wisdom of the USPTO, the better. (More specifics on this appear within the following pages.) We have put this logic to the test when working for patent-holding plaintiffs and accused infringers in patent infringement matters. Parties who criticize the USPTO's judgment and decision-making, even subtly, tend to alienate at least a subset of the jury.

At the same time, many jurors believe so much in the credibility of the USPTO that they expect the agency to be both the monitoring body and the enforcement authority when a patent is infringed. Some jurors expect the patent examiner to testify on one party's behalf at trial. The updated and more complete version of the Federal Judicial Center's patent tutorial video helps many jurors better understand the key realities that the USPTO is busy, examiners are not testing inventions in a lab, and the process can involve human error. Still, patentees should communicate clearly that the issued patent, not the USPTO, gives them the authority to enforce their ownership rights. Depending on the case facts, one or both parties are likely to benefit from clarifying that the USPTO will not testify at trial on behalf of either party.

F. The (Sometimes Fleeting) Celebrity Status of the Inventor

For most jurors, named inventors share a status similar to published authors of good books. Many people think they have potential to write the next great American novel, much like many believe they have the next great invention in their own mind's workshop. However, very few ever put pen to paper in either scenario. The fact that an inventor took his or her idea to the patent phase greatly impresses many people. To then have that application blessed by the USPTO is a clear endorsement indeed. Of course, the named inventor can lose that celebrity status fairly quickly if it appears that he or she was not the first legitimate inventor of the product. The inventor's character matters a great deal as jurors assess claims of infringement and invalidity.

Stories of even passing interactions between the named inventor and the defendant or between the named inventor and those involved with the prior art hold great interest for jurors. We have consulted on cases in which a lunch meeting, held before the filing of a patent application, between the named inventor and the alleged infringer holds as much import for the jury as does the claim language at issue. A memo that indicates the alleged infringer knew of and considered the claimed invention as it developed its own product often serves as

5. A national juror survey we helped develop first asked jury-eligible participants for their perceptions of federal governmental agencies in 2005. However, we have collected this information during private mock trial research beginning in the early 1990s and with the same results, where the USPTO earned the top slot in favorability.

the filter for viewing the defendant's behavior with suspicion.[6] This suspicion can be overcome if the accused infringer can show it took great pains to design around the claimed invention; however, the defense will have the burden of overcoming inherent misgivings about seemingly coincidental overlap between the claimed invention and the allegedly infringing device or process.

G. The Inability to Fit the Case Facts to the Verdict Form

> *"They were trying to hide that they infringed. . . . It was a patent case and in my notes I had written to myself, 'What does all this have to do with a patent case?'"*
>
> —Patent juror who found infringement

It is (a little) understandable, when you think about it. You put a great deal of effort into preparing your infringement case, you prepare your witnesses, you have good days and bad days in trial, and then you get toward the end of trial with issues *still* before the court on the phrasing of the verdict form. Given such uncertainty, how can you be expected to be specific with the jury about the verdict form questions before closing argument? Even then, it is the rare closing argument that puts significant focus on the verdict form questions. Rather, the best face of closing that often appears in front of a jury in final arguments is a cursory run-through of the verdict questions, with counsel quickly requesting a "yes" to this question and a "no" to that one. Ultimately, this foreperson's sentiments are echoed across too many patent juries:

> *"I spent three months of my life [on a patent jury], and I felt used because I didn't know what the verdict meant. It was almost as if, here the attorneys are, doing it to us again with this questionnaire."*[7]
>
> —Jury foreperson

There are significant negative ramifications on jurors who hear too few connections between the evidence and the law. Trial consultant Beth Bonora interviewed this jury foreperson and describes well what we have repeatedly heard from jurors at the conclusion of patent trials:

> After a three-month patent trial, I went to a hospital to interview a doctor who had served as the foreperson on a trial involving cutting-edge technology. The first words out of his mouth were, "I'm going to talk to you on one condition—tell me what it is we decided." He described

6. A memorandum in the *Apple v. Samsung* patent trial was significant in jurors' judgments. *See* Seth Weintraub, *Interview with* Apple-Samsung *Jury Foreman: How He Applied His Patent to Break Stalemate*, 9TO5MAC (Aug. 27, 2012), http://9to5mac.com/2012/08/27/interview-with-apple-samsung-jury-foreman-how-he-applied-his-patent-to-break-stalemate-video/.

7. From an interview conducted with actual jury foreperson by trial consultant Beth Bonora.

> the jury's painful struggle to understand the complex verdict form. The jurors were diligent, several were college-educated, and they worked hard, in a cooperative fashion—for weeks—to answer 18 very specific questions, which they had never expected to see on the verdict form.
>
> They read the jury instructions over and over, they looked carefully at many of the 560 exhibits. The sad irony is that they mostly agreed at a global level as to what had happened and what a just result would look like for the companies. They were shocked that no one had adequately explained to them ahead of time just what it was they were actually going to have to decide. They grappled with the relationship between the specific questions on the verdict form and the larger issues in the case. They were baffled and frustrated by their inability to bring their hard work to fruition. Some were angry.
>
> This is not an isolated case—juries continue to be hobbled by inadequate efforts to educate and instruct them. It's not easy to educate a patent jury. Smart and successful litigators often underestimate how much they must do to keep a jury from getting lost in the woods with no way out. It also takes a judge willing to adequately pre-instruct to give jurors the tools they need for effective learning and deliberations.[8]

Even pre-instruction is not enough (but we certainly advocate its use). In fact, the most powerful way to equip your jurors with the tools they need to answer the verdict questions is to effectively link patent law to the evidence in opening, with witness testimony, and in closing. You may not know the precise wording of a number of verdict questions at the point of opening statement; however, you do know the law of infringement. Later in this chapter, we will suggest (1) a very specific structure for your infringement case that incorporates the law, and (2) a framework for making a complete argument within an issue that makes the link between the law and your evidence more overt. In our experience, using these approaches makes a dramatic difference in jurors' ability to understand the law when it comes to completing the verdict form.

In addition, Bonora reminds us of the following:

> The [following] tools have been available for years, endorsed by the [American Bar Association], and many other organizations—let's use them!
>
> - Tutorials for the jury
> - Liberal allowance for graphics and simulations
> - Table of contents to the trial exhibits
> - Organized binders with exhibits
> - Allowance for jurors' questions, and full answers
> - Interim summaries by the attorneys
> - Thorough pre-instruction[9]

8. *Id.*
9. Email Interview with Beth Bonora, Trial Consultant (2012).

H. Jurors' Predominant Focus on Firstness

In the era before the America Invents Act, many jurors struggled with the fact that the "first to invent" was the standard for determining the rightful inventor. Those who struggled felt this standard was "patently unfair" to the person who finally filed for the patent, especially in light of their own inventive experiences where bright ideas often ended up a dim memory. In the words of patent mock jurors:

- "The basic idea was the plaintiff's. . . . I'm sure a lot of people thought about it, but plaintiff is the one that [sic] got the patent."
- "Who runs with the idea? Who takes it to fruition? That is key to the whole thing. People dream all the time with these things."
- "The idea may have been out there, but he [the patentee] put it together and he presented it."

Still today, in a different environment we continue to observe jurors who care about who acted first, who has proof of the earliest development, and who "wins" the timeline. This is yet another example of how jurors' frequent struggles with the complexity of patent cases translates to a search and a reliance on shortcuts they can understand and use to decide a fair result. Trial attorneys must continue to recognize and address jurors' tendencies and present a case that speaks to them.

I. Jurors' Struggle with the Lack of a Requirement to Prove Intentional Copying

Unless willfulness is part of your case, patent law is unique in the way law professors and attorneys Christopher Cotropia and Mark Lemley describe:

> Patent law is virtually alone in intellectual property (IP) in punishing independent development. To infringe a copyright or trade secret, defendants must copy the protected IP from the plaintiff, directly or indirectly. But patent infringement requires only that the defendant's product falls within the scope of the patent claims. Not only doesn't the defendant need to intend to infringe, but the defendant may be entirely unaware of the patent or the patentee and still face liability.[10]

Now, at first blush, this fact would seem to benefit only the patent-holding plaintiff. As plaintiff, why not underscore the fact that it is not your burden to prove the defendant intended to copy your client's patent? After all, some jurors do mistakenly look for evidence of intent in cases where willfulness is not even being claimed. It would be important to clarify that for a jury. However, there exists a bit of a "bad guy" problem here for plaintiffs. To some jurors who hear this for the first time, their reaction is, "You mean, even I could be held liable for accidentally copying someone else's patented idea?" The vulnerability

10. Christopher A. Cotropia & Mark A. Lemley, *Copying in Patent Law*, 87 N.C. L. Rev. 1421 (2009).

attached to that sentiment could place the accused infringer in a sympathetic position (and some jurors may want to acknowledge that with their verdict). It surprises us to some degree that more accused infringers do not capitalize on this inclination to sympathize. However, the lion's share of jurors recognize that they would need to nullify the law in order to vote for an infringer out of sympathy. In this situation, the plaintiff should clarify that it is the jury's mandate—not the USPTO's—to enforce the plaintiff's patent rights. Contemplate for jurors the downside of not enforcing your patent, even if the defendant's infringement is accidental.

J. Your Judgment Regarding What *Not* to Teach in Your Case

This may be the single most difficult decision a patent trial attorney must make. As tricky as it can be to teach others about the complex legal and technical issues in any patent case, it may take greater courage to determine what *not* to include in your case. More than any other kind of case, we find that patent jurors absorb far less than attorneys present. The more you include, the less control you have over what jurors absorb. We will get specific about teaching technology later in this chapter, but suffice it to say that less is more. Not sure what to include or exclude? Finding the answer to that question is the single best use of mock trial research in patent litigation. Do not limit yourself to simply testing *jury* comprehension. Judges and arbitrators also struggle with complex information when the issues are foreign to them. Consider research that factors into mock judges' or mock arbitrators' comprehension of your case as well.

II. Persuasion for the Patent Infringement Plaintiff

A. Choosing the Right Infringement Theme

It is easy to become enamored with a clever turn of phrase in choosing a theme. However, the right theme for a party in any case must be carefully chosen because it has the potential to become the primary filter for jurors' interpretation of your argument. Choose well and you can direct jurors' focus where you want it to go. Choose poorly and you may alienate jurors from your client's position.

1. Criteria for Determining the Right Theme

Irrespective of jurisdiction, criteria exist for patentees with regard to themes that work well for the infringement phase of the case. Following are the most prevalent criteria.

1. **Choose a theme that appeals to your tougher audience**. Your easier audience (the pro-infringement juror) does not need your theme to direct them as much as your noninfringement-prone jurors do. First, understand the characteristics of these noninfringement jurors. (See Chapter 5 for a more thorough discussion of these jurors.) In short, our research finds that noninfringement jurors tend to be more rules-oriented and more logical rather

than emotional in their thought processes. If you choose a theme that focuses on the law (i.e., what is legal according to the letter of the law), it will resonate far more with these jurors than if you choose a theme based on fairness (i.e., what is fair at jurors' gut level).

2. **Contrast your client's legitimate behavior with the defendant's illegal infringement**. Resist the inclination to immediately go on the offensive regarding your opponent's poor behavior. You will be more persuasive if you first underscore what the patent holder did well in this case. In addition, by using phraseology that points to your hard work to invent the concept, you lay the groundwork for a validity defense that focuses on novelty.
3. **When possible, set the theme (with accompanying silver bullet) as the structural framework for your opening statement**. The silver bullet comprises the first one to two minutes of your opening. Besides setting the tone for your argument, it is also a good opportunity to introduce the skeletal framework of your argument. You may find you need two themes—one for your infringement case and one for your validity case. Use good judgment in introducing the theme in either two different parts of your argument or all at once.

2. Wording the Right Theme

As one example, consider a simple theme that has applicability across any number of patent cases for the patentee plaintiff:

> *They say imitation is the highest form of flattery. But this defendant's illegal imitation infringes the patent we legally and painstakingly obtained, pure and simple. Needless to say, we are not flattered.*

Another approach that focuses on the validity case shows how you can acquire a dual advantage by focusing on novelty:

> *To say that this patent was an easily found pot of gold at the end of a short path would be misleading. The true path to this invention was a long, frustrating one, full of more bumps and detours than the inventors could even recall. To allow the defendant to take a shortcut and infringe this patent is patently unfair.*

B. Teach the Vital Need for Litigation to Protect Inventors' Rights . . .

Many jurors tell us they were completely unaware at the onset of a case (and often further in) that the patent holder must initiate civil litigation to enforce its patent rights. Unless you tell them otherwise, many jurors believe the USPTO is the enforcement authority. Why does that matter? Because this role of enforcing one's "patent-given" rights makes patent infringement plaintiffs begin at a more credible level with jurors in comparison to, say, personal injury plaintiffs. Patentees are not seeking monetary gain for the sake of its dollar value, they are (often) seeking to enforce their rights, prevent unfair business conduct, and reclaim the value of their hard-earned rights that motivated their patent strategy in the first place. This enhanced legitimacy affects your jury profile (see Chapter 5, Jury Selection) and your case strategy.

C. . . . Even When That Means the Plaintiff Has a Legal Monopoly

While most jurors agree that the patent holder has the right to the legal monopoly afforded by the patent, a minority of jurors see the patent as harmful to the economy (and, ultimately, to themselves).

Interestingly, the percentages change dramatically when we looked at a subset of jury-eligible respondents who believe patent infringement cases against a corporation "almost always" have merit. This shift tells us that a question about this in jury selection is important to identify pro-infringement jurors.

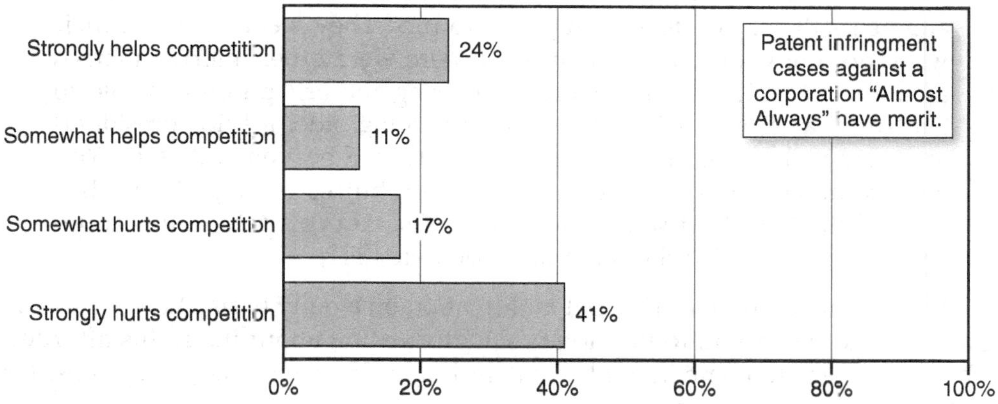

Source: Persuasion Strategies/K&B National Research, National Juror Survey (2011) (N=400)

Your job as plaintiff's counsel is to persuade the pro-defense jurors that society should care about protecting the inventor's rights because his or her patent provides a necessary "boost" for innovations to follow. A few examples from history make this point effectively:

- Since Eli Whitney's cotton gin invention was patented in 1774, 79 additional patents were issued that were innovations on his original design.
- Since Samuel Morse's telegraph patent issued, 807 additional, related patents followed.
- Since Alexander Graham Bell's telephone patent issued, 350 related patents issued.

D. In a World of Legal Monopoly, Choices Are Critical to Jurors

Aside from the important need to persuade jurors who fear that patent rights are akin to unfair monopoly, all jurors will pay close attention to your overt point that the defendant always has legitimate choices besides infringing the patent. This argument carries the double advantage of making the alleged infringer look worse for not capitalizing on its choices while underscoring the fact that patent rights are *not* a dead end for would-be innovators. Every time we run mock trial research or talk to jurors after actual patent trials, they raise the issue of choices both parties had, as is evidenced by this quote from the jury foreman in the *Apple v. Samsung* patent trial that resulted in a verdict in excess of $1 billion for Apple in 2012. The last line of his quote makes clear the importance of Samsung's choices to the jury's decision.

> What was put into evidence was two things. Minutes of a meeting that was held in Korea and Google was present and it had to do with the tablet. Google demanded in their minutes they [Samsung] were too close to Apple and they needed to pull back because they were worried about their operating system. . . . Overall they [Google] wanted everything to be less like Apple. There were other approaches they [Samsung] could have used. They chose not to pass that information down to the engineers that were developing the product. They went on about their work not knowing the decision. And there were other internal memos after that in evidence that were comparing the cell phones, Apple to Samsung, and the individual on the Samsung side, a [vice president] at a very high level, said the difference is that of heaven and earth. You need to move closer. They did move closer, but in moving closer, they crossed the line. That was unnecessary. You can compete in this country, be similar, and at the same time compete fairly.[11]

When you are immersed in patent litigation on a daily basis, it is easy to forget that juries need you to provide basic information about the rights afforded those who want to compete with a patent holder in the marketplace. Consider using this simple analogy:

> A patent is not a stop sign for competitors. It is a "proceed with caution" sign. Competitors can proceed in a legitimate way that builds upon or works around the patent rather than imitates it. The defendant in this case chose to break the law and take an illegal shortcut when other legitimate routes existed. That's what this jury needs to protect—the rules of the road.

E. "Accidental" Infringement Is Still Infringement

When assessing literal infringement or infringement under the doctrine of equivalents, it is not uncommon for jurors (at least initially) to insert their own inaccurate standard of intent into their analysis. Consider overtly making the point that accidental infringement is still infringement by addressing it in your opening statement or by introducing the concept during oral voir dire, especially when you suspect the accused infringer will be likeable. Some jurors may feel that it is unfair to hold a party responsible for unknowingly infringing.

11. *Id.*

Analogize to an out-of-state driver unknowingly breaking a traffic law in jurors' local jurisdiction. That driver's actions are still prone to being ticketed.

F. Jurors' Judgments of the Importance of the Claimed Invention Color Their Perception of the Plaintiff's Infringement Claim

On a number of occasions (and especially when more than one patent is at issue in a case), we have watched jurors filter their view of the strength of the plaintiff's case through their judgment about the relative importance of the claimed invention. In those instances, jurors have frequently criticized the plaintiff for being petty against the defendant or, worse, anticompetitive. The presence of more than one patent creates an inherent tendency on jurors' parts to compare their importance against one another. One remedy for this risk is to create as strong a case as possible that focuses on the problem that needed to be solved and the remedy to the problem via the claimed invention. The more clearly jurors understand the need, the more they can be persuaded about the patent's significance. If necessary, overtly grant that the invention's utility may seem less significant at first blush, but that its meaning in the industry (and, if possible, to the consumer) is greater than meets the eye.

G. Licensing Behavior Speaks Representatively of Competitive Intent

We have seen it over and over again. When evidence of a patent-holding plaintiff's licensing options comes into a case, jurors place great focus on how the patent holder behaved. Did the patent-holding plaintiff offer licensing to the accused infringer and to others? To others but not to the accused infringer? Jurors place a great deal of weight on the past behavior of a party, and often to a greater extent over your key fact witness's testimony. If the plaintiff offered licensing options on its own invention, jurors want to know if they were offered indiscriminately or if plaintiff appeared to use them as an anticompetitive tool by discriminating among a pool of potential licensees. When you can trumpet the plaintiff's good behavior in offering a license, especially if it was offered to the accused infringer, you should do so. It matters to the fact finder.

H. Create a Framework That Sets the Context for Your Infringement Case

Social science and brain science research continue to find that we need context (in this case, story) to learn and connect seemingly disparate pieces of information, especially when that information is complex. For that reason, astonishment is the most apt word to describe our reaction to the number of sophisticated patent litigators we see who organize their opening statement in a claim-by-claim (or patent-by-patent) structure. It may have served you well in the *Markman* hearing, but it will fail in front of a jury (or even a judge fairly new to patent litigation). A claim-by-claim structure fails to teach jurors in a way they will retain your persuasive point or the technology behind your client's invention.

In addition, that topical approach will lose you the opportunity to tee up your validity defense within your infringement case. (See rows II, III, and IV in the following table.)

Instead, consider the following for the body of plaintiff's infringement opening.

Plaintiff's Infringement Structure

Structural Point	Logic Behind the Structural Point
I. The Problem That Needed to Be Solved	Many plaintiffs' arguments jump too quickly to the patented technology without first making the case for its value. Psychologically, you want jurors to *want* to fight for the patent holder's technology in order to vote in favor of infringement. Build jurors' enthusiasm for the patented technology by first selling them on the problem. In addition to describing the problem, explain the harm (or, at a minimum, the downside) to the consumer (and to the plaintiff/the industry) of keeping the status quo. This explanation does not need to be lengthy. If a compelling story accompanies the problem, incorporate that story here. Any story anywhere in a patent case is a welcome event for jurors.
II. The Effort That Went into Solving the Problem	Just as "inventor lore" focuses on the fact that it took Edison more than 9,000 attempts to invent the lightbulb, *explain your inventor's attempts*, both failed and successful, to invent the technology. (Doing so also tees you up for the validity defense that this technology was far from obvious.) In addition, explain the *length of time* it took to finally achieve the current invention, especially if the "invention time" was protracted. Great effort deserves great reward. If the *monetary expense* of achieving the plaintiff's invention and patent was great, consider introducing the amount of money spent to the jury. However, take care in making this decision. While the number may be impressive, it could also provide an unintended "anchor" for the jury in any damages discussions.
III. The "Aha" Moment When the Inventor(s) Achieved the Right Design	Whether subtle or dramatic, jurors love a good "aha" moment to help solidify the fact that the invention was legitimate and hard-fought. For some jurors who never come to appreciate the technical details, this part of the story sticks with them in a way that the technology never will. Even when the "aha" moment is a collection of hours or days that occur over time, introduce the emotion that accompanied the sense of accomplishment and/or the inventor(s)' pleasure when the patent issued. Jurors tend to place greater trust in "in-the-moment" emotions and behaviors over "after-the-fact" testimony.
IV. The Benefit to the Consumer of the Plaintiff's Patent(s)	Just as you defined the problem that needed to be solved from the consumer's perspective, underscore the effect of the solution on the consumer. This sets the scene for making a significant damages argument in addition to motivating jurors to understand the technical case. This applies whether or not the patent was commercialized.

Structural Point	Logic Behind the Structural Point
	If the patent at issue was commercialized: Explain how your inventor's innovation affects our daily lives. Use concrete examples to which you can return as you explain the technical side of each claim term or patent. By focusing on consumer use, you can reduce the number of analogies to which you refer. Too many disparate analogies can confuse rather than clarify. If this patent was not commercialized: At a minimum, this invention is now in the public domain via the patent's disclosures. There is no telling how this patent may advance knowledge for the next iteration (or for whom). Consider contrasting this inventor's contribution via public disclosure with Coca-Cola's decision not to do the same with its secret formula for its cola product. Doing so adds interest to your inventor's story by "associative contrast."
V. The USPTO's Reward for Plaintiff's Disclosure of Its Secret Formula	Underscore the fairness aspect of patent disclosures and inventions to set the stage for the unfairness of defendant's infringement. Once patented, the secret formula is now a public but protected formula. It allows those who want to improve upon the disclosed innovation to do so without copying the public, but protected, formula. Briefly educate jurors about the fact that, contrary to popular belief, the USPTO is not an enforcement agency that proactively seeks and prosecutes infringers. Rather, the jury in this civil case holds the legal monopoly on that authority, just as the patent holder holds the legal monopoly on the claimed invention.
VI. The Technology Behind the Plaintiff's Patent(s)	The prior five points of context will prepare jurors to finally begin to understand and appreciate the technical side of your case. This stage should now be easier given the context provided by the prior five points. Your best chance of motivating jurors lacking technical proficiency to learn your technology is to set the technology within your invention story. Once jurors have that context, they are more likely to learn and retain the key technical aspects of each patent. (Read on to review more recommendations on teaching technology in patent litigation.)
VII. The Damage to Plaintiff from Defendant's Patent Infringement	At a minimum, you will want to make a general statement about the degree of damage, if not the monetary damage to the patent-holding plaintiff. When dealing with multiple patents, consider testing in a mock trial whether you can separate out the damages arguments by patent, thereby doing as many damages segments in the opening as you have patents, or whether it is more effective to do one comprehensive damages argument at the end of your argument. If applicable, explain how this field is crowded with competitors. This immediate explanation accomplishes two things. First, it sets the stage for making the argument that a small innovation can be a big deal and worthy of a patent in the USPTO's eyes. Second, it lays the groundwork for assigning motive to your defendant competitor to steal your invention.

I. Avoid Being "Just a Number"

For good reason, patent attorneys refer to patents using the last three digits of the issued patent number (e.g., the '123 patent). However, this practice literally turns the inventor into a number. It may never be practical to eliminate the three digits, so we suggest adding the inventor's name instead (e.g., the Smith '123 patent). For the plaintiff, making this small addition personalizes the patent and gives jurors a second shot (name plus patent number) at remembering which one you are covering when more than one patent is at issue in a case.

In situations where a descriptive label or phrase can help to emphasize the patent's novelty and distinction from other art, we have also seen descriptive labels help patent holders as well (e.g., the Triple Camera '123 patent).

J. Use Concrete Language

Trial consultant and colleague Ken Broda-Bahm urges our patent clients to "move down the 'ladder of abstraction' when choosing jury-friendly language."[12] (His blog post from *Your Trial Message* comprises the bulk of content for this section on using concrete language.)

Based on the work of the only U.S. senator who was also a renowned communication theorist, S.I. Hayakawa, the idea of a ladder of abstraction is a recognition of the fact that language can range from broad abstractions ("liberty," "power," "good") down through several levels to specific identifiable concepts ("a day off," "a traffic ticket," "a chocolate cake"). Applied to the practical needs of communication, the lesson is that you can often improve communication by moving down the ladder. Using more concrete language increases the chance that the thing you think of when you use a word comes closest to the thing your audience thinks of when they hear that word.

Still, communicators have a tendency to creep up the ladder because we think it makes us sound educated, or formal, or broadly inclusive. (In our experience with patent litigators, it also seems to occur because you communicate so frequently with other patent litigators who know your meaning at a much more abstract level than a jury or a judge new to the patent world ever could.) But better communication in most cases is found at the other end, down in the nitty-gritty of identifiable things and actions.

IP cases are difficult by nature. Compared with other kinds of cases, like personal injury, parts of your argument necessarily lack the sense of place, event, main character, and visceral harm when you are in the midst of a technical dispute over precise meanings. For the many lawyers who have spent time in the field of academic debate, it can be more like the sterile world of "topicality" rather than the flesh-and-blood narrative of advantages and disadvantages.

But that is not inevitable. One way to move your patent case down the ladder is to tell a compelling invention story, in the form of either your client's

---

12. Ken Broda-Bahm, *Climb Down the "Ladder of Abstraction" in Patent Cases (and All Cases)*, Your Trial Message (Apr. 23, 2012), https://yourtrialmessage.com/climb-down-the-ladder-of-abstraction-in-patent-cases-and-all-cases/.

own story if you're claiming infringement or a prior-art story if you're claiming invalidity. Nothing breathes life into abstract issues like a human story. Another way to increase concreteness is to more minutely scrutinize your language and adapt to the frame of reference jurors are likely to carry. While you cannot always use the jurors' language, you can often base your themes on their concepts.

For example (as Broda-Bahm suggests):

You May See It As . . .	But Jurors Understand It As . . .
Infringement	Theft
Invalidity	Someone's blunder
Prior art	Somebody got there first
Obviousness	I could have done that
Licensing	Pay to play

Instead of satisfying yourself with the knowledge that your words are legally accurate, ask yourself whether you are using words that would allow jurors to draw a picture of what you are talking about—literally. A good test of whether you are truly at the bottom rung of the ladder is whether your fact finder could pick up a pencil and create an image showing the setting, character, and action that you are describing. For example:

- *No picture*: "The law allows remedies for the infringement of our patent."
- *Picture*: "Right here in this courtroom, you can draw a line in the sand that says theft of this invention is not okay."

Broda-Bahm makes another interesting comment about jurors' fixation on "copying" despite the rarity of this claim in patent cases:

> *Patent cases based on allegations of outright copying tend to be rare. According to one study,*[13] "a surprisingly small percentage of patent cases involve even allegations of copying, much less proof of copying. Copying in patent law seems to be the exception, not the rule." The authors [sic] analysis of cases found only 1 in 10 patent cases include an allegation of copying, and most of those are pharmaceutical cases. Despite the relative infrequency of copying claims, patent juries nonetheless tend to equate the issue to simple cheating, like stealing the answers from your neighbor at school.
>
> This is why the patent invention story plays a critical role. As Chuck Kauffman, a consultant at Cap Analysis Group, put it, jurors tend to have a "romantic" view of invention, drawing from the classic examples of Thomas Edison and Alexander Graham Bell. In that mindset, an item proves its uniqueness, shows non-obviousness, and highlights the egregiousness of infringement through a compelling story. Looking at the patent issues themselves, it is a definitional jumble until it gets down to

13. Cotropia & Lemley, *supra* note 10.

the point of someone cheating or stealing something. Relevant or not, that is the filter jurors tend to use.[14]

K. Teach the Law

One of the biggest challenges patent jurors face comes with understanding the *significance* of a given argument. More often than not, they struggle because counsel has not made a clear enough link between the evidence and the law.

1. Literal Infringement

Because jurors often struggle mightily with what does and does not constitute infringement, your best chance of helping them understand often occurs by three steps: (1) teaching the requirements of literal infringement; (2) explaining how the accused infringer meets those requirements; and then (3) translating parts (1) and (2) through contrast.

Step 1: Teach the Requirements of Literal Infringement

Jurors understand easily that meeting every element of a given claim means *every element*. What is often less clear is jurors' understanding of how two competing technologies might match element for element when a side-by-side visual comparison is not feasible or simply does not demonstrate an immediately clear match. Jurors need more than a technical explanation to understand how you meet your burden.

Step 2: Explain How the Accused Infringer's Device/Method Meets Each Element

Using the simplest technical explanation you can, explain how the accused infringer's device or method meets each element. (Later in this chapter, we discuss approaches to teaching technology.) This step risks losing some jurors but is a necessary setup for step 3.

Step 3: Translate Through Contrast

Many cases (patent or otherwise) benefit immensely through teaching by contrast. When you "contemplate the alternative," you get the advantage of a "double whammy" of teaching. We call it the "Say and Show" model of argumentation. To make a complete argument on any specific issue, take jurors through the five steps included in the following graphic. The description to the right of each point explains the goal of the given step.

For steps 2 and 4, the critical demonstratives would be ones that compare/contrast reality with fiction on the same demonstrative. We have seen jurors place heavy emphasis on these points during mock deliberations when the technology or claim language was particularly dense.

---

14. Ken Broda-Bahm, *Tell Your Patent Invention Story in a Way That Is Worth Copyrighting*, Your Trial Message (June 9, 2011), https://yourtrialmessage.com/your-patent-invention-story/.

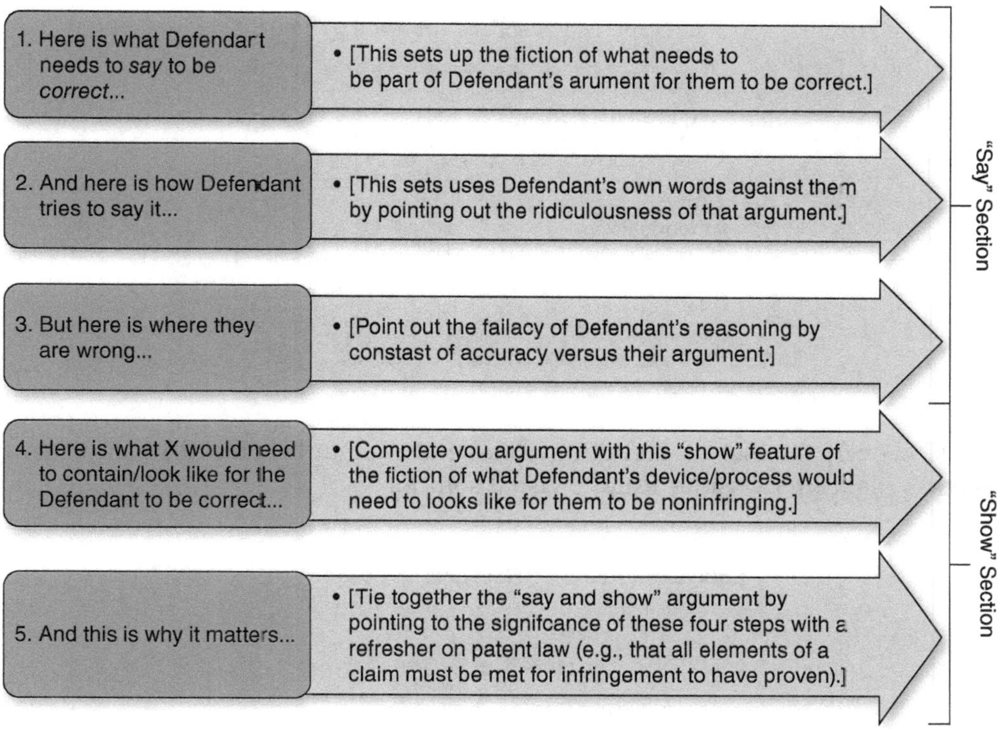

2. Infringement Under the Doctrine of Equivalents

The fascinating part of watching jurors deliberate in mock trials about the doctrine of equivalents is the fact that they frequently seem to feel more grounded (compared to assessing literal infringement) in evaluating whether the accused device or process performs substantially the same function, in substantially the same way, to achieve substantially the same result. The words "function," "way," and "result" are more jury-friendly, and many jurors seem comfortable comparing the accused device or method to the claimed invention (although they frequently miss the fact that the standard is to assess "element by element" rather than the patent as a whole).

The challenge you face with jurors when proving infringement under the doctrine of equivalents begins with the fact that, for many jurors, the "street definition" of "equivalents" equates to "identical." Therefore, unlike the term "literal infringement," you often start with jurors who have a preconception of equivalents from their own experience. As plaintiff, job one is to talk them out of those preconceptions.

Now, you could create a demonstrative that lays out the difference in black and white (defined in the figure as a poor example by G. Christopher Ritter):

"Equivalent" and "Identical" Are Not the Same

According to Merriam-Webster's Dictionary:

Equivalent
equal in force, amount, or value; equal in area or volume but not superposable; corresponding or virtually identical especially in effect or function

Identical
being the same; having such close resemblance as to be essentially the same

Source: G. Christopher Ritter, Creating Winning Trial Strategies and Graphics (2004)

However, this set of definitions does not accomplish the distinction you need as plaintiff. Consider Ritter's visual solution:

Equivalent Items Do Not Have to Be Identical

Source: G. Christopher Ritter, Creating Winning Trial Strategies and Graphics (2004)

With only written words in the title to supplement your verbal explanation, this demonstrative makes a simple but dramatic point and enlightens jurors regarding the key difference between "equivalent" and "identical."

Consider jurors' translations of this legal theory from across a few different cases as they tried to make sense of the concept of the doctrine of equivalents. As you can tell, those who found for the plaintiff placed their common focus on function. Whether or not these jurors were technically correct, their logic is worth noting. For example, in the words of patent mock jurors:

- "They [the plaintiff's claimed invention and the defendant's device] don't do the same thing, but they accomplish the same thing . . . under the equivalent clause."
- "It's more sophisticated, but it's doing the exact same thing. The result is the exact same."
- "The systems are working pretty much exactly the same. You got a mousetrap, it's got a small spring in it and a guy designs a mousetrap

with a bigger spring in it, and one works quicker than the other, but they're both working exactly the same."

- "They do exactly the same thing except one is a Cadillac and one is a Chevy."

III. Persuasion for the Accused Patent Infringer

A. Choosing the Right Noninfringement Theme

A defendant needs to acknowledge where the jury will be when the plaintiff "sits down" in terms of both opening statement and case-in-chief. A good theme is part of that acknowledgment but also takes the jury effectively into the defendant's perspective on how to view the issues in dispute.

1. Criteria for Determining the Right Theme

1. **Choose a theme that appeals to your tougher audience**. As with the choice of theme for the plaintiff, you should aim for your tougher audience as defendant. Your tougher audience will focus more on *fairness*. Frame your party's actions as ethical (in addition to legal) from your theme in opening to your last words in closing. (Chapter 5 will give you more information about the high-risk juror for the noninfringement defendant.)
2. **Underscore your fair, noninfringing behavior**. Your theme *and* your story should both emphasize the fair options of dancing in the same arena without stepping on your opponent's toes. For example, one small change may first strike your jurors as unfairly splitting hairs.
3. **Convey a "consumer-protective" stance**. Many patent infringement plaintiffs take a "patent-protective" stance. As a defendant, it can be tempting to respond in a defensive, "no we didn't" manner. To some degree, this may be necessary. However, the better, more complete approach is to take a proactive, "consumer-protective" stance. (We will return to this key thought in Chapter 7.)
4. **Highlight differences**. Whether you do it through specific thematic language or as a component of your case message, make room for the jury to identify and argue all the differences between your client and the patentee. The more different jurors perceive the parties in seemingly small or less relevant ways, the easier it is for jurors to perceive and identify differences in the ways that lead to a noninfringement verdict.

B. Wording the Right Theme

A noninfringement theme that emphasizes ethics, fairness, and consumer protectiveness might be:

> *Small as the differences may appear, we designed our technology to make a big deal of supporting the plaintiff's legitimate patent rights and, ultimately, the consumer's rights.*

If you had no awareness of the plaintiff's patent(s) before designing your own technology, a simple variation could be:

> *Small as the differences may appear, our technology does the right thing by creating a big distance around the plaintiff's legitimate patent rights and an even bigger protection of consumers' rights.*

C. Beginning Your Argument

Juror attention is never better than in the first few minutes of your opening statement. To open pro-plaintiff jurors to your defense position, your first moment of the opening will need to accomplish three key things. First, you will need to jolt plaintiff-oriented jurors into listening to you. Recalcitrant jurors are often best persuaded through the unexpected.

Second, you will need to get them to care about your client's innovation(s). To do so, start with something that both inspires jurors to understand that small innovation is important and to understand quite simply how a seemingly small innovation can make a difference in (if possible) the consumer juror's own life. Doing so may require you to start with something other than your client's allegedly infringing design if that design is not something with an immediate appearance of value to the typical juror.

Third, and important, *many jurors do not understand that it only takes one difference from the plaintiff's claimed invention to qualify as noninfringement.* Some jurors see evidence of any overlap (or, at a minimum, broad overlap) as evidence of infringement. Therefore, your strongest position—and one taken early in your argument—is to acknowledge overlap between your product and the claimed invention before you start to fight about the differences. Then, overtly note that your degree of overlap is allowed within the law. For you, this is Patent Law 101; for many jurors, it is a revelation. You cannot be too overt about teaching this point.

Try something like this: In silence, hold up a paper clip. Then, start your argument.

> *The paper clip. A simple enough invention, wouldn't you say? Would it surprise you to know that it took several patents covering versions that didn't work to finally get to a paper clip that did? The first patent for a crude paper clip was granted in 1898. In 1921, an inventor named Clarence Collette was granted a patent for a paper clip with "sharply pointed projections for penetrating and engaging the sheet material." The inventor's goal was to keep the clip from slipping off the page. The problem was, it also shredded the paper it was clinging to. After a few more patented versions, a man named Henry Lankenau patented the modern-day clip in 1934—just like this one.*
>
> *A simple design with small changes, all recognized by the Patent Office. As you can imagine, there was a great deal of overlap across the various versions over the years. But still the Patent Office granted patents on this small innovation. Why? Because small changes can make a big difference. And, thank*

goodness for the Patent Office's wisdom in granting patents that should be granted for those changes. Progress often comes in small steps.

Now, we're talking about something more complicated here with our design. But the principle holds true that a few changes can make a big difference. And in this case, the plaintiff made changes to technology that had come before and we made changes to our own as well, just as the final inventor of the paper clip did. There were others in this race to a workable design besides the plaintiff and us. Both the plaintiff and our company had a legitimate right to try to improve what existed in the first place. That's not infringement. That's progress. And that is ultimately good for the consumer.

The more complex the design in your case, the more powerful this paper clip analogy (or something simple like it) can be. If a small change to a simple design can be patented or deemed noninfringing, it only follows that the USPTO would view a small change to a complex design in the same way.

D. Distinguishing Fair Competition from Anticompetitive Behavior

Even when no claim of unfair competition exists on the verdict form, the thought of it exists in many jurors' minds. This notion of anticompetitiveness in a patent case typically takes two forms with jurors. First, some jurors see the *fact* of patents themselves as anticompetitive. We have found a strong correlation between jurors who feel patents are inherently anticompetitive and jurors who begin a case in the accused infringer's corner. Second, some jurors will take a less concrete position about the anticompetitive nature of patents in general but will watch for anticompetitive *behavior* on the plaintiff's part. However, no matter where your jury fits, we recommend that you allow jurors to draw their own conclusions about a plaintiff's anticompetitive behavior (or not) rather than overtly claiming a plaintiff's behavior is anticompetitive. Under this scenario, you can certainly lay out the evidence that a plaintiff is trying to control the market unfairly without making the argument overtly. It can, in fact, be more persuasive if you endorse fair competition with patents but lay out the evidence that the plaintiff's behavior has been lacking.

E. Structure with the Fairness Theme and Fair Competition in Mind

After you have established your theme and embedded it within a silver bullet (see previous example at Section III.C), consider the following noninfringement structures to entrench your focus on fairness, ethics, and consumer protectiveness. The first structure is a candidate for cases where invalidity is a defense. The second structure addresses a pure noninfringement defense.

In most cases on which we have consulted, the accused infringer is also arguing patent invalidity as a defense. When infringement and invalidity claims are not bifurcated, we urge a structure that interweaves the accused infringer's defense based on both theories.

Defendant's Noninfringement Structure (When Invalidity Is Also a Defense)

Structural Point	Logic Behind the Structural Point
I. Correctly Issued Patents Protect the Consumer Through Fair Competition	It is critical that your argument start with an endorsement of the USPTO. Without this, jurors may believe your criticism of plaintiff's patent(s) is a castigation of the entire patent system. Given jurors' strong belief in patents and the USPTO, you stand a far stronger chance of persuading them your way if you begin from a position that is consistent with their belief systems. Talk to jurors about the genius of the patent process when executed correctly, including the fact that patents protect a legitimate inventor's rights while educating the public on the invention and while giving innovators a road map to either (1) design around or (2) advance beyond the current invention.
II. Fair Competition with Patent Rights Requires Two Things: A. A Legitimately Issued Patent B. Noninfringing Behavior on Competitors' Parts	*Briefly* note that the patent must be valid and *then*, to persuade jurors that your position is more reasonable than plaintiff's, demonstrate that you are the grown-up in the case by overtly establishing that your behavior must be appropriate to stay within the law.
III. The(se) Patent(s) Was/Were Not Legitimately Issued	Educate jurors about the information the USPTO needs in order to issue a valid patent. Then explain why and how the USPTO was hamstrung in this case, thereby erring in issuing this/these patent(s).
IV. You Cannot Infringe an Invalid Patent	Make this point briefly and then move quickly to the next one. If you belabor this point too much, it can sound defensive.
V. Even if the Patent Was Valid, We Did Not Infringe	Demonstrate a reasonable stance by educating the jury about what infringement would look like in this case and then contrast it with your noninfringing behavior. (See Section III.G in our description of the "Say and Show" internal structure for a more detailed discussion of this point.)
VI. We Were Motivated *Not* to Infringe	To cap off your argument in a manner that underscores your noninfringing behavior, speak to your motive *not* to infringe. When that motive can be self-serving (e.g., hurting one's own reputation), jurors are especially likely to trust what you say.

And when invalidity is not a defense or when you are required to bifurcate your invalidity case from your noninfringement case:

Defendant's Noninfringement Structure (When Invalidity Is Not a Defense/Not in This Phase)

Structural Point	Logic Behind the Structural Point
I. Patents Protect the Consumer Through Fair Competition	It is critical that your argument start with an endorsement of the USPTO. Without this, jurors may believe your defense represents a castigation of the entire patent system. Given jurors' strong belief in patents and the USPTO, you stand a far stronger chance of persuading them your way if you begin from a position that is consistent with their belief systems. Talk to jurors about the genius of the patent process, including the fact that patents protect a legitimate inventor's rights while educating the public on the invention but also while giving innovators a road map to either (1) design around or (2) advance beyond the current invention. These outcomes of the process create innovative products and processes for the consumer. When you have patents of your own, use this first point to introduce your company and your respect for the USPTO borne out of your own (valid) patent experience.
II. We Were Motivated *Not* to Infringe in Three Ways:	Speak to your motive *not* to infringe. When you note that infringing would have been the *wrong thing* to do and when that motive can be self-serving (e.g., hurting one's own reputation), jurors are especially likely to trust what you say.
A. Infringing Would Have Been the Wrong Thing to Do	Considered optional by some litigators, this step is actually quite important for persuading jurors. This step allows you to make a succinct case about your *behavior* (above and beyond claim elements), which matters greatly to jurors.
B. Infringing Would Have Hurt Our Reputation	For those who may not quite trust your stated ethics of doing the right thing, be clear about the self-serving *harm(s)* to yourself of infringing. For example, infringing behavior could hurt your reputation in the industry.
C. We Do/Did Better if Our Device/Process Is/Was Different from the Plaintiff's (and, Therefore, Noninfringing)	If possible, provide the self-serving corollary of the *benefit(s)* to yourself not to infringe. For example, is a better or different device more marketable?
III. What Infringement Would Look Like (and How Our Device/Process Is Noninfringing)	Demonstrate a reasonable stance by educating the jury about what infringement *would* look like in this case and then contrast it with your noninfringing device/process. (See Section III.G in our description of the "Say and Show" internal structure for a more detailed discussion of this point.) This step often includes a side-by-side "contrast graphic" that compares the plaintiff's patent embodiments contrasted with your process/device.
IV. Our Simple Request	The last thing you should ever do in a patent case in particular is to utter the statement, "This is complicated." The intimidating effect of this statement is the exact opposite of what jurors need to hear in order to learn well. Instead, you need to make this case simple, beginning with how you structure your argument, then on to how you teach the technology, and ending with a "simple request." In this request, ask jurors to give you the simple right to continue to produce/use your noninfringing product/process. At the end of the day, that is all this is about.

F. Addressing the Plaintiff's Patent Stretching

In the right factual circumstances, accused infringers can deploy a common rhetorical strategy using prototypical "if . . . then" logic to argue either the accused products do not infringe the patent-in-suit or, if they do, the patent must be found invalid. It is effective to present this argument to jurors in the form of patent stretching, or the simple and visual argument that the patentee plaintiff has a right to its patent in the form it was granted by the USPTO—an ownership deed on property with clear boundaries demarcated by the fence afforded by the patent. But, in this case, the accused products are outside the fence—clearly distinct from the patented claims and, therefore, noninfringing. In this scenario, the accused infringer is not infringing because its products are not within the patent's claims.

A Patent Defines the Invention's Boundaries

Credit: M'Lynn Phillips, Jill Kustner, and Patrick Paulin at IMS Legal Strategies

So, to attempt to "cover" the accused products with the patent claims, the patentee plaintiff is trying to move the fence, or stretch its ownership rights beyond the bounds of its actual property line. By trying to move the fence, the plaintiff stretches patent law too far. By trying to move the fence and expand its property, the plaintiff finds itself claiming ownership over public property—a place where the public (including the accused infringer) has free use of the ideas the plaintiff is now trying to claim it invented. This renders the patent invalid, and justifies the accused infringer's use of the ideas in the event jurors believe the accused products "practice" the ideas the plaintiff stretches its patent to cover.

The Patent Holder Is Improperly Trying to Expand the Invention's Boundaries

Credit: M'Lynn Phillips, Jill Kustner, and Patrick Paulin at IMS Legal Strategies

Using simple and powerful visuals to help present this argument can help to set up a strong defense position that wins whether on noninfringement, or in the event the jury finds the accused products practice the patent claims, a better chance of finding those claims invalid for being outside the bounds of the patent and preempted by prior art.

Special thanks to M'Lynn Phillips, Jill Kustner, and Patrick Paulin at IMS Legal Strategies for sharing their visual depiction of this concept that works well to communicate a somewhat complex concept in a simple way.

G. Making a Complete Contrast in Your Internal Structure

We introduced the "Say and Show" model of argumentation to the plaintiffs earlier in this chapter. However, it need not just be the domain of the patent infringement plaintiff. Complete argumentation is critical to educating and persuading your jury. To make a complete argument on any specific issue, take jurors through the five steps in the following figure. The description to the right of each point explains the goal of the given step.

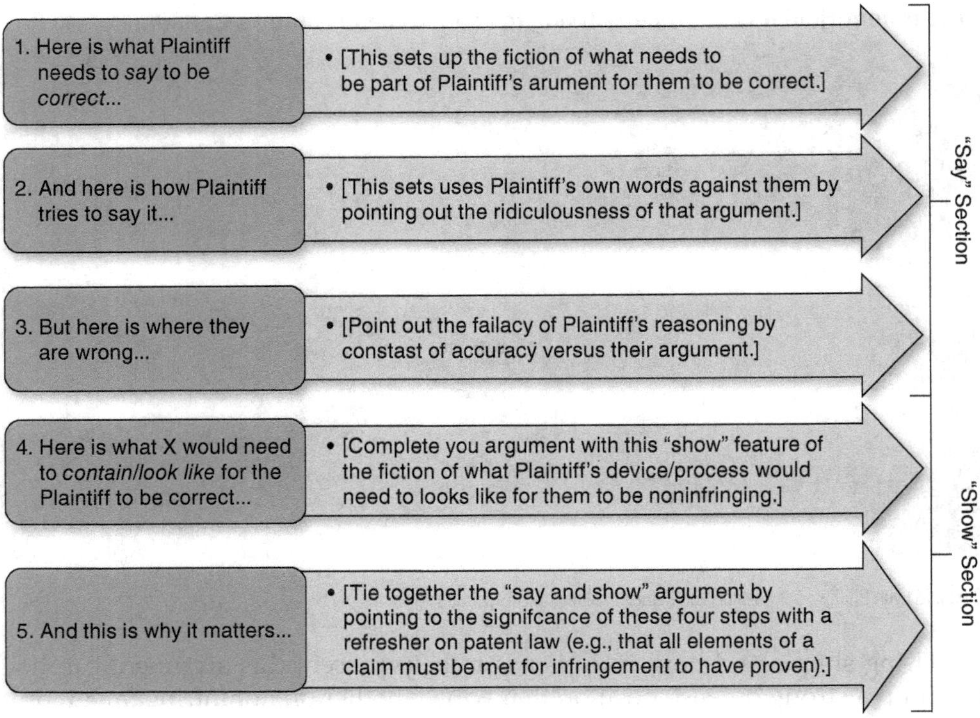

For steps 2 and 4, the critical demonstratives would be ones that compare/contrast reality with fiction on the same demonstrative. We have seen jurors place heavy emphasis on these points during mock deliberations when the technology or claim language was particularly dense.

H. The Defendant's Challenge of Not Having Its Own Relevant Patents

> *"One thing that struck me, if defendant's product is so dramatically different, then why didn't they go out and get their own patent?"*
>
> —Patent mock juror

In the specific mock trial referenced in this juror quote, the fact that the defendant could not point to its own patent supported many jurors' belief that defendant's concept was not novel and patent-worthy, making it an infringing product. These jurors questioned defendant's decision not to get its own patent, which suggested theft of something the accused infringer did not earn. Knowing that this risk exists, it behooves you to consider how/whether to address the reasoning behind *not* acquiring your own patent. Two approaches come to mind:

Approach A: Note that the law does not require you to get your own patent to prove noninfringement of someone else's. First, and most obviously, you should underscore the fact that you do not bear the burden to prove noninfringement. You might fold that point into the wisdom of the law that pairs this "non-burden" with a "non-requirement" to get your own patent on a design that has small differences from someone else's patent. Patents are a choice of protection, not a requirement of production.

Approach B: When relevant, add the logic behind your client's decision not to seek a patent for its product. After you make the point described in Approach A, add in the story behind your client's choice not to seek a patent. Too readily, many jurors assume the absence of a patent behind your client's device/method means it tried and failed to get one precisely because the differences between its device/method and the plaintiff's patent were nonexistent (and, therefore, infringing).

I. Overtly Claim Your Motive Not to Infringe

In a world filled with copycats, the cynical juror often assumes that the accused infringer's greater motive is to take the easier path of copying rather than to innovate. This assumption puts pressure on the accused infringer to dig out of a hole of suspicion. Take this on by explaining your motive *not* to infringe *and,* if possible, your motive not to infringe out of a self-serving perspective. Why self-serving? Because we find that a self-focused motive on the part of a defendant is often more trusted by jurors than an other-centered one. Your key witness (whether the owner or the innovator) should speak to this motive (foreshadowed by you in your opening statement). For example, wanting a better mousetrap could come from a motive of being excited by inventing something new or by finding it boring to copy the old. Both are simple motives, but they help jurors appreciate the fact that copying is the opposite of what the accused infringer ever wanted.

Representing a corporate defendant? Use jurors' preconceived or strongly held beliefs to your favor. We know that most jurors, including even the most pro-business people, believe corporations act with one primary goal: profit. Embrace this motive in a way that helps jurors believe you are being honest and direct about motives, which in this case include the motive not to infringe since that is ultimately a poor choice for the bottom line.

J. A Defendant's Behavior in Taking a License Speaks to Belief

When we addressed the issue of licensing for plaintiffs, we made the point that when evidence of licensing options by plaintiff comes into a case, jurors place great focus on how the plaintiff behaved. That same focus comes into play when an infringement defendant introduces the fact that the individual or company has taken licenses in other technologies. Specifically, jurors often conclude that a defendant who pays money for other licenses would have taken a license in the patent-in-suit had he believed it was warranted. Trial consultants Julie

Blackman, Ellen Brickman, and Corinne Brenner note this logic path by many jurors: "If a company routinely paid for licenses from others when it was warranted, why would they start infringing now?"[15] They cite this mock juror quote from a past patent case:

> *"I don't think [defendant company] feels like they owe him [the inventor] anything. Otherwise, they would have paid. They paid everyone else. They paid $75 million [to license another technology]! It's not like they can't afford to pay it. They don't feel like they owe it."*
>
> —Patent mock juror

K. Teaching the Law

1. Literal Infringement

> *"They had to violate all of the claim limitations, and I don't think they violated all of them."*
>
> —Patent mock juror

Drawing upon rhetorical theory and modern-day debate techniques, one can appreciate the fact that a complete argument is far more effective than an incomplete one. In the previous quote, this juror appreciated the juxtaposition between the law and the evidence. However, many jurors are not as adept at drawing that link, especially as the evidence or the law becomes more dense. The common villain that prevents jurors from making crucial links between the evidence and the law is typically incomplete argumentation.

Modern-day philosopher Stephen Toulmin identified a six-part model of argumentation[16] (which we are simplifying here into three steps) that demonstrates the coupling of the evidence with patent law. When you read this, you may feel a reaction of "but of course." However, we caution you to take seriously the need to make the warrant (see the following image) explicit. In our experience, the biggest reason jurors lack the ability to translate the significance of the evidence or to understand an argument is because counsel believed the warrant could be left implicit.

---

15. Julie Blackman et al., *East Texas Jurors and Patent Litigation*, 22 Jury Expert 5 (2010).
16. Stephen Toulmin, The Uses of Argument (2003).

For the defense, consider this simple (but complete) argument:

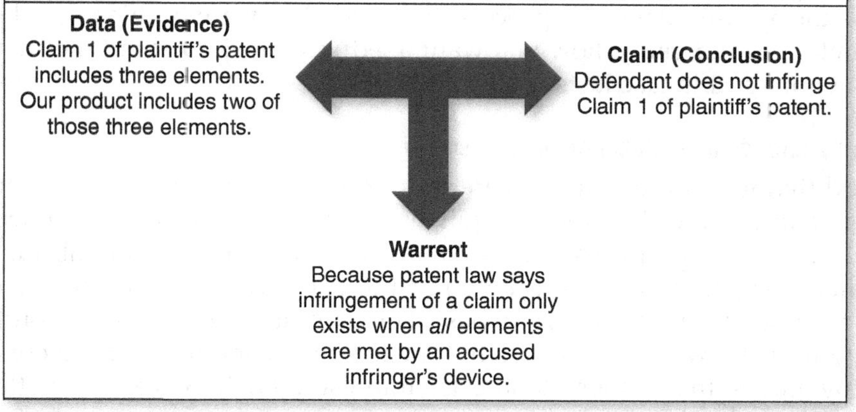

The (Simplified) Toulmin Model of Argumentation

Again, the failing of most arguments is the exclusion of the warrant. What is clear to you given your knowledge of patent law is often confounding to jurors. You will not insult their intelligence by including this linking sentence (and more than once, potentially). You will only make them feel smarter if they understand the warrant, and you may bring some confused jurors along who failed to follow your conclusion or evidence absent that critical sentence.

2. *Infringement Under the Doctrine of Equivalents*

> *"If they [plaintiff] used prior art to get where they are at, why couldn't [defendant] do the same thing? The information was already out there. If something made a product better, is that infringement or not?"*
>
> —Patent mock juror

This mock juror made this statement while the group was considering infringement under the doctrine of equivalents. It became readily apparent that he wanted to consider the patent as a whole when considering the equivalents standard, rather than through an "element by element" manner as the standard requires. In our experience, this desire to look at the patent as a whole is at least a common starting point for many jurors, especially when the invention is a device. The USPTO summarizes the standard on its website as follows: "The essential objective inquiry is: 'Does the accused product or process contain elements identical or equivalent to each claimed element of the patented invention?'"[17]

17. *Glossary*, USPTO, https://www.uspto.gov/learning-and-resources/glossary (last visited Feb. 5, 2025).

We can provide you no "black and white" wisdom regarding which side this potential tendency for jurors to consider the patent overall hurts more; it clearly depends on the given patent as a whole and the elements juxtaposed against the accused device or process. However, be aware of this possible misinterpretation, and gauge how you want to educate the jury about the standard within your specific case facts.

a. The "Triple Identity" Function-Way-Result Test

We find that jurors often take greater than normal notice that a claim may be infringed under the doctrine of equivalents if some element of the accused device or process performs substantially the same function, in substantially the same way, to achieve substantially the same result. Two factors make this so. First, the legal standard has a mnemonic quality, and second, the repetition of the word "substantially" makes this standard more likely to be cited by jurors than other standards. Interestingly, however, even though the doctrine of equivalents may seem to require a lower standard of proof (to them) of "substantially close enough" compared to literal infringement, we have observed jurors frequently place greater scrutiny on the elements of proof when they are spelled out as three hurdles: (1) function, (2) way, and (3) result. Most jurors find those three words to be very accessible and may not rely as heavily on the jury instructions as they do their own "street definitions" of those words.

L. Teaching the Technology

Too often, jurors find the technology phase of opening statements or witness testimony to be ideal nap time. While it may not be possible to translate all of the technology-related aspects of your case into something invigorating, we find it is indeed always possible to make it more relevant and engaging.

1. Teach from the Consumer's Perspective, Not from an Engineer's

The first tenet of good persuasion is good teaching. Good teaching meets jurors where they live. Where most jurors lack engineering knowledge, they have much consumer knowledge. When the dispute is over something consumer-driven, start there. For example, we recently worked on a case where the fight was over key-cutting machines like those we all encounter in hardware stores when we want to make a copy of our house key. The accused infringer claimed noninfringement by first noting that its machine did not require the user to insert the entire key into the machine while copying, unlike the plaintiff's technology taught. While it helped to be able to vaguely visualize that difference, it helped even more to go one step further and note that the consumer benefits because the accused infringer's machine allowed the consumer to keep the original key on her key chain, while the plaintiff's technology would require removing it. Handling key chains daily as we do, that difference was much more salient to the typical juror.

M. Wave Your Patents as Often and as Loudly as Possible

> *"One thing that struck me—If defendant's product is so dramatically different, then why didn't they go out and get their own patent?"*
>
> —Patent mock juror

The fact that an accused infringer cannot point to its own patent often supports many jurors' beliefs that the accused infringer's concept was not novel and patent-worthy, making it an infringing product. Some jurors even believe that an accused infringer must have had deceptive motives for increasing its bottom line when it developed and sold an unpatented product that is so similar to the patent-holding plaintiff's idea. These jurors question an accused infringer's decision not to get its own patent, seeing the behavior more as theft of something the accused infringer did not earn rather than as a competitive idea allowed under the law.

In the words of one patent mock juror, "If they were really more advanced, why didn't they start out the right way by getting their own patent?" This argument helped convince some jurors that the accused infringer had the most power to avoid this dispute. If the accused infringer had patented its product, "then there would have been no question about infringement" (patent mock juror).

N. Use a Timeline—But Use the *Right Kind* of Timeline

A timeline can be quite useful in any case *if* it makes more of a persuasive point than simple chronology. The vast majority of timelines make three key mistakes:

Mistake 1: Most timelines are greedy. They include too many entries, thereby burying critical events among less important ones.

Mistake 2: Most timelines default to a horizontal, purely chronological layout without visually laying out a persuasive case.

Mistake 3: Most timeline entries along a horizontal line have entries appear above the line or below the line based on layout demands versus strategic, persuasive ones.

An example of a technically accurate but not very persuasive timeline appears in the following figure.

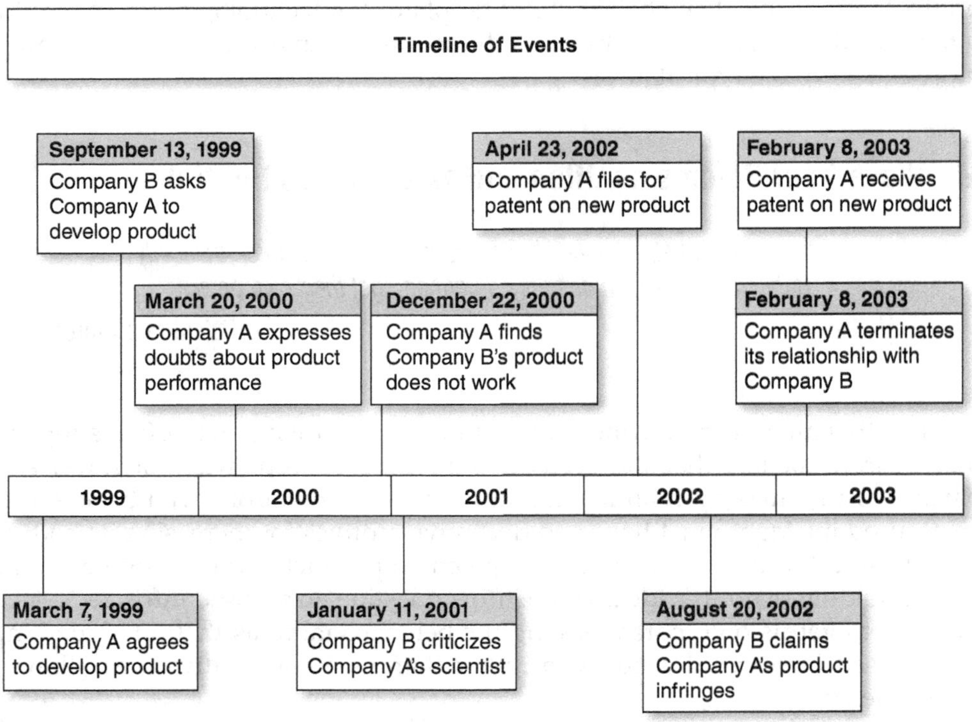

A well-designed timeline should aim to make your persuasive point as self-evident to the fact finder as possible. For example, if you follow a traditional timeline layout with a horizontal line that cuts your page in half, think hard about entries you place above the line versus below the line. As infringement plaintiff, your entries above the line might demonstrate the industry problems the right invention needed to solve. Below the line, you could demonstrate the developmental steps by which your invention accomplished that objective. As infringement defendant/invalidity plaintiff, the entries above the horizontal line might show the chronology of the prior art, while entries below the line demonstrate the claimed inventors' redundant steps in replicating that prior art.

The following sample timeline demonstrates what we mean. This particular timeline demonstrates the events that would have put the defendant on notice above the line and the defendant's knowledge below the line. The point this party wanted to convey to the fact finder was that the inventor was proactive in following the necessary steps to protect its invention while the defendant was fully aware of those actions even though they denied it when litigation ensued. The Focal Point LLC provided these two views of the timeline.

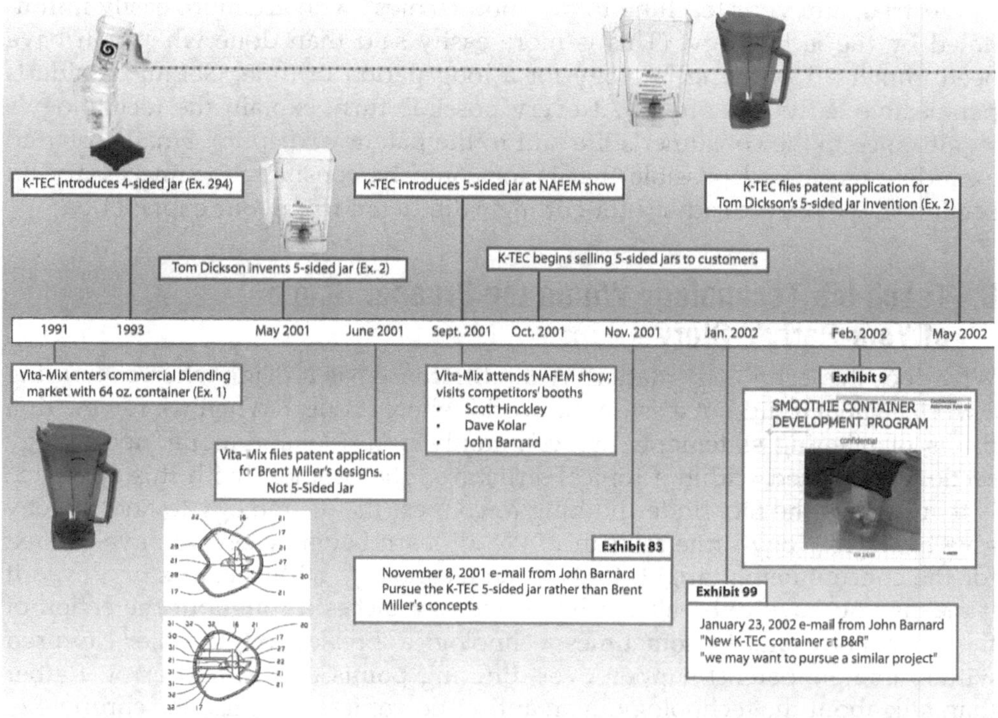

The first view of your timeline should be one that orients the jury to the "on notice" events above the horizontal line. The second view should orient jurors' to evidence of defendant's clear awareness below the line.

IV. Teaching the Technology Well

Whether you represent the plaintiff or the defendant in a patent matter, the manner in which you teach the technology can make or break your case.

A. Achieve the Lowest Common Denominator of Technical Simplicity

Three key barriers typically exist to keeping any of us from understanding technology. (Not one of those barriers is stupidity. Even highly intelligent fact finders struggle with technology.) First, when we feel intimidated by information, we shut down our own ability to learn. Jurors who self-identify as "techies" embrace the information more readily than those who do not. Second, too much detail too soon in the introduction of an unfamiliar technology can overload the learner. Third, jurors who cannot figure out *why they should even care* about the technology are typically less motivated to pay attention to you or your expert.

At trial, aim your teaching to the "non-techies" who are more easily intimidated by the technology. (This is more easily said than done when you have been immersed in the technology for a long period of time. Get an outsider's perspective early and often.) At every possible turn, explain the technology's significance to the consumer's life and to the patent in dispute. Finally, plan to exclude every detail possible that is (or could be considered) unnecessary. In Section C, we provide advice for cutting extra detail from your explanation.

B. Teach the Technology Within the Broader Scope of Your Party's Story

Why does the technology matter? What difference has it made when comparing a world where it did not exist to the world where it does? When we review first drafts of opening statements, we commonly find a "stand-alone" technology section embedded within a topical structure. The problem with this approach is that it gives the fact finder nothing to connect the technology to and thereby give the technology some relevance. We all learn better when we have context for the concept being taught. Embed the technology within your story, even if it means you have to break up the technology pieces throughout the action of the story. For example, sometimes technological breakthroughs (later captured within a single patent) happen over differing points of trial and error. Rather than talk about the technology in an antiseptic, topical way, use the chronology of the story to intersperse the breakthroughs as the technology evolved.

C. Technical Detail to Keep or Cut

When your goal is to thoroughly orient the jury to the technology in the case, you are already in trouble. Too much detail befuddles most jurors and waters down your critical teaching points. When that occurs, you have lost control of where, amidst the morass of details, the jury will place its focus. Instead, conduct focus group or mock trial research to determine where and how to narrow the technical detail to the most abbreviated teaching possible. We recommend that you use the following criteria to determine what to keep. If the detail(s) you *could* teach do not fit at least a few of these criteria, *cut those details*.

Five Criteria for Keeping or Cutting Technical Detail

Criterion 1:	Does the technical detail help the consumer (juror) understand the relevance of the technology to him or her?
Criterion 2:	Does the technical detail underscore the key strengths of your client's innovation?
Criterion 3:	Does the technical detail demonstrate a key area of overlap with or distinction from the allegedly infringing technology?
Criterion 4:	If you had only 15 minutes to teach the technology, is this technical detail so key that you would include it in that abbreviated time?
Criterion 5:	Can you explain the technical detail so that a junior in high school could understand?

D. Translate "Magic" to Your Best Advantage

As discussed earlier in this chapter, patentees should look to retain the perceived magic in the invention without making it completely inaccessible to jurors. Accused infringers want to demystify the claimed invention by removing the magic. In both instances, one technique we have seen work effectively is tantamount to translating a foreign language to the native language. For patentees this means retaining both as critical halves to a complete explanation and understanding. Jurors need the foreign language of the technical and detailed explanations of the technology (e.g., the claim language or expert description of the technical process) as well as the translation (i.e., the layperson way of describing or saying the same thing). Accused infringers may emphasize only the translation and all the prior art and similar technology that appears to accomplish what the translation describes. In both instances, the translation of the claimed invention's magic and how it relates to jurors' interpretations of the innovation are key.

E. Four Ways to Make the Technology More User-Friendly

Once you have determined what to keep in your technology tutorial, consider this advice from senior trial consultant Theresa Zagnoli and the tips that follow: "Make sure your expert witness reports/disclosures/deposition testimony leave room to turn technical language and charts into jury friendly demonstratives. On occasion we have been held so closely to the drawings and presentations in the reports that it was nearly impossible to accommodate more understandable versions for trial."[18]

We often talk about leveraging "the familiar" to help jurors understand and interpret new and complex concepts that feel and sound foreign. "The familiar" can take many forms. In our experience, mock jurors and trial jurors frequently tell us they try to understand new technology by thinking about things they see on a daily basis—kitchen appliances, technology in their cars, or something specific to their occupation. Look for linkages to these familiar technologies and products and carefully consider how, and to what extent, you want them to apply those comparisons.

a. When it comes to using analogies, do it sparingly, and be careful. Since an analogy is a play on words, opposing counsel gets to play with your words too.
    1. When you can concretely refer to the technology from the consumer's perspective, do so rather than using an analogy.
    2. When you use analogies, use as few different ones as possible. The ideal approach is to use one analogy that can be interwoven throughout the components of a given technology. When that is not possible, more analogies might actually serve to confuse the jury.
b. Teach jurors in the way you learned the technology yourself. This can often be powerful since it uses social proof and allows the attorney to take more

18. Personal Communication with Theresa Zagnoli, Senior Trial Consultant, Zagnoli McEvoy Foley (2011).

ownership and a role in the teaching: "[A]n opening statement should present the scientific evidence the jury will hear incrementally and step-by-step, the same way the attorney learned it and the same way it will be presented by the expert."[19]

c. Create animations to better teach a simplified model of processes too difficult to demonstrate in court or devices whose inner workings are too difficult to imagine.
d. Repeatedly use a similar formula for showing/describing each patent's technology in order to make the technology seem more familiar and less intimidating.

F. Keeping Track of Duplications and Distinctions: Universal Formula for Animating Your Technology

Jurors can struggle with the fact that every case that includes claims of infringement and invalidity requires them to appreciate duplication (used figuratively, not literally, given legal requirements) *and* distinctions surrounding the same technology. For each patent, we recommend a three-step animation that should significantly increase jurors' ability to understand these duplications and distinctions. This animation serves the dual purpose of showing *distinctions* between the prior art and plaintiff's innovation and *duplications* between the plaintiff's innovation and the accused infringer's allegedly infringing device/ method. Ironically, the *sequence* of steps is the same for either party. However, the visuals and the goals are diametrically opposed.

	As Patent-Holding Plaintiff	As Accused Infringer
Step 1	Animate the technology *before* the plaintiff's patent came to be (from a consumer-friendly perspective). [Top half of the animation] *For instance, the way a mobile phone camera used to perform.*	
Step 2	Animate the technology described by the plaintiff's patent (again, from a consumer-friendly perspective). [Bottom half of the animation] The goal is to show the *distinctions* between the two. *For instance, the patented phone camera has distinct differences from past patented ideas.*	Animate the technology described by the plaintiff's patent (again, from a consumer-friendly perspective). [Bottom half of the animation] The goal is to show the *duplication* between the two or obviousness to combine two prior art concepts. *For instance, the patented camera phone is strikingly similar to known prior art.*
Step 3	Demonstrate plaintiff's technology (from Step 2 but now moved to the *left* half of the screen) and defendant's infringing technology (on the *right* half of the screen) to show the *duplication* between the two. *For instance, the accused infringer's mobile phone camera duplicates the plaintiff's patented product.*	Demonstrate plaintiff's technology (from Step 2 but now moved to the *left* half of the screen) and defendant's infringing technology (on the *right* half of the screen) to show the *distinction* between the two. *For instance, the accused infringer's camera phone is visually distinct from the plaintiff's patented product.*

19. Douglas E. McCann & Scott M. Flanz, *How to Present a Persuasive Opening Statement in a Patent Jury Trial*, Fish (Aug. 12, 2020), https://www.fr.com/insights/ip-law-essentials/how-to-present-persuasive-opening-statement-patent-jury-trial/.

G. Sometimes Low Tech Is Best

When you can, tell your invention story so simplistically that jurors find it a "no-brainer" that your invention was authentic. Animations are not always critical—sometimes something as simple as a household item can work. In this instance, one of the authors worked on a matter more than 20 years ago where we have been allowed to disclose the specific strategy used to persuade jurors from the plaintiff inventor's perspective.

The manufacturer of the anti-AIDS drug, AZT, was suing generic drug manufacturers for infringing their product. As well-known as the drug was, the story of chemical invention was dull and dry. In the mock trial, it was quickly apparent that most jurors could not follow all of the scientific detail. So we worked with the inventor—a lab technician named Marty St. Clare—to determine what she could convey about her "aha" or "eureka" moment of invention that made the discovery of AZT so significant. It turns out that her discovery of the compound was profound because it took such a miniscule amount of the compound to make the AZT effective. So, during her witness prep, we asked her to show us what the amount would look like if she used a pencil. It was so small she could not draw it—but she could use the writing implement itself to demonstrate the power of the chemical. She said that if you started with the eraser, that would equal a mole of compound (something many who took high school chemistry could relate to), and if you took the tip of the eraser, that would equal a millimole. If you then looked at the sharpened point of the pencil, that represented a micromole of compound. And, finally, if you put the sharpened tip of the pencil under a microscope and magnified it, that magnification represented a nanomole. And that was the amount of compound necessary to make AZT effective.

We watched the jury pay rapt attention to Ms. St. Clare's testimony. After the case ended in a directed verdict for our client, we interviewed some jurors who noted how memorable her testimony was and how impressed they were by her invention. Imagine a jury calling chemistry "cool"!

V. Willful Infringement and the Jury

Even though willful infringement is often the purview of the judge, we want to note some brief thoughts here when willful infringement touches the jury. Willful infringement sets a high bar in most jurors' minds. They need to see very concrete evidence of willfulness before finding against an accused infringer. Following the 2007 *In re Seagate Technology*[20] decision requiring jurors to find "objective recklessness" by the alleged infringer, it was a logical leap to assume that the high bar would move to an even loftier position. However, logic has not met reality, because recent research has found that willful infringement post-*Seagate* decreased a mere 10% compared to pre-*Seagate* findings of willfulness, a finding that is not even statistically significant.[21]

20. 497 F.3d 1360 (Fed. Cir. 2007) (en banc), *cert. denied*, 552 U.S. 1230 (2008).

21. Christopher B. Seaman, *Willful Infringement and Enhanced Damages After* In re Seagate: *An Empirical Study*, 97 Iowa L. Rev. 417 (2002).

Law professor Christopher Seaman studied predictors of findings of willfulness or no willfulness over a six-year period (split three years before *Seagate* and three years after). According to his research:

> From the collected data, a "substantial" or "legitimate" defense to infringement is the most significant predictor of a finding of no willfulness. In contrast, evidence of copying by the accused infringer is highly correlated with willfulness. Surprisingly, however, neither opinions of counsel nor evidence that the accused infringer had attempted to "design around" the patent were statistically significant in willfulness decisions. In addition, whether a patent-in-suit has been reexamined by the U.S. Patent and Trademark Office (PTO) appears to have little impact on willfulness. Finally, bifurcation of willfulness at trial also does not have a statistically significant impact on willfulness.[22]

Seaman also found several interesting distinctions between judges and juries when willful infringement was before different fact finders, including:

- Juries find willful infringement substantially more frequently than judges do in a post-*Seagate* world.[23]
- However, when judges do find willful infringement, they almost always award enhanced damages, and they award more in willfulness damages than jurors do.[24] Contrary to the popular image of the runaway jury and damages awards, this differential between judges and juries is consistent with what frequently occurs in types of litigation other than in the patent world.[25]

A. Strategies for Willful Infringement Plaintiffs

Depending on whether or not willfulness is bifurcated from other claims of infringement in the trial (and whether or not the following evidence is admissible), determine your earliest opportunity to convey to the jury (1) that the defendant was aware of the patent at issue and (2) that other defendants (or would-be defendants) acted by taking a license or settling. Jurors are highly influenced by the behavior of comparable companies to the defendant. The demonstrative, in the following figure, was illustrative in showing that other companies paid their fair share when confronted by the patentee.

22. *Id.* at 420.
23. *Id.* at 417.
24. *Id.* at 420.
25. Karen Lisko, Proven Jury Arguments and Evidence (2012).

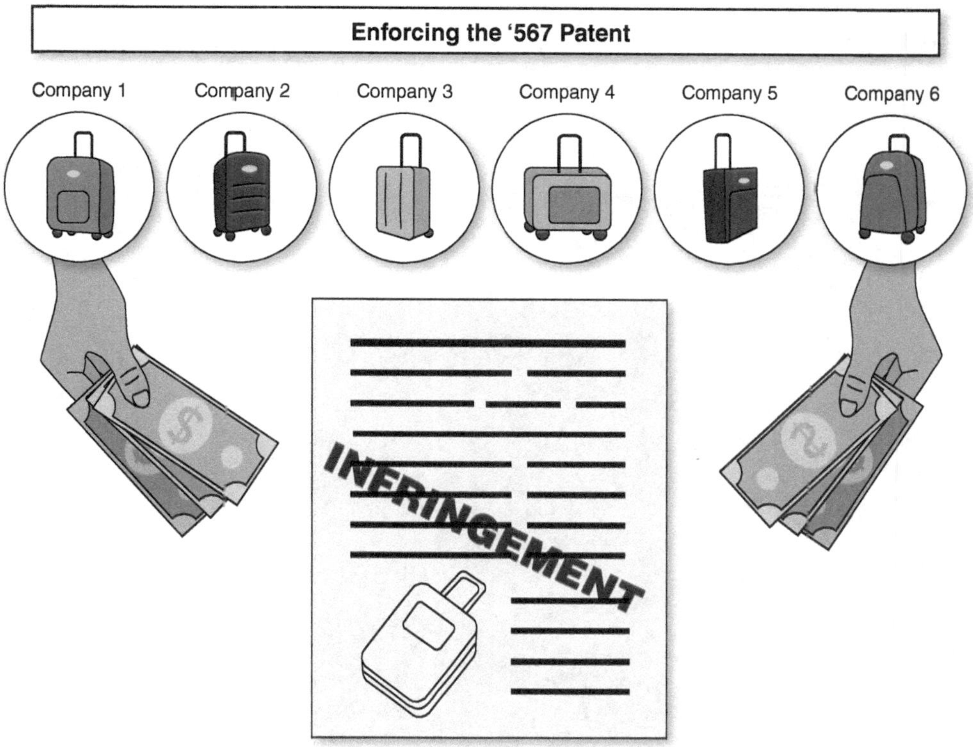

Credit: Jason Bullinger

B. Strategies for Willful Infringement Defendants

Bear in mind that jurors do tend to want to see clear proof of willful infringement rather than find for the patentee simply because of an assertion of "theft" or "willfulness." We have consulted on cases where the patentee's accusation of "theft" worked to the defendant's benefit because jurors felt the patentee provided too little proof; without enough proof, jurors saw the claim as an anticompetitive move rather than a sincere claim of willfulness. If such a defense is possible, it is worth using or, at a minimum, testing in a mock trial.

Earlier in this chapter, we discussed the key benefits of focusing on the accused infringer's motive to avoid infringing. When the patent is well known and/or the accused infringer was aware of the patent at the time of its product or process development, it behooves the defense to take a proactive stance and address its own self-serving motives to avoid infringement of plaintiff's (or anyone else's) patents, including the central desire to differentiate oneself in the marketplace.

CHAPTER 7

Invalidity

"In any invalidity case, the patent itself is on trial. If the jury understands that the patent is like a fence staking claim to property, then they can be counted on to do the right thing; even lay jurors understand a property owner cannot use a fence to take for itself property that was previously freely available to the public."

—Denise DeFranco, global head, IP litigation, Johnson & Johnson[1]

I. Patent Invalidity and the Jury

Without question, jury attitudes toward patent litigation can vary both by region of the country and by certain demographics. We have witnessed that phenomenon firsthand many times during our jury research throughout the country. However, even as new patent cases are accompanied by their own unique jury attitudes, we never cease to be amazed by how many attitudes patent jurors share in common, regardless of geography or background. The first section of this chapter identifies some of the key patterns we repeatedly find regarding patent invalidity perceptions in our private research with actual and mock jurors in patent litigation.

A. A Psychological Presumption of Validity

"Obviously it was valid. [The patentee] was given a patent number and the whole works."

—Patent mock juror

It is law that issued patents carry with them a presumption of validity. But we also continually witness a strong *psychological* presumption of validity from a jury perspective. For just a moment, consider the presumption of validity as a corollary to the presumption of innocence in criminal law. Many jury researchers

1. Personal Communication with Denise DeFranco, Global Head, IP Litigation, Johnson & Johnson (2013). At the time of this communication, DeFranco was a partner at Finnegan, Henderson, Farabow, Garrett & Dunner, LLP.

(including us) will tell you they have seen jurors much more likely to perceive the U.S. Patent and Trademark Office (USPTO) as having issued a valid patent than they are to perceive criminal defendants as innocent until proven guilty. If you have made a claim of invalidity in past litigation, you know the invalidity plaintiff's burden of proof is not an easy one. This burden goes beyond the fact that the standard of proof is higher for invalidity (clear and convincing evidence) than for proving infringement (preponderance of the evidence). The fact that many jurors see an invalidity claim as a castigation of the USPTO explains much of why invalidity plaintiffs face a tough (but not impossible) task in proving their case.

How Detailed Is the USPTO in Evaluating Patent Applications?

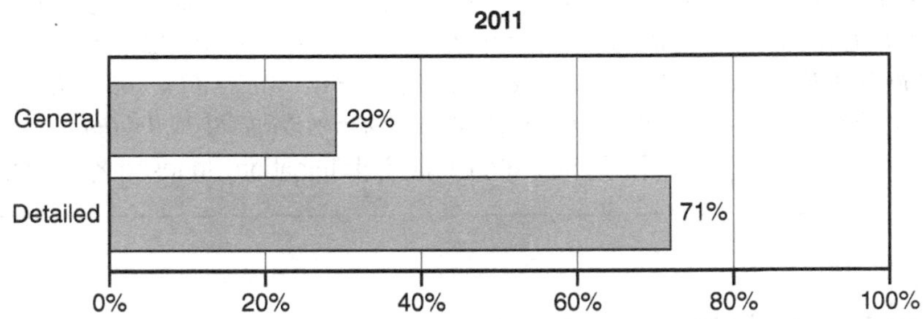

Source: PERSUASION STRATEGIES/K&B NATIONAL RESEARCH, NATIONAL JUROR SURVEY (2011)

Historically, jurors tend to believe the USPTO spends a substantial amount of time conducting a detailed review of patent applications, but those opinions have shifted over the years. When we have surveyed jury-eligible adults nationwide concerning their attitudes about the USPTO, a strong majority respond that they believe the USPTO is "somewhat" or "extremely" detailed in evaluating patent applications, contrasted with a minority proportion who believe the USPTO is "somewhat" or "extremely" general (or "broad brush") in their evaluations.

How Easy or How Difficult Would It Be for You to Find a Patent Invalid After It Was Issued by the USPTO?

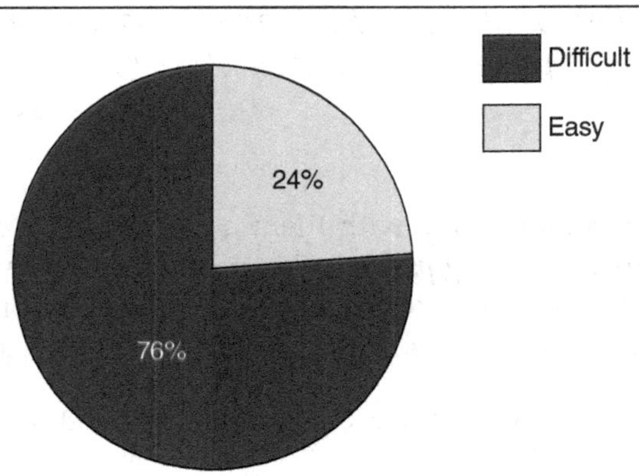

Source: 2023 Mock Jury Research Data from the Eastern District of Texas, Northern District of California, and District of Delaware (N=101)

When asked a slightly different question in 2023, 59% of more than 100 mock jurors across three different common patent venues reported the perception that it was somewhat likely or extremely likely that the USPTO would make a mistake in issuing a patent. Fully 76% of this same sample of mock jurors said it would be somewhat difficult or very difficult to find a patent invalid after it was issued by the USPTO.

While this data is venue-specific rather than a national sample of respondents, it confirms some potential shifts in the perceived fallibility of the USPTO that we have also seen reflected across venues and cases in the 2020s. It also coincides with a great deal of data confirming Americans' decreasing trust in federal government, institutions, and a variety of entities once perceived as national authorities. While we continue to observe the USPTO receiving the most favorable ratings of all the federal agencies we evaluate in our research, there is a trend toward decreasing trust and faith that the USPTO and its agents will do the yeoman's work of prosecuting patents without making some mistakes.

The pro-USPTO attitude still exists, particularly in certain venues where jurors are less sophisticated or less technically skilled, and is especially typical for jurors who have had little to no direct experience concerning the inner workings of the USPTO. Therein lies one strong explanation for why the USPTO enjoys such a strong reputation among many jurors. Research finds that upwards of 35% of jurors' deliberation time across a variety of cases is spent on jurors talking about themselves and their own experiences. (We have also been fascinated to observe mock arbitrators and mock judges—typically recruited from among retired federal judges or senior counsel—talk about themselves and their own experiences in mock deliberations as well.) However, in patent cases, few jurors have any tales to tell of their own experiences with the USPTO in comparison to their (often negative) experiences with other federal agencies, such as the Internal Revenue Service (IRS) or the Occupational Safety and Health Administration (OSHA). Instead, patent juries talk far more about having an idea stolen or thinking of the next great invention but never acting upon the idea. When you couple the absence of negative USPTO experience with typically high-level respect for inventors, the invalidity claimant's task is a tough one indeed. As one patent mock juror put it:

> I would really defer now to the Patent Office. If they have determined twice that it was a valid patent, they have a level of expertise far beyond what we have and it's unfair to come back around to a layman and find that the patent office made a mistake.

In addition, at least a few jurors on every patent jury believe the patent examiner takes a proactive role in practicing or at least testing the patented invention, much like cookbook authors follow recipes in test kitchens. Many jurors also assume that the patent examiner takes it upon himself or herself to do an extensive amount of independent research about the claimed invention and the technology behind it. Still other jurors expect to see the patent examiner take the stand at trial to describe in great detail how he or she came to the conclusion that the patent should issue. It is typically a disappointment to jurors with these expectations when no such patent examiner appears at trial.

B. Certain Demographics Can Correlate with Patent Jury Attitudes

Even though we have said more than once in this book that demographics are typically lousy indicators of juror leanings, we have found certain exceptions. Political affiliation is often the "best of the worst" demographic indicator, largely because those affiliations often reflect many of our life values. Over the past ten years, political affiliation has become an even stronger signal for people's beliefs, and as so much research and experience prove, political affiliation is a clear and divisive flag in American culture. (However, be mindful of the fact that a Democrat in the Eastern District of Texas can look very different from a Democrat in the Northern District of California.) When asked how easy or difficult they think it is to mislead the USPTO, most Americans believe it to be more difficult than simple, a trend that holds over time and that remains consistent in our 2023 observations and is increased in some venues after jurors observe the Federal Judicial Center video.

C. The Patent Jury "Flip"

When we talk about the patent jury "flip" in Chapter 5, we address the fact that *certain* jurors who are pro-inventor on infringement actions can also be anti-inventor on invalidity claims *in the same case*. Political affiliation is one characteristic that exemplifies that flip. As noted, Democrats can be more likely to report that the USPTO can be misled, a factor that correlates with more easily finding patent invalidity. Democrats are also more likely to favor patentees in their infringement claim. When present in your particular case, this fact represents a clear quandary at the time of jury selection. How do you decide whether to keep or jettison a more liberal juror in this specific circumstance? Our advice is to be clear about which of your cases is stronger, your infringement/noninfringement case or your validity/invalidity case. If you feel that call is tough to make in a particular case, strongly consider conducting a mock trial to test the waters in your venue or in a venue closely matched to yours.[2]

D. Views of the USPTO Affect Views of Invalidity

Now, even though the great majority of jurors hold favorable views of the USPTO, there exists just enough variability in attitudes to enable us to determine whether jurors who hold a more favorable attitude toward the agency think differently about invalidity claims than those who are not as sold on the agency. It turns out, not surprisingly, that jurors who hold a favorable view of the USPTO are much more likely to support the validity of a patent than those who do not have as favorable a view.

---

2. At the time of publication of this book, mock trials are strongly discouraged (i.e., banned in practical terms) in the Eastern District of Texas, due to exhaustion of the jury pool from so much pretrial research. The order banning research in this jurisdiction, however, does allow research to be conducted in other, similar venues.

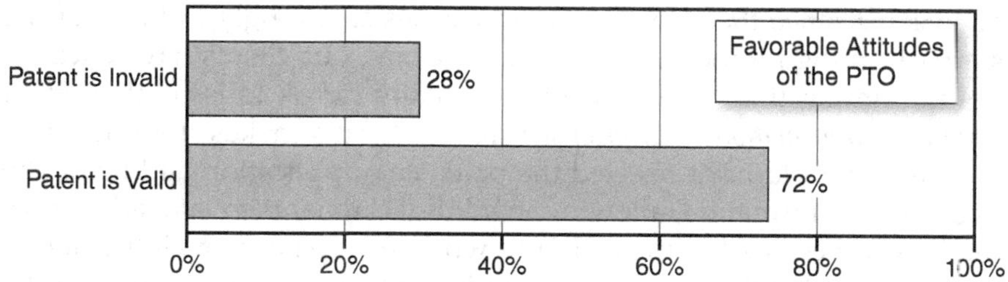

Source: Persuasion Strategies/K&B National Research, National Juror Survey (2010) (N=200, p=.024)

E. The Federal Judicial Center Video (Slightly) Influences Views of Invalidity Claims

Many courts make use of a 17-minute patent orientation video produced by the Federal Judicial Center in 2013 titled *An Introduction to the Patent System*.[3] The video is often shown to potential jurors before jury selection begins or immediately preceding opening statements. We find that the video is most commonly seen at the request of one or more parties in the case. Theories abound regarding whether the video has a biasing effect on jurors and in which direction. The dividing line appears to fall between instinct (that the video helps the patent holder slightly more) and research of mock jurors' reactions (that the video helps the accused infringer slightly more). See Chapter 4 for a more complete discussion of our research where we found mock jurors were mildly influenced by the video to believe that patent examiners must be overwhelmed by the large stacks of applications in their offices, thereby causing more risk of human error in the process. However, we also found no real effect of watching/not watching the video on mock jurors' ultimate verdicts. Other research firms that report having studied the effect of the video on mock jurors have found the same.[4] Despite this mild biasing effect, the video is quite useful for orienting jurors to the patent process and key legal terminology.

F. Endorsing the USPTO as a Strategy for Both Sides

As we noted in Chapter 1, the USPTO has enjoyed the top slot among federal agencies in favorability among jury-eligible respondents for at least as long as we have been collecting national data on jurors' views of numerous federal agencies.[5] We made this exact point in the infringement chapter (Chapter 6), so why make it with regard to invalidity actions? The reason is simple: *No matter which side* you represent in an invalidity action, our jury experience tells us that you must somehow

3. This video can currently be viewed at U.S. Courts, *The Patent Process: An Overview for Jurors*, YouTube (Nov. 22, 2013), https://www.youtube.com/watch?v=ax7QHQTbKQE.

4. These firms whose findings mirror our former group, Persuasion Strategies, include TrialGraphix and Trial Behavior Consulting.

5. Our first national survey whereby we asked jury-eligible participants for their perceptions of federal governmental agencies was in 2004. However, we collected this information during private mock trial research long before then and with the same results, where the USPTO earned the top slot in favorability.

embrace the USPTO, since the tide of opinion washes so strongly in favor of the agency. As a party bringing the patent invalidity claim, our clients have encountered success in arguing that the USPTO was actually *correct* to issue the patent *given the incomplete information (i e., prior art) before it.* This makes the point that the patent examiner would have rejected the patentee's application had he or she been given complete information, allowing invalidity claimants to take advantage of most jurors' presumed trust in the USPTO's work. As a patent invalidity defendant, you might argue that the patent examiner is a subject matter specialist in the given technology and had ample background information to make an informed decision. Later in this chapter we discuss both approaches in more detail.

G. Jurors' Focus on Behavior over the Technical Details

Do not forget the reality that the vast majority of jurors primarily focus on process and behavior over technical differences. An engineering mind may be fascinated by how a piece of machinery works, but jurors are much more likely to care about how it came to be, how others respected the innovation (or not), and how it ultimately affects jurors' own lives (if at all). This is true when comparing the patent to an infringing device as well as when comparing the patent to the prior art. It is *the* common denominator that spans infringement and invalidity cases. We see it every single time we work on a patent case. Once you satisfy jurors' interests, then they can be more amenable to processing the details around claim language, and so on.

As one juror put it, "We don't know enough to speak intelligently about the product," suggesting instead that the more important goal was to determine "who is the good guy and who is the bad guy." In this particular case, one of the main heuristics (or inferential leaps) that jurors applied was the perception that the accused infringer was trying to promote innovation and superior technology, while the patent holder was buying patents in order to stop that innovation.

H. Jurors' Need for Story Within Your Invalidity/Validity Case

You may feel you have a compelling story to tell surrounding your invalidity/validity case. Leading off with your invalidity or validity story is a fine idea. However, telling a story at the beginning of your invalidity/validity argument and then leaving it altogether for your technical case is like listening to a keynote speech where the speaker leads off with a joke and then does not say another funny word. It is a big disappointment to your listener, and it can hurt both your credibility and their ability to learn. You must interweave story *throughout* your argument while incorporating technical explanations or descriptions of claim language as support for your story. Throughout this chapter, we make recommendations for making story and technical teaching compatible.

I. Jurors' Deep Need for Primers on Patent Defenses

When you consider the vast amount of brain power that has gone into formulating jury instructions across every type of litigation over the years, one would hope and expect that jurors would place intense scrutiny on the instructions given them for use in deliberations. Our research with thousands of jurors over the years only bolsters our respect for the hard work most jurors generally put into reaching what they believe is the correct outcome. We have had the privilege of interviewing actual jurors post-trial (when allowed) and observing thousands of hours of (mock) deliberations. We are always intensely curious about jurors' use (or non-use) of jury instructions. In our observations, most jurors *do* rely on instructions when they feel they need to translate an unfamiliar term on a verdict form or when they feel they need to break a deadlock on an issue in their collective decision-making process. As a result, jurors often spend less time reviewing instructions (or their notes about instructions) in cases where they feel their own "street definitions" of terms (such as "breach" or "negligence") suffice.

In patent litigation, where many terms are less user-friendly than in other types of cases (with perhaps the notable exception of the term "obviousness"), does it not follow that jurors would be more diligent in their reliance on patent jury instructions in comparison to other types of cases? We find that jurors rely on key jury instructions slightly more in patent litigation than in other types of litigation (though they still may not rely on them nearly as much as the drafters would hope).

We also observe differences in how certain types of jurors make use of jury instructions. Pro-plaintiff jurors who may take a more simplistic view of the case facts tend to ignore instructions in most case types, and patent litigation is no exception for them. Pro-defense jurors are more likely to rely on instructions; especially in patent cases, they rely on instructions that are more difficult for pro-plaintiff types to rebuff (i.e., it is more difficult to discount a definition provided in an instruction when you are completely unfamiliar with the term being defined).

But, more importantly, patent juries need as much help as you can give them in "translating the translations" or jury instructions themselves. This area of litigation runs so far afield of their daily experience that they often skip over narrow invalidity defenses in broader deference to the USPTO's judgment in issuing the patent in the first place (as noted earlier in this chapter). However, when jurors find the defense understandable, the majority of them will try to apply that understanding to the facts of the case. Confusion on the law usually benefits one party more (as does clarity). Aiming for confusion is both dangerous and unethical. Instead, when you aim for clarity by teaching the connection between the law and your case facts, you garner more influence over jurors' use of that information. If we could place a subheading on each page of the book, it would read, "In patent litigation, better education better influences." The pages that follow offer some examples of tying the law to the facts in a way that should increase your influence with the jury. No matter what your approach, do not hesitate to do two things. First, repeat yourself in what you teach. It often takes more than a few attempts to ensure that jurors get the connection you want them to get. Second, spend the time necessary to explain *why* the law makes sense and *why* the law is fair, instead of relying too heavily on the fact that the law is the law.

J. Handling Confusion Between Anticipation and Obviousness

To get even more specific, let us look at the dilemma that often occurs with jurors' understanding of anticipation and obviousness, especially when both defenses are raised in the same case. Jurors are not alone in this confusion. Even patent litigators and district court judges have been known to confuse these two invalidity defenses. Jurors often look at the two as interchangeable and, therefore, confuse the requirements between them. Stemming from this confusion, the Federal Circuit has described the differences. Attorney Kevin McBride synthesizes the differences:

> In two Federal Circuit Court cases, *Comaper v. Best Buy* and *Therasense v. Beckton Dickinson*, the district courts below erroneously applied patent law defenses of "anticipation" and "obviousness." The Federal Circuit's discussion of each case provides a useful framework to understand these interrelated defenses.
>
> The Federal Circuit Court explained:
>
> "Anticipation" [under 35 USC § 102] is a patent defense that must be based on a single prior art reference. For a claim to be anticipated, each claim element must be disclosed, either expressly or inherently, in a single prior art reference, and the claimed arrangement or combination of those elements must also be disclosed, either expressly or inherently, in that same prior art reference.
>
> "Anticipation" requires only one step to prove, if a single prior art reference is available. If a single document teaches all elements of a patent, in the same arrangement, the single prior art reference can invalidate the target patent. (Subject to a clear and convincing evidence standard for issued patents)
>
> "Obviousness" [under 35 USC § 103] is a patent defense that may be based on multiple prior art references. Determining obviousness requires considering whether two or more pieces of prior art could be combined, or a single piece of prior art could be modified, to produce the claimed invention. This analysis typically invokes the familiar teaching-suggestion-motivation ("TSM") test, asking whether a person having ordinary skill in the art would have found some teaching, suggestion, or motivation to combine or modify the prior art references.
>
> "Obviousness" requires two steps to prove. Even though multiple patents can be used as prior art references, there must also be a "teaching" that suggests a "motivation" to combine the prior art references into a single new invention (the "TSM" test). The "suggestion" to combine can be provided by the references themselves, through another document, or via affidavit or declaration testimony of a person of ordinary skill in the art of the invention.[6]

6. From "*'Obviousness' v. 'Anticipation'—Similar but Different Patent Law Defenses*," retrieved in 2013 at http://www.mcbride-law.com/2010/03/02/obviousness-v-anticipation%E2%80%94similar-but-different-patent-law-defenses/.

While the foregoing description is indeed helpful, it requires more explanation complete with examples for the typical juror to fully understand and apply the legal requirements to a given case. These examples matter because jurors are willing but not necessarily qualified to look at a case as a person of ordinary skill in the art. Left to their own devices, we see them use their own "street definitions" of obviousness and anticipation. Concrete examples and/or analogies specific to your case interrupt that inclination to a large degree. Mock trial research is an ideal way to test and determine the most persuasive examples or analogies specific to your case.

II. Persuasion and the Accused Infringer

A. General Invalidity Strategies

1. "Dethroning" the Patent Holder (Even When the Patent Holder Is a Non-Practicing Entity)

Most jurors' *initial* loyalty in a patent infringement dispute defaults to the named inventor or patent holder. After all, the inventor went to the trouble of inventing something (awe-inspiring to many jurors) to solve a problem, whether obscure or overt. She then received the recognition of the USPTO by being awarded a patent (one of the few federal regulatory bodies for whom jurors have high regard). To win on invalidity, you now have to dethrone both the claimed inventor *and* the USPTO in jurors' eyes unless you can figure out a way to help both the inventor and the USPTO save face while still achieving a win on your invalidity claims.

Alleged infringers can make the mistake of taking a dismissive tone toward non-practicing entity (NPE) plaintiffs. As we note in more detail in Chapter 4, our research regarding jurors' views of NPEs is that many jurors still afford them legitimacy for having lawfully acquired the patent. It can backfire against accused infringers to adopt a derisive tone with these plaintiffs. That said, it still bears noting to a jury that the plaintiff is *not* the inventor. By putting that information in front of your jury, they can draw their own conclusions about them.

As we recommended before, if you position the USPTO as having made the *correct* decision to award the patent at issue based on *incomplete* information, jurors will struggle less with your request that they invalidate the patent the USPTO issued. Once that persuasive seed is planted, you will be in a position to take a more aggressive position against the patent applicant and its responsibilities to disclose a valid invention.

2. Dealing with the Heightened Standard for Burden of Proof

Akin to endorsing the USPTO (before you point out they were hamstrung with inadequate information when they allowed the patent to issue), consider endorsing the burden of clear and convincing evidence. You know the patentee will make a big deal of it, so preempt them by overtly expressing your respect for the reasoning behind a heightened standard for proving invalidity, followed by your expressed confidence that they will find you have met or exceeded this standard. For example, you might say:

> *The law says we must clear a higher burden for proving a patent to be invalid. The standard* ***should*** *be higher. To earn a patent, you must clear a lot of hurdles to convince the patent examiner that your invention is worthy of a patent. In kind, we need to prove that the claimed inventor fell short of its responsibility. We are confident we will prove exactly that.*

3. *Pointing to the Patent Holder's Invalidity by Starting with What* Validity *Looks Like*

It may seem counterintuitive for an accused infringer to talk validity before invalidity. However, adopting this approach will accomplish two things. First, it will help jurors more easily understand the concept posed in a positive way rather than first proving the negative. Second, it allows you to present the patent holder's options had she gone through the patent process in a legitimate manner. The more options jurors see the patentee as having squandered, the more they will criticize her. Consider a demonstrative for your case titled "How to Ensure a Patent Is Valid." Take jurors through this primer in an abstract way first, and then introduce them to the components the patent holder met and failed to meet. (By granting that the patent holder did meet some steps, you allow jurors to see more reasonable "gray" in the case while still finding fault with the patentee.)

4. *Introduce the Fact (or Remind Jurors) That Litigation Is the Legitimate Method for Determining Invalidity*

If the patent holder was smart in presenting his infringement case, he would have explained that litigation is the legitimate method for determining infringement. Even if that occurred, grab this fact for yourself in your invalidity case. Explain the fact that the USPTO is *not* the arbiter of patent disputes once a patent has issued. This fact will surprise many jurors.

If possible, link this fact to the reality that the USPTO is already overburdened. Clarify for jurors that, just because it takes a few years for a patent to issue, no one should think a patent examiner is spending anything close to that amount of time on any single patent. This is the U.S. government. Some tax returns take months to process because the IRS has so many other tax returns to process. In kind, patent examiners review hundreds of patent applications every year and spend an average of 18 hours on each application.[7] When you emphasize the fact that those sparse hours span months or years in the patent review process, this news can be stunning to jurors. The agency cannot be expected to serve as an appellate body on top of its overburdened responsibilities.

---

7. *See* John R. Allison et al., *Extreme Value or Trolls on Top? The Characteristics of the Most-Litigated Patents*, 158 U. Pa. L. Rev. 1, 32 (2009).

Now introduce the fact that the patent examiner cannot be expected to research and identify complete prior art for each applicant. Just as a professor needs to know he can rely on each graduate student to provide a complete list of references for a master's thesis, the patent applicant carries the legal and ethical responsibility to disclose the full prior art.

5. Define Your Invalidity "Aha" Moment

When litigators think of the "aha" moment in a patent case, they typically think it is the province of the patent holder at the moment of invention. We would argue that this view is too limiting. In many cases, the accused infringer also has an opportunity to present its own "aha" moment in its invalidity argument. Is there a moment in time to which you can point when you discovered the patent holder's patent was invalid? If so, build this "aha" moment into your story. Your goal would be to counter the perception that many jurors see an accused infringer's invalidity arguments as nothing more than a legal ploy to "weasel" out of the case. If you can point to an "aha" moment when you discovered patentee's patent was invalid, jurors are likely to trust you more—even if that discovery occurred during the work-up of the defense in this case.

6. (Perhaps) Allow the Patent Holder to Be Mistaken

There are those cases where the evidence points to the fact that the patent holder may have missed (some or all of) the critical prior art through error rather than through bad intent. If the evidence points in that direction *and* you want to point it out, educate jurors that the patent holder is still on the "validity hook." For example:

> *Could [the patent holder] have simply missed the key prior art related to his patent? Anything is possible, I suppose. However, mistaken or not, it was his legal responsibility as an applicant to find it and disclose it to the Patent and Trademark Office. The evidence will show that this necessary disclosure didn't happen, and the law will tell you that whatever the reason, he is still required to possess a valid patent.*

7. When the Defendant Has Its Own Patents While Attacking Plaintiff's Patents

Some jurors fail to understand how an accused infringer who holds its own patents can claim that the plaintiff's patent is invalid. "If the Patent Office screwed up in awarding the plaintiff its patents," the logic goes, "then how can we know the defendant's own patents aren't invalid too?" This is why it is better to protect the USPTO as having gotten it right but based on faulty information. Be prepared to defend your own patents and how the process of disclosure differed for them, enabling the USPTO to have the necessary information in those circumstances to make the right decision.

8. When the Defendant Tried a Design-Around and Still Claims Invalidity

In our research, we find that jurors struggle with defendants who have attempted to design around the claimed invention only to later claim the patent is invalid.

Absent greater context, these two facts together make the accused infringer look greedy and insincere in its invalidity claim. It is critical that you add more detail for credibility's sake. For example:

- If the accused infringer *first* concluded that the patented technology was invalid and *then* decided to design around the patent anyway, make that sequence of events clear. Explain the sequence of events and the thinking of the defendant in going to the trouble to design around a patent it believed to be invalid. Was it not worth the risk of being sued? Was it somewhat gray to determine independently that the patent met invalidity standards? Have your key witness testify to the rationale behind this thinking and action.
- If the accused infringer *first* tried to design around the patent and *then* concluded that the patented technology was invalid, grant to the jury that these two actions appear inconsistent. Then truthfully explain why the information you have now is superior to what your client understood at the time of the design-around. If true, link the accused infringer's absence of knowledge to the patent examiner's lack of knowledge. Doing so makes it more palatable to the jury to understand both that the patent examiner may well have gotten it right (like your client now is) had she had more complete information at the time of examination.

9. Tying Noninfringement to Invalidity

Given the foreign nature of patent litigation to the average juror, it is not surprising that jurors often see your noninfringement case as something separate from your invalidity case (with the exception of the point that follows). Simple as it is, you can often educate them about their inherent connection by making the point—sometimes more often than once—that "you cannot infringe an invalid patent" to supplement your other noninfringement points. We will make more recommendations about framing this defense later in this chapter.

10. Positioning Invalidity as a Legitimate Defense Rather Than as a Noninfringement Dodge

> *"They [accused infringers] went through every claim on there, and said, 'We didn't infringe,' but why are they bothering to say that the patent is invalid? They are trying to make an excuse. If it was really true, they would be bringing this up with the patent office, not as a defense in a lawsuit."*
>
> —Patent mock juror

Unless your noninfringement and invalidity cases are bifurcated at trial, you are likely in a position to try your invalidity case adjacent to your noninfringement defense. As a result, jurors are sometimes susceptible to believing the invalidity defenses you raise are simply a dodge around your infringing action. (A mock trial is an excellent vehicle to identify the prevalence of that risk.) If you determine you have legitimate claims to make on invalidity, jurors will need to understand that you see your case that way as opposed to an attempt at a fall-back position in the event they reject your noninfringement case.

Use story as a vehicle to explain the legitimacy of your invalidity case to the jury while also tying your invalidity case to your noninfringement position. Too often, litigators leapfrog to building discrete legal defenses (e.g., anticipation or obviousness) when they should first develop a credible motive for bringing invalidity claims into the suit in the first place. As a result, jurors often view invalidity defenses as discrete arguments that are merely a "checklist of loopholes" for the accused infringer to dodge responsibility. To form a persuasive foundation for your invalidity defense, start broadly with the filing of the suit against you and narrow to the specific invalidity defenses in a logical, step-by-step manner. See the "Beginning Your Proactive Invalidity Story" graphic in Section III.B. (Remember to relay the story in the present tense. Doing so keeps the story more immediate to jurors and keeps them from feeling like they missed all of the action.)

B. Telling Your Proactive Invalidity Story

Beginning Your Proactive Invalidity Story

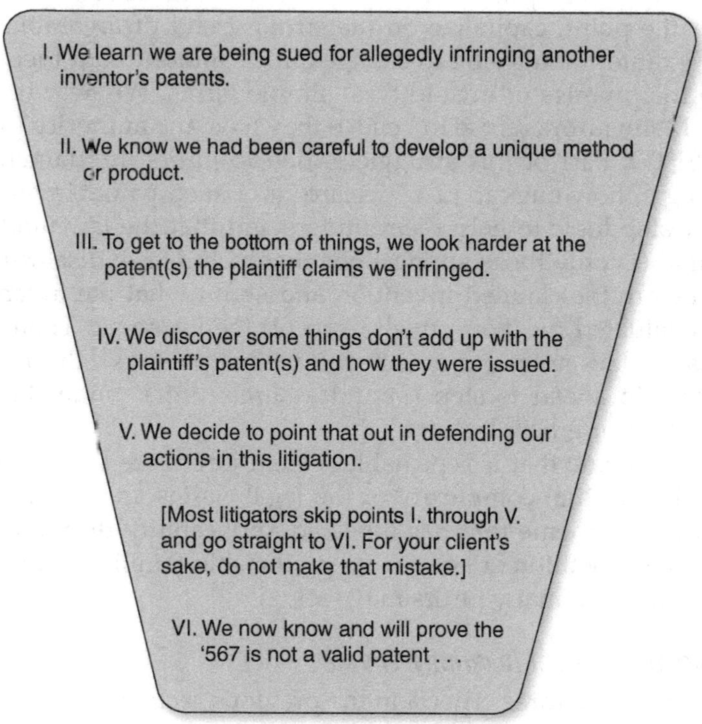

When you look at Elements I and II, you may be tempted to skip those if you have already argued your noninfringement position. Do *not* make this mistake. It is important to frame Element III as a reasonable investigation rather than as a defensive witch hunt. In our view, that reasonableness is more evident juxtaposed against Elements I and II. If you have spent time already arguing that you do not infringe, you certainly may want to keep Elements I and II brief, but do not abandon them altogether.

C. Choosing the Right Invalidity Theme

As we noted in Chapter 6, it is easy to become enamored with a clever turn of phrase in choosing a theme. However, the right theme for a party in any case must be carefully chosen because it has the potential to become the primary filter for jurors' interpretation of your argument. Choose well and you can direct jurors' focus where you want it to go. Choose poorly and you may alienate jurors from your client's position.

1. Criteria for Determining the Right Theme

Knowing the "must have" criteria for determining the right theme is more important than offering you a "one size fits all" wording of the theme. When you know the three key criteria, the wording becomes a more flexible task best fit around your unique case facts.

1. Use positive perceptions of the USPTO to your advantage. Without belaboring the point, capitalize on the strong trend of favorability toward the USPTO rather than trying to change jurors' minds about their competence.
2. Teach the premise of invalidity in simple terms. We hear it over and over again: Many jurors refuse to believe they have the authority to second-guess the USPTO. Part of this struggle is tied to jurors' fundamental misunderstanding of how one can just "declare" an issued patent invalid. Jurors need step-by-step logic to help them understand that the law (and fairness) dictates that (1) only those applications that include full disclosure about what came before the claimed invention and about what the invention is can be fairly evaluated for their novelty and (2) then granted. Then, (3) if that full disclosure does not occur or is not clear, that patent's validity is in question. Do not skip ahead to step (3) and assume jurors' understanding of steps (1) and (2) is implicit. It is not.
3. Make it a theme that is repeatable. Patent jurors are frequently intimidated by the intellectual complexity of the legal claims and patent details. When you choose a theme that has repeated applicability throughout your argument, that repetition creates some predictable familiarity that helps reduce the intimidation many jurors may feel.

2. Wording Your Patent Invalidity Theme

Bearing in mind the three criteria in the previous section, consider this potential theme as one example for setting the tone for your invalidity case:

> *We are here to tell you that it turns out the plaintiff's patents should not have been granted. However, we are **not** here to tell you the Patent Office got it wrong. In fact, based on what the patent holder told them, the Patent Office*

got it right. But a patent issued on inaccurate or incomplete information cannot be valid.

3. Framing Your Patent Invalidity Silver Bullet

To at once embrace the USPTO *and* make your argument that the patent(s) should not have issued, consider this as one way to begin your opening statement:

> *We are here to tell you that it turns out the plaintiff's patents should not have been granted. However, we are **not** here to tell you the Patent Office got it wrong. In fact, based on what the patent holder told them, the Patent Office got it right. Unfortunately, it was not given complete and accurate information during the application process. You will learn that the Patent Office relies heavily on the truthfulness of the patent applicant to determine if the patent should issue. The patent examiner does not run experiments on the claimed invention in a lab; she relies primarily on her desk reading of the material contained in the patent application. If that information is questionable, granting the patent is not the answer. Unfortunately, the patent examiner cannot always know that the information in front of her is, in fact, partial and questionable. And the legal burden is on the applicant to be thorough and accurate in its disclosures.*

4. Delivering a "Consumer-Protective" Closing

Even though many jurors may have a leaning going into the closing argument, you still have an opportunity to persuade. Consider an approach that takes a slightly different angle from what you have advanced by this point in your case. For example, anytime you can frame your case around the jury, you are engaging them in a manner not often tapped by patent litigators. Consider this "consumer-protective" closing as one example (and much credit for this sample closing goes to trial consultant Shelley Spiecker of Persuasion Strategies):

> *The purpose of the patent process is to help the marketplace. How do patents help the marketplace? Good patents help the marketplace by protecting ideas that are original, unique, and new. That provides the incentive to innovate, to "build a better mousetrap," and that helps competition, and that ultimately helps consumers.*
>
> *But just like a good patent can promote that system, a bad patent can pervert it. When a patent application gets through and ends up offering false protection to an idea that is not original, not unique, and not new, then the patent ends up limiting the freedoms of others in the marketplace, without creating any incentive to innovate. That hurts competition, and it hurts consumers.*
>
> *Thankfully, in the great majority of cases, patents work out fine. Those applying for patents supply the information that they're supposed to, the information that proves that their idea really is original, unique, and new. Occasionally, however, an improper patent slips through—and it may be more obvious than original, and it may be already public, already practiced well before the patent is ever filed. And it may slip through only because of what the person applying for the patent left out. You'll hear that this is what we*

have here today: a good patent process, but a bad patent. But the process isn't yet complete, because you haven't yet made your decision. As a juror, you are a vital part of the patent process because you decide whether this good process has nonetheless let a bad patent slip through.

D. Persuading Through Specific Legal Defenses

1. Prior Art Invalidity

a. Overarching Approach

When you claim invalidity because the invention was anticipated by prior art, your key job is to prove to jurors that the patent holder invented nothing of significance that was new. After you have taken jurors through the "Proactive Invalidity" story progression described in Section II.B, consider the following elements as a way to both teach and persuade jurors about your invalidity claim.

Continuing Your Proactive Invalidity Story (Prior Art Invalidity)

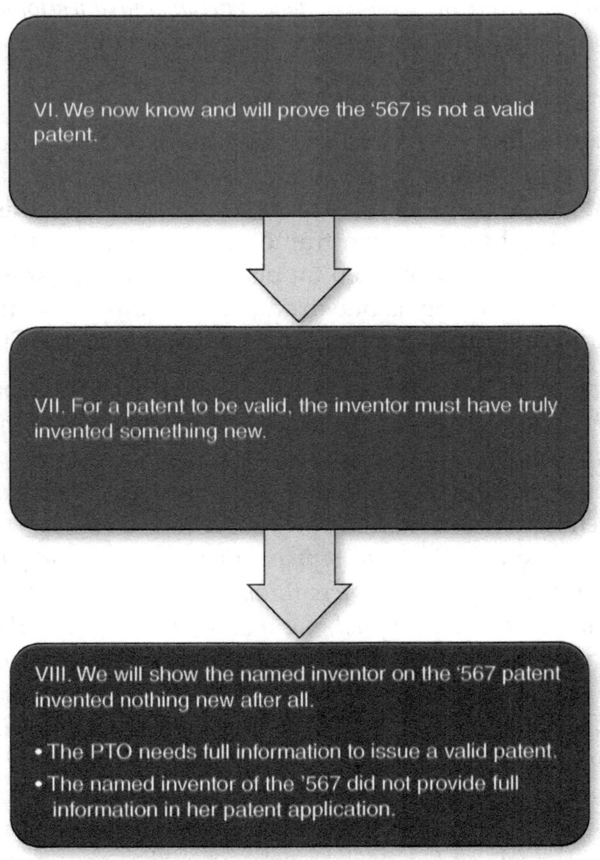

One strong caution: at first glance, you may consider some of the steps unnecessary to say aloud because they seem so obvious, at least to you. Your legal training makes implicit a logic path that most jurors desperately need you to make explicit. It is natural for jurors to become intimidated by dense technology or the technical law so prevalent in patent litigation. As a result, they can mentally shut down and are more likely to miss connections between your persuasive point and the evidence or the law. In our experience working with patent juries, no jurors will judge you for being overt in your logic, no matter how basic it feels to you. Most will appreciate you for it, *and* they may be better persuaded by your argument and evidence as a result.

To understand each of these points in greater detail, let us look at these one at a time.

VI. We (now know and) will prove the '567 is not a valid patent.

Remember that you want to introduce this point in a way that flows naturally from your research into the patent you are accused of infringing as opposed to a "knee-jerk" defense simply because the invalidity defense is a legal option for an accused infringer.

VII. For a patent to be valid, the inventor must have truly invented something new.

Empower jurors to make a determination of invalidity by overtly arguing that a finding of invalidity is often the most fair outcome even though the USPTO issued the '567 patent. For the patent process to work for all, there must be a "double-check" system in place to ensure that issued patents are legitimate. Litigation is that "double-check," contrary to many people's belief that the USPTO has its own wholly contained "double-check" system in place. Many jurors erroneously believe the USPTO will take action of its own volition if it thinks something was amiss with the patent application, much like an employer might go back and look at its background check of a new hire.

Acknowledge that a jury's finding of invalidity in this case serves you. This admission will give you credibility. But then point out the fact that discovery of an invalid patent also serves the consumer (juror). If invalid patents stay in circulation, they hold back legitimate innovation and competition based on incorrect (or incomplete) information within the patent that was erroneously issued.

If you are allowed, make your proof of the jury's power to invalidate a patent concrete through enumeration. Have your patent expert testify to the number of patents found invalid either over the course of a given period of time or in a certain category or field. In order to assert this number, your expert will need to grant that many more patents were not found invalid in that category or during that time frame (before your opponent makes that point), but differentiate the patent holder in your case as having a clearly invalid patent.

VIII. We will show the named inventor on the '567 patent invented nothing new after all.

And, now, the hard work of educating the jury about the fallibility of the patent examiner begins.

VIII. We will show the named inventor on the '567 patent invented nothing new after all.

- The USPTO needs full information to issue a valid patent.

Consider framing this issue in a way that gives the patent examiner the benefit of the doubt:

> *The patent examiner can do his job well if he has all of the necessary information provided to him. He must rely on the claimed inventor to be thorough in disclosing all of the relevant information to enable the examiner to ensure the invention is novel.*

Explain to jurors that the patent examiner relies on the electronic (or in limited circumstances, paper) application and drawings provided to him by the applicant, but this was not always the case. From 1770 to 1890, patent applicants were required to submit small models of their inventions.[8]

When the practice of requiring the submission of small models was discontinued in 1890, applications became only paper and drawings, which is what patent examiners must rely on today (albeit electronically submitted). Help jurors understand that application review typically occurs at the patent examiner's desk, not in a laboratory or somewhere in the field. As a result:

- The patent examiner *does not* get to see a physical device.
- The patent examiner *does not* run experiments to see if the device works.
- The patent examiner *does* read the file provided to him by the applicant. The requirement is that the applicant provides complete information for the examiner to do his job.

Remind jurors that ever since the Patent Act of 1832, accused infringers have been allowed to challenge the validity of a patent issued by the USPTO in part because applicants do not always disclose all the relevant prior inventions and the patent examiner cannot be expected to conduct independent research to double-check patents once they have issued. *This litigation is part of that double-check.*

VIII. We will show the named inventor on the '567 patent invented nothing new after all.

- The USPTO needs full information to issue a valid patent.
- The named inventor of the '567 did not provide full information in her patent application.

(1) Endorse the Patent Applicant

In any type of litigation, you have many choices regarding how you describe your opponent. In patent litigation, you can describe the patent holder as either inept or powerful. We often find that patent litigators are inclined to frame the patent holder as incompetent. However, we find in our jury research that the more powerful a party (in the jurors' eyes), the more responsibility jurors typically ascribe to that party. Under cross-examination or in deposition, press the

8. Teresa Riordan, *Patent Models' Strange Odyssey*, N.Y. Times, Feb. 18, 2002.

named inventor to acknowledge that she is the expert regarding her own invention (and, if possible, on the technology surrounding her invention). Once you gain that admission, endorse the named inventor's expertise at trial.

(2) Focus on the Applicant's "Soft Requirements"

Secondarily, build upon that technical expertise by additionally focusing on the "soft requirements" of the patent applicant's character (again, ideally through the testimony of the patent holder). While establishing character may seem ancillary to proving your invalidity case (and, therefore, optional), this piece can prove critical to jurors. They place prominent focus on the behavior of parties to patent litigation.[9] Establish that trust must be a vital cornerstone of the patent application process. To a large degree, the patent examiner must trust the applicant to be forthcoming. When relevant, contemplate aloud a scenario where the patent applicant might be trustworthy but mistaken at the same time. Be clear that even if a critical piece of prior art is mistakenly omitted, it is still the legal responsibility of the applicant to include it and the legal right of the jury to find a patent invalid.

Once you have focused on the patent holder's role and responsibilities, contrast those qualities with those of a patent examiner who cannot be expected to be a subject matter expert on all nuanced technologies, especially in these days of ever-changing innovation in specialized, obscure fields of expertise.

(3) Address Obscurely Cited or Missing References

To jurors, prior art references are mere footnotes on the patent unless you can make them come alive in the story of what came before the claimed invention. Now that you have endorsed the patent holder's expertise, you have laid the groundwork for establishing the vast amount of what she should have disclosed and in what manner. We consulted on one case where a cited reference for particularly relevant prior art arguably rendered the patent obvious. However, its manner of citation by the patent applicant was so obscure that we framed it as being akin to a "footnote within a footnote" in a research paper. Just as with missing references, consider framing motive to obscure references with a rhetorical question: "Now, what would have been the harm to the applicant of citing/making more prominent this particular reference?" Rhetorical questions can be particularly powerful with jurors because it requires them to mentally engage in providing their own answer. If you have laid the proper groundwork, you should have strong influence over the answer they mentally provide on their own.

(4) Point Out Missteps by the Patent Examiner

When necessary, highlight evidence that the examiner was less than thorough in her research of the references. For example, if the examiner's file shows that she researched some but not all references, make this point clear both verbally and visually. In this case, jurors' typically high expectations of patent examiners in general should feed their disappointment in an examiner's clear misses.

9. *See* Seth Weintraub, *Interview with* Apple-Samsung *Jury Foreman: How He Applied His Patent to Break Stalemate*, 9TO5MAC (Aug. 27, 2012), http://9to5mac.com/2012/08/27/interview-with-apple-samsung-jury-foreman-how-he-applied-his-patent-to-break-stalemate-video/.

b. Obviousness

> *"I don't think [the patent] should ever have been issued. I side with [the accused infringer] for the fact that they made a better machine, with different inputs, and [the patentee] would never have gotten the patent if he had included those prior arts [sic]."*
>
> —Patent mock juror

Demonstrate "consumer protectiveness" by pointing out that being the "first to file" is not adequate to get a patent. You need to be original, unique, and new. If something is obvious or already out there in the market, then there are good reasons why it should not get a patent. Allowing a patent on an obvious method or device hurts the consumer because it robs the patent process of its purpose. It grants protection to ideas that are not innovative, and *that* restricts a consumer's choice. Restricted incentive to innovate and be protected makes innovation secretive, thereby slowing down progress.

Continuing Your Proactive Invalidity Story: Obviousness

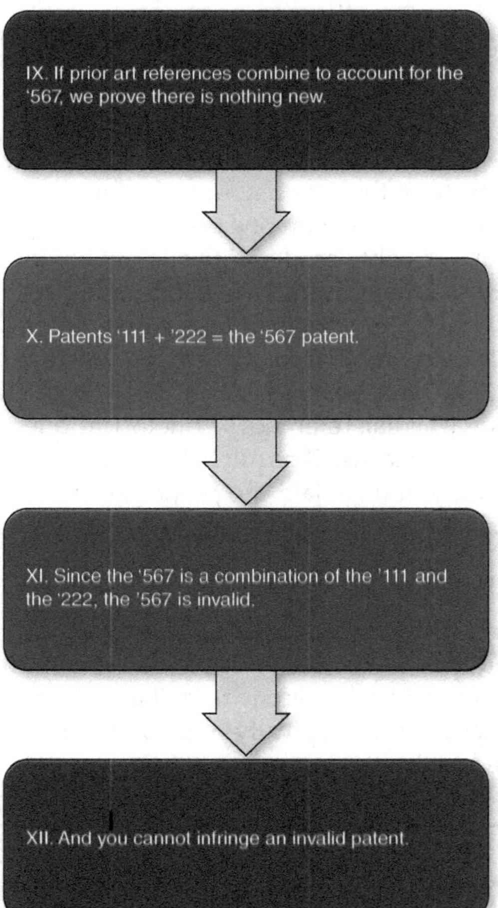

At the risk of repeating ourselves, if this structure seems basic and obvious to you, it should. However, we have seen jurors struggle mightily when they do not have a simple logic path and structure like this one to follow. If, on the other hand, they follow this logic because you have made it overt and simple, you will empower them to believe they can fathom how a patent could be deemed invalid. In patent litigation, like in no other field, the better teacher often prevails.

In a 2020 panel presentation on effective jury communication in patent litigation, U.S. District Court Judge Alan Albright of the Western District of Texas concurred, saying:

> I think more now than I did before—the quality of lawyers matters a great deal. . . . Now that I'm sitting there as a referee, watching, and evaluating from having tried a fair number of cases myself, I think almost without exception in every trial I have had, the lawyers I would have perceived to be the better lawyers have won the case. And that can go the other way too. . . . In several trials I have had, the lawyers who were not very good lost the case. . . . In every case where the disparity of lawyers was palpable, the better lawyers have won even in cases when I didn't think they were going to.[10]

Let us take on the steps in the "Continuing Your Proactive Invalidity Story: Obviousness" graphic one at a time:

IX. If prior art references combine to account for the '567, we prove there is nothing new.

Immediately focus on both the logic and fairness of this requirement and help jurors understand that this tenet is something fundamentally known to those who help inventors file patent applications. To allow a patent to issue *when it was obvious to combine two preexisting prior art references (without changing their properties once combined) would be cheating* (the fairness issue) and redundant (the logic issue). On the flip side, *acknowledge that it would be unfair to randomly find two unrelated references that make no sense to combine*. By contrast, the two references to which you are referring make a great deal of sense.

Jurors sometimes struggle with trusting that someone of ordinary skill in the art (e.g., your expert) would know to combine two separate patents when the combination seems illogical or foreign, especially if the prior art references have not been combined in the past. Trust your jury by explaining why it would have been obvious to combine the '111 and '222 patents to get to the '567 patent. Then, for good measure, help make that combination more user-friendly by analogizing to something different from the actual patent at issue, if need be. The USPTO has offered several examples, such as:

> Consider the '567 patent that covers the four-wheeled suitcase. If no one had ever strapped a suitcase to a portable wheeled cart, it would make sense to say, "not obvious to combine." By contrast, for those of us who are old enough to have flown many times with a carry-on and

10. Magna Legal Service, *Effectively Communicating with Jurors in a Patent Case*, YouTube (Dec. 21, 2020), https://www.youtube.com/watch?v=De29Gj_GYNw.

a portable set of wheels, it seems obvious to have combined those two items into one, much like someone finally put peanut butter and jelly in the same jar.

From the USPTO website:

Sundance, Inc. v. Demote Fabricating Ltd., 550 F.3d 1356 (Fed. Cir. 2008), involved a segmented and mechanized cover for trucks, swimming pools, or other structures. The claim was found to be obvious over the prior art applied.

A first prior art reference taught that a reason for making a segmented cover was ease of repair, in that a single damaged segment could be readily removed and replaced when necessary. A second prior art reference taught the advantages of a mechanized cover for ease of opening. The Federal Circuit noted that the segmentation aspect of the first reference and the mechanization function of the second perform in the same way after combination as they had before. The Federal Circuit further observed that a person of ordinary skill in the art would have expected that adding replaceable segments as taught by the first reference to the mechanized cover of the other would result in a cover that maintained the advantageous properties of both of the prior art covers.

Thus, the *Sundance* case points out that a hallmark of a proper obviousness rejection based on combining known prior art elements is that one of ordinary skill in the art would reasonably have expected the elements to maintain their respective properties or functions after they have been combined.[11]

Then return to your case-specific allegations of obviousness:

The same goes for the elements of the '567 patent. The technology covered by the '111 patent was known in 2003. The technology covered by the '222 patent was known as of at least 2007—four years before the '567 application. To anyone skilled in the art, it is and was obvious that you could combine these elements. (That does not mean it would have been obvious to the patent examiner unless she was given easily accessible information to consider them in combination. She wasn't given the accurate information to do that.) Now, don't let the patent holder say, "But no one combined them before us." That is not the law. The law is that it would have been obvious to someone skilled in the art to combine them, not that they were not combined before.

X. Patents '111 + '222 = the '567 patent.

So it is a matter of simple math (introduce the "empty" demonstrative that follows). If the '111 prior inventions plus the '222 prior inventions (both of which came at least four years before the '567 application) equal the '567, the '567 is not a new and novel invention and should not have been patented.

---

11. USPTO, Manual of Patent Examining Procedure §2143 (9th ed. 2024), http://www.uspto.gov/web/offices/pac/mpep/s2143.html.

If Prior Art (Patents) Combine to Account for the '567, the '567 Invented Nothing New						
Element One of the '567 Patent	+	Element Two of the '567 Patent	+	Element Three of the '567 Patent	=	The '567 Patent
Element X of the '111 Patent	+	Element Y of the '111 Patent	+	Element Z of the '222 Patent	=	The '567 Patent

Present the story of the '111 patent here. Build the visual case within the framework of the thematic graphic. After you have established the two elements present in the '111 patent, build out the graphic to show that all necessary elements are present in the '222 patent as well, to combine to the '567 patent. For example:

The fact that the examiner looked so carefully at the '111 patent, which the patent holder disclosed, is evidence that when the applicant cites the correct references, the examiner evaluates them. But there is absolutely no evidence in this case that the examiner gave any consideration to the second prior art patent that is relevant in this case (the '222 patent)—let alone the same level of consideration and evaluation of the '111 patent—especially since the patent holder never disclosed it to the Patent Office.

XI. Since the '567 is a combination of the '111 and the '222, the patent is invalid.

Emphasize "why it matters" that the three claims found in the two prior art patents means the '567 patent is invalid:

The '567 has already been invented. The fact that this prior invention was memorialized in two parts beforehand doesn't change that fact. Had the patent examiner known the two parts, we argue the patent would not have issued. You now know more and you can do the right thing. No one ever intended the patent process to reward redundancy. In this case, the issue is that the '567 is not worthy of a patent because we have clearly shown that the combination of two prior patents already invented the elements in the '567 patent, and that combining them would have been obvious. The fact that it was obvious means it was not worthy of a patent.

XII. You cannot infringe an invalid patent.

At this stage, keep it simple so that jurors can understand the nexus between invalidity and noninfringement:

At the end of the day, you can only infringe a valid patent. The '567 patent is not valid, and therefore we do not infringe.

(1) Create a Persuasive Obviousness Timeline

Without question, timelines are jurors' favorite demonstrative. If you do not have one, they want it. If you have it, they scrutinize it. However, many timelines used in trial lose their persuasive power when you include a greedy amount of entries along a traditional horizontal line (if persuasiveness was ever achieved at all).

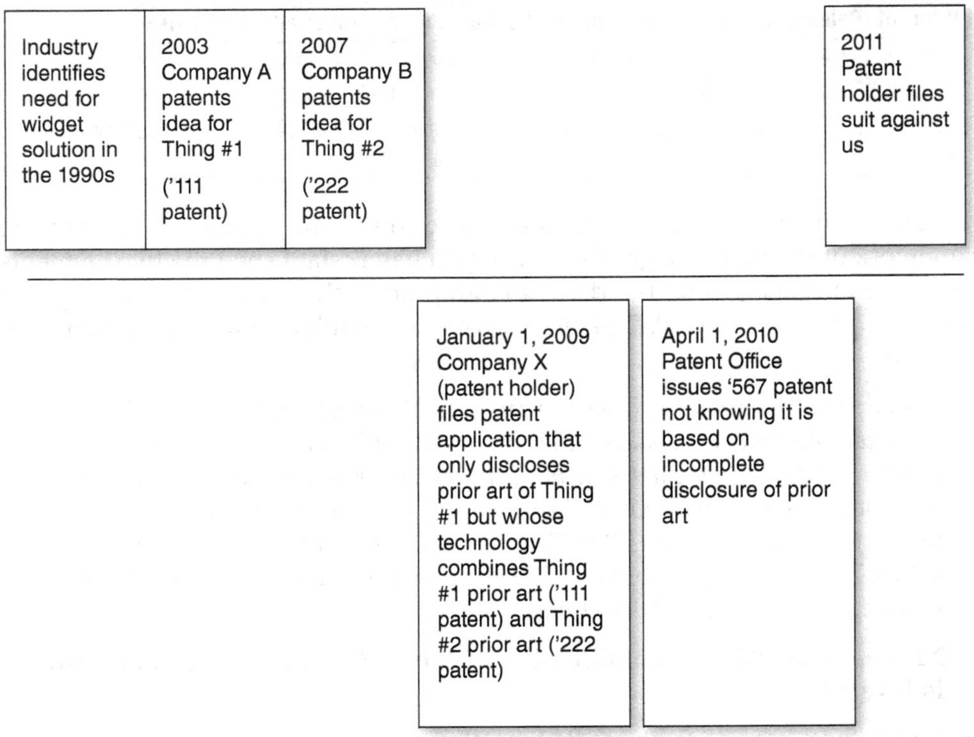

Now, technically, this timeline does the trick. Its intent is to make an obviousness argument on behalf of the accused infringer. It shows the relevant dates and makes it clear that the patentee failed to disclose the relevant prior art in his patent application. However, it misses the persuasive mark on two fronts. First, it is likely to look just like any timeline the other side creates. It will not stand out like it should. Second, it fails to make the persuasive point that your invalidity case needs—that the patent holder applied for and was granted a patent based on incomplete disclosures of the prior art.

The following timeline is quite simple in design but stands out from other traditional timelines and should make the persuasive point that the claimed inventor failed to fully disclose and that the USPTO issued the patent with partial information.

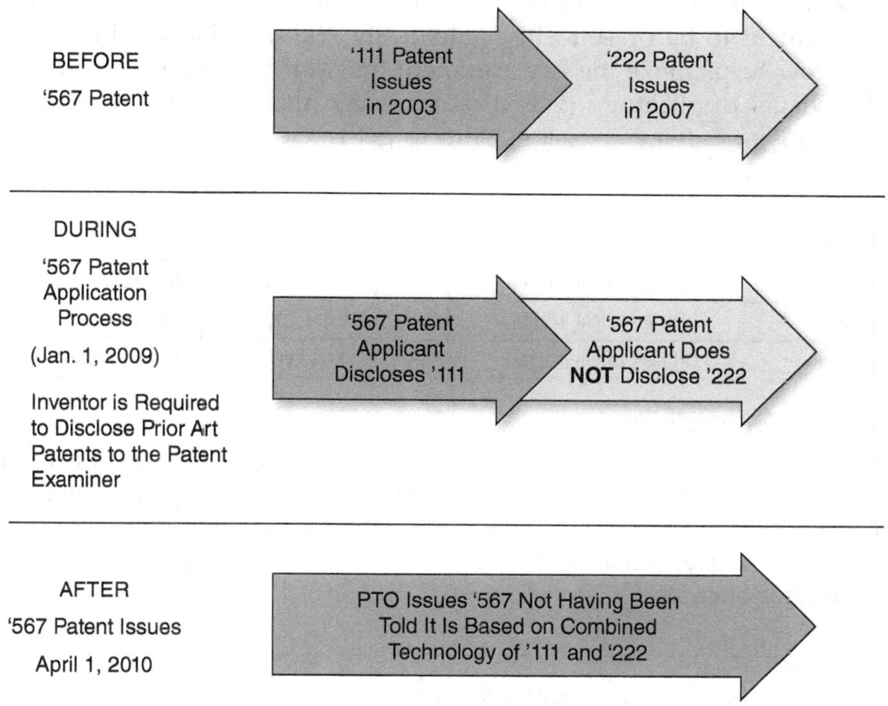

c. Anticipation

When a single piece of prior art anticipates the claimed invention, jurors often expect anticipation to be a literal duplication or a carbon copy. Start with that erroneous assumption and help jurors understand how far the law allows you to deviate from the "carbon copy concept" and still prove that prior art anticipates the claimed invention. We have observed mock jurors visually scour two side-by-side patent drawings (the prior art and the patent at issue) typically looking for differences, not similarities, in an effort to make their jobs easier. Once they eliminate differences, they find the patent to be anticipated. However, as any accused infringer knows, it is very tough to find duplication all around, not to mention the fact that carbon-copy duplication is not the standard. It is your job to know that jurors often start with that misapprehension and to educate them about what the law requires in order to find anticipation.

(1) Conceptual Duplication

Most anticipation arguments that we have tested appeal to jurors on a more "broad view" level, thereby educating jurors that carbon copy is *not* the standard but that each element must be present in a single prior art reference for anticipation to exist. Use a checklist to help jurors keep track of the fact that the key elements are all met. If you can also insert relevant imagery next to each element (even though the imagery will not precisely duplicate the prior art element), you will help diffuse any fiction that the imagery must match for a given element to be present. Psychologically, the fact that the images share the same row helps make the key argument that anticipation exists without the need for visual duplication. (We also appreciate that the one-to-one imagery comparison is not always possible. Aim to get as close as you can by creating this "lack of contrast" graphic.)

Patent at Issue		**Prior Art**	
Element One	[Insert patent image]	[Insert prior art image]	Element One
Element Two	[Insert patent image]	[Insert prior art image]	Element Two
Element Three	[Insert patent image]	[Insert prior art image]	Element Three

2. Non-Prior Art Invalidity

When you claim invalidity not connected with prior art, your key job is to prove to jurors that the patent holder failed to follow the fair and proper steps in its patent description. After you have taken jurors through the story progression described previously, consider the following educational steps that could apply to any number of cases.

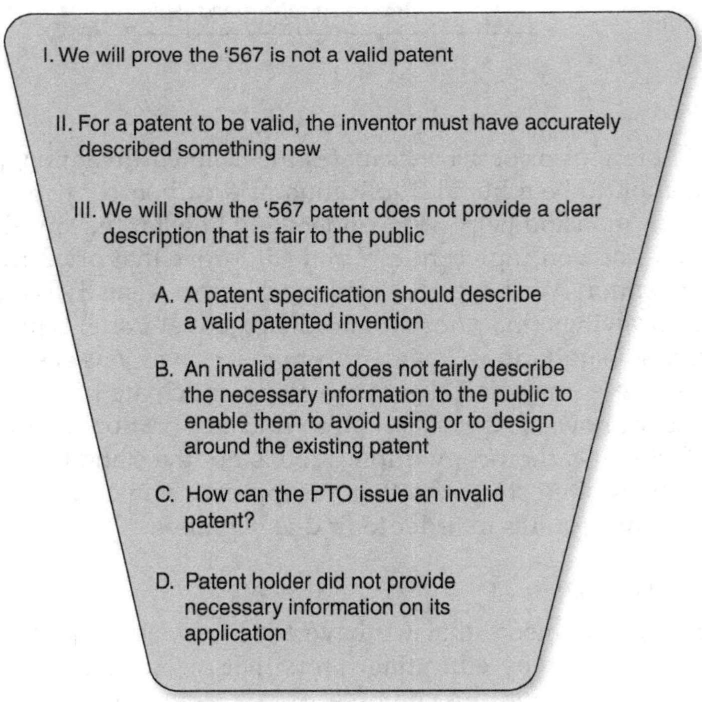

Then get specific about the information the patent holder should have provided. It may be tempting to jump past the elementary steps and move to the legal claims, but we advise strongly against making that leap. Patent juries constantly struggle with trying to understand the context for a legal defense. After you provide the necessary context, then they can better understand the legal points you are about to make.

a. Blurring Between Written Description and Enablement Requirements

Jurors can struggle with what they find to be a blurring of the lines between the written description requirement and the enablement requirement. The Federal Circuit has reaffirmed that the two requirements are separate and distinct.[12] The Federal Circuit offered an example:

> An invention may be described without the disclosure being enabling (e.g., a chemical compound for which there is no disclosed or apparent method of making), and a disclosure could be enabling without describing the invention (e.g., a specification describing a method of making and using a paint composition made of functionally defined ingredients within broad ranges would be enabling for formulations falling within the description but would not describe any specific formulation).[13]

However, as attorneys Vanessa LeFort and Mary Boyle note,[14] much consternation exists about the blurring of the lines between the written description and enablement requirements. (As non-lawyers, we provide no opinion about the legal similarities or differences, but we have repeatedly observed that plenty of juror confusion abounds around these terms.) LeFort and Boyle state:

> Section 112, in relevant part, provides that "[t]he specification shall contain a written description of the invention, and of the manner and process of making and using it, in such full, clear, concise, and exact terms as to enable any person skilled in the art to which it pertains . . . to make and use the same."[15] To satisfy the enablement requirement of § 112, a patentee must "describe the manner and process of making and using the invention so as to enable a person of skill in the art to make and use the full scope of the invention without undue experimentation."[16] To satisfy the written description requirement, the patentee must "convey with reasonable clarity to those skilled in the art that, as of the filing date sought, he or she was in possession of the invention, and demonstrate that by disclosure in the specification of the patent."[17]

---

12. *In re* Barker, 559 F.2d 588, 194 U.S.P.Q. 470 (C.C.P.A. 1977), *cert. denied*, 434 U.S. 1064 (1978); Vas-Cath, Inc. v. Mahurkar, 935 F.2d 1555, 1562, 19 U.S.P.Q.2d 1111, 1115 (Fed. Cir. 1991).

13. *See In re* Armbruster, 512 F.2d 676, 677, 185 U.S.P.Q. 152, 153 (C.C.P.A. 1975) ("[A] specification which 'describes' does not necessarily also 'enable' one skilled in the art to make or use the claimed invention.").

14. Vanessa LeFort & Mary Boyle, *Written Description and Enablement: The Pas de Deux Continues, in* PATENT LITIGATION 2009 (Practising Law Institute 2009).

15. 35 U.S.C. § 112, ¶ 1 (2006).

16. LizardTech, Inc. v. Earth Res. Mapping, Inc., 424 F.3d 1336, 1344–45 (Fed. Cir. 2005), *reh'g denied*, 433 F.3d 1373 (Fed. Cir. 2006).

17. Ariad Pharms., Inc. v. Eli Lily & Co., 560 F.3d 1366 (Fed. Cir. 2009).

The overlap of these two standards has been roundly discussed inside and outside the Court. "[T]he legal criteria of enablement and written description are related and are often met by the same disclosure."[18] The Federal Circuit has explained that "[t]hose two requirements usually rise and fall together."[19] As one justice sitting on the Federal Circuit's predecessor court put it, "I cannot see how one may in 'full, clear, concise and exact terms,' enable the skilled to practice an invention and still have failed to 'describe' it."[20] Criticizing the written description requirement as lacking an administrable standard, Federal Circuit Justice Rader has argued that the written description standard "seems to fall back on enablement, using the latter as a proxy for the former."[21] As construed for biotechnology inventions, where it has been most often applied, the written description seems to go beyond enablement—it has been described as a "super-enablement" standard that requires the specification to disclose more than is required to enable the invention.[22]

b. Lack of Written Description

As the USPTO website notes, the first paragraph of 35 U.S.C. § 112 provides:

> The specification shall contain a written description of the invention, and of the manner and process of making and using it, in such full, clear, concise, and exact terms as to enable any person skilled in the art to which it pertains, or with which it is most nearly connected, to make and use the same, and shall set forth the best mode contemplated by the inventor of carrying out his *invention*.[23]

Jurors typically find this definition easy to understand. They understand that there is to be no "secret" in the "formula" of the patent description. Jurors use words like "recipe" and "blueprint" to analogize to the written description requirement. However, even when they feel they have a grasp of the legal requirement, they still struggle with understanding whether a specific claim meets this requirement. Quite often, they default to broader conclusions, which results in less control by counsel over the criteria jurors use to resolve this question.

To be even more effective arguing lack of written description, consider the persuasive power of contrast by contemplating how the specification language *would have to read* for the written description requirement to be met. While some jurors may not fully appreciate the technical nature of the language or even the nature of the claimed invention, those same jurors can likely appreciate the fact

18. Capon v. Eshhar, 418 F.3d 1349, 1360 (Fed. Cir. 2005).

19. *LizardTech*, 424 F.3d at 1345.

20. *In re* Barker, 559 F.2d 588, 595 (C.C.P.A. 1977) (Markey, J., dissenting).

21. LizardTech, Inc. v. Earth Res. Mapping, Inc., 433 F.3d 1373, 1380 (Fed. Cir. 2006) (denial of petition for rehearing) (Rader, J., dissenting).

22. LeFort & Boyle, *supra* note 14.

23. *Design Patent Application Guide*, USPTO, https://www.uspto.gov/patents/basics/apply/design-patent (last visited Feb. 5, 2025) (emphasis added).

that a difference exists between inadequate language and the existing specification language (which is arguably adequate). Start by describing language that meets the written description requirement (or one option for it, if more than one option exists) in the left-hand column. (The language in the right-hand column is intentionally grayed out at this stage.)

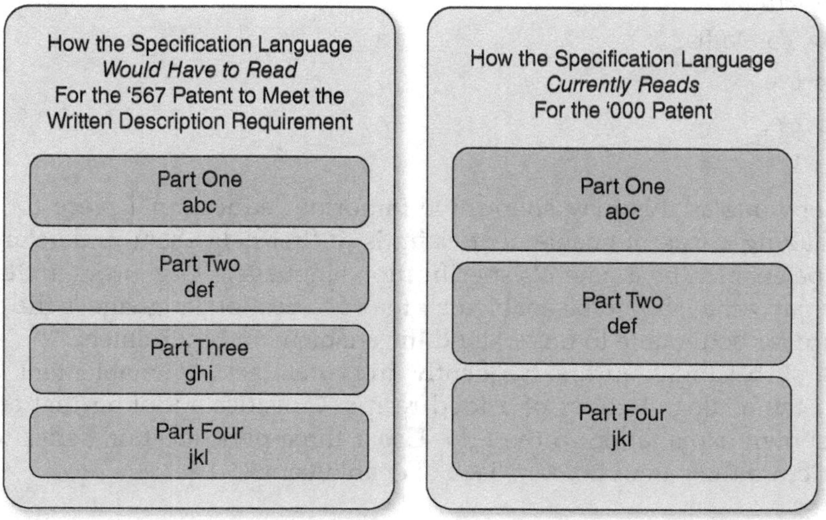

Then, to sharpen the contrast, reveal the inferior language of the patent holder's specification language.

It may not always be easy to convert the specification language into "parts" as described. However, illustrating what is missing should be a teaching point that will help you prevail on lack of written description.

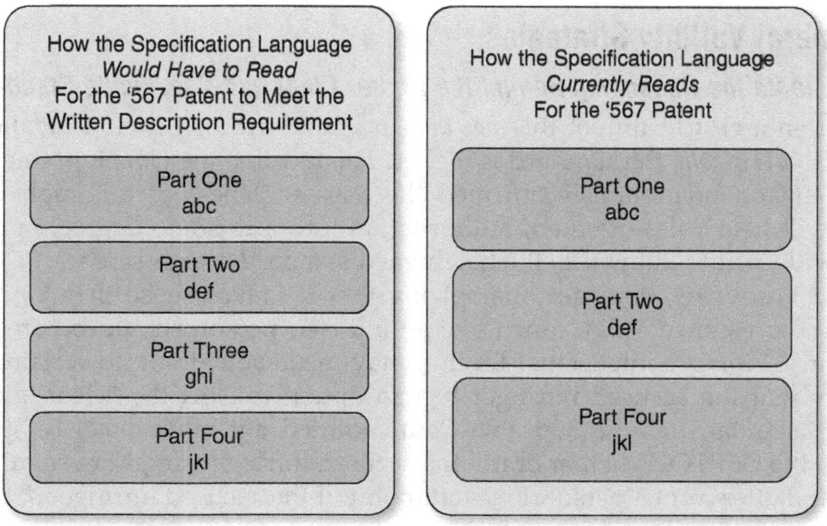

c. Lack of Enablement

The patent enablement requirement refers to the requirement of 35 U.S.C. § 112, first paragraph, that the specification describe how to make and how to use the invention. The website the Business of Patents, http://www.the-business-of-patents.com, makes the concept exceptionally simple and visually clear:

Enablement

How To Do It

Step 1 . . .

Step 2 . . .

Step 3 . . .

As obvious as this may sound, the important educational piece for jurors when making a lack of enablement claim is to first help them understand *who* should be enabled by a patent's specification language. Once jurors understand that the party that should be enabled by the specification language is the public, jurors are far better able to understand the enablement requirement.

Not surprisingly, jurors frequently interpret lack of enablement claims through the analogous filter of a food recipe. Consider adopting that analogy for your own explanation to the jury. Use a three-part question series to help jurors picture the patent holder's lack of enablement.

Question One	Where is the patent holder's specification language lacking?
Question Two	If someone attempted to replicate the patent based on the language, why would it be impossible to complete the task?
Question Three	What could go awry if someone of ordinary skill in the art attempted to replicate the patent based on the published description?

III. Validity Persuasion and the Patent Holder

A. General Validity Strategies

1. Illuminate the Reasoning Behind the Higher Clear and Convincing Standard

It is not enough to trumpet the fact *that* the standard for proving invalidity is higher. Explain *why* the standard is higher. The fact that the U.S. Supreme Court evaluated and unanimously affirmed the reasonableness of this higher standard[24] will help rules-oriented, authoritarian jurors to some degree, but other jurors will want to know *why* the heightened standard makes sense.

At a base level, consider analogizing that it makes sense that the patent should be presumed valid, much like an indicted person should be presumed innocent. At a more intellectual level, it may mean something to certain jurors to know that the accused infringer has an option to skirt the "clear and convincing" standard (as the Supreme Court pointed out in its majority opinion) through the USPTO. Whether or not the accused infringer sought reexamination does not matter from a persuasion standpoint. If the accused infringer *did* seek a

24. Microsoft Corp. v. i4i Ltd. P'ship, 564 U.S. 91 (2011).

reexam and was shut down, this information will be meaningful to jurors. If the accused infringer *did not* seek a reexam, jurors will wonder why. Both positions put the accused infringer in a defensive position of needing to explain.

2. Educate Jurors About the Sophistication of Patent Examiners

The accused infringers may try to make headway by overtly or implicitly casting patent examiners as overburdened bureaucrats who sit at their computers all day. If that occurs in trial, make it clear that patent examiners are well educated. Jurors may be interested to know that Clara Barton, the founder of the American Red Cross, was one of the first female patent examiners to hold the position.

Many examiners tend to specialize in their field of review. Much like physicians, many tend to be specialists rather than generalists. However, be careful in making too much of this analogy. We continue to find that the more powerful a character is in any litigation story, the more jurors expect of that person. You will want to feel comfortable that the patent examination was well done and highly defensible.

3. Ensure You Have Laid Validity Groundwork in Your Noninfringement Defense

The novelty of your invention should be well established if you do your job right in your noninfringement story. (Of course, this assumes you argue noninfringement at all, and, if so, first. Mock trial research is a powerful way to make some of those strategic calls. Our experience has found that the order of your arguments can often have a strong impact on jury persuasion.) Dwell on the novelty and hard work that went into the inventive process. Jurors pay close attention to stories of trial and error, in part because this evidence carries the human element of the patent story that they crave (and understand) as well as persuasive evidence that more trials and more errors point to a nonobvious invention.

4. Watch the Carryover Effect of a Weak Infringement Case on Your Validity Defense

> *"[The accused infringer's product is] not just an improvement on what [the patent holders] did. It's a different way to do what they did. That's like saying that the guy with the Cadillac is stepping on an old beat-up Yugo or something. Because the Yugo had four wheels and they made it before the Cadillac. It's just not really true. It disadvantages the actual intent of patent protection [which] is to protect your investment in developing new technologies or improvements and that's 100% valid. But what these guys [patent holders] did was not that new. They didn't disclose all the information, so it looked like they were trying to pull a fast one."*
>
> —Patent mock juror

5. (Perhaps) Allow the Accused Infringer to Be Mistaken in Its Invalidity Claim

When the facts call for it *and* when you believe the accused infringer to be a sympathetic character, consider a "perhaps" defense (which we develop in greater detail in Section III.D, Continuing Your Validity Story), which pulls together infringement and validity. The point is to educate jurors about the accused infringer's options and to put the infringer in the position of needing to either respond to or ignore those options during their argument. (Of course, if the defendant *did* opt for any of these actions, you would delete reference to those. We submit it is still worthwhile to point out the options they *did not* choose. We continue to find that the more jurors understand options available to a party, the more they hold that party accountable for having capitalized on them or for explaining why they chose not to proceed.) For example:

> *Perhaps the accused infringer didn't consider other available options before being sued and before responding to the suit with invalidity defenses.*
>
> *Perhaps the accused infringer had its own reasons to stop short of seeking a license from us.*
>
> *Perhaps they decided against designing around our patent.*
>
> *Perhaps they opted out of asking the Patent Office to reexamine our patent for their own reasons.*
>
> *At this stage, we don't know their reasoning for "opting out of some of those options." All we know is that they opted to leapfrog over those options and responded to our infringement claim against them by stating that our patent is now invalid.*

B. Telling Your Proactive Validity Story

We understand that you do not want to assume the legal burden in defending your validity case, since you have no obligation to do so. However, the more compelling story wins even when, technically, your validity defense is more like an accused infringer that fails to lose. One approach makes this abstract concept more concrete.

Beginning Your Proactive Validity Story

I. We catch the defendant infringing our patent and we sue to enforce our patent rights.

II. Instead of simply defending their actions, they attack the patent process and they attack us.

III. We are proud of how hard we worked for our novel invention.

- A. We worked hard to get it to the point of a workable invention.
- B. We worked hard to ensure it was novel and disclosed what came before it to show that fact. (prior art validity)
- C. We worked hard to describe our innovation clearly in our patent application. (non prior art validity)

IV. The PTO appears to agree by granting a patent.

C. Choosing the Right Validity Theme

1. *Criteria for the Right Theme*

1. **Give a nod to your infringement theme**. The best invalidity theme is one that transitions well from your infringement theme. Even if your invalidity theme comes at a later time, draw the link for jurors.
2. **Use positive perceptions of the USPTO to your advantage**. It is no accident that this criterion is the same for both the invalidity claimant and the validity defendant. As we have mentioned numerous times throughout this book, the positive esteem with which jurors hold the USPTO is something to endorse, not something to resist.
3. **Be clear that you do not hold the burden to prove validity**. You will need to make this point very quickly so as not to sound defensive, but it should be done.
4. **Focus on having done the right thing**. It may be tempting to default to a "legal-logical"-sounding defense, especially since the heightened standard is in your favor. However, jurors need to hear your focus on doing the right thing to achieve a valid patent. Patent juries care deeply about a party's behavior and ethics. Making that characterization part of your case is worth the energy.
5. **Make your wording memorable**. There is nothing more gratifying than knowing you landed on the perfect theme because jurors repeat the theme during deliberations. The right theme is more than mere words. It is the filter through which your story and evidence make winning sense.

2. *Wording Your Theme*

One example of the right theme might look something like this:

> *The bigger the innovation blessed by the Patent Office, the bigger the attack waged by the competition.*

It is simple. It conveys the fact that the USPTO approved your client's patent, and the word "competition" implies motive on the alleged infringer's part to claim invalidity.

3. *Wording Your Silver Bullet*

Your silver bullet is the first 90 seconds to two minutes of your opening statement. Attorneys Brett Foster and Mark Miller of Dorsey & Whitney represented K-TEC and prevailed in a patent infringement matter against Vita-Mix[25] while at Holland & Hart. They have shared their winning silver bullet for our use as an example here. (This silver bullet merges both the infringement and validity cases into one.)

> This case can best be understood through three sayings that you have probably heard before:
>
> - One: If you build a better mousetrap, the world will beat a path to your door.

25. K-TEC, Inc. v. Vita-Mix Corp., No. 2:06-CV-108-TC (D. Utah May 24, 2010).

- Two: Actions speak louder than words
- And three: If you can't beat them, join them.

Let's look at the first saying: "If you build a better mousetrap, the world will beat a path to your door." It means that innovation is, and should be, rewarded. In this case, K-TEC built the better mousetrap. A blender container, called a "jar," that dramatically increased the speed and efficiency that drinks could be blended. If you think about the way products develop, then you know that there are sometimes small steps—little advantages that don't make a huge difference but still improve a product, like a radio that needs fewer batteries to work. Then sometimes there are big steps—innovations that change the nature of the market—like the iPod. K-TEC's blending jar in the high-performance commercial-blending market was a very big step. It could more efficiently blend a greater number of drinks in a quarter of the time, and that is a very big deal if you're in the business of selling blended drinks. It was so clear that K-TEC built the better blending jar that initially the commercial blender buying world did indeed beat a path to K-TEC's door. Ruby Tuesdays said that K-TEC's five-sided container "beat the shoot"—(but they didn't say "shoot")—out of the industry leader, Vita-Mix. Baskin Robbins made K-TEC its approved supplier, and Caribou Coffee said they loved the new container. And customers were not the only ones to recognize the superiority of K-TEC's design. Vita-Mix saw it as well. Their Director of Sales said the K-TEC design "blows ours away." Clearly, this was the better mousetrap.

Let's look at the second saying: "Actions speak louder than words." In this case, it means that Vita-Mix's actions at the time speak louder than their attorneys' words today. At the time, when Vita-Mix first learned of the K-TEC container, their actions were to treat it as patentable. The [chief executive officer] of Vita-Mix recognized the value of K-TEC's five-sided jar and the likelihood that it would be patented. Their actions, first, were to try to work around K-TEC's idea to develop their own idea that would work as well. They couldn't. What Vita-Mix didn't do at the time was treat K-TEC's design as something that was obvious, or already done. What Vita-Mix didn't do at the time was treat K-TEC's design as just a version of something they themselves had invented. No, at the time, Vita-Mix treated it for what it was: an important new innovation that had a good chance of cornering the market. But the words of Vita-Mix's lawyers today will be that K-TEC's design was obvious, or anticipated by its own inventions—words that don't reflect Vita-Mix's actions at the time. Their actions then will speak louder than words today.

And let's look at that third saying: "If you can't beat them, join them." In this case, that means that when your best efforts to compete don't work, then try something else. It has to be said in this case that Vita-Mix gave it their best to find some product that would blend as well but wouldn't infringe on K-TEC's design. They tried fourteen prototypes to design around K-TEC, but in the end, none of these designs were as good. So they tried something else. But instead of trying to join K-TEC by buying or licensing their design, they simply used K-TEC's design. Vita-Mix must have interpreted the saying as "If you can't beat them, then cheat them."

K-TEC built the better mousetrap. And the world did start to beat a path to their door. Vita-Mix recognized that it was a valid and patentable idea, and their actions at the time speak louder than their words now. Vita-Mix tried with fourteen different mousetraps, but none were better. And when Vita-Mix couldn't beat K-TEC, they settled for cheating them. That is what this case is about.

There is one more saying that might apply to a case like this: *Imitation is the sincerest form of flattery*. Well, Mr. Dickson is here today asking for your help because he is tired of being flattered by Vita-Mix.

D. Continuing Your Validity Story

The following potential points provide a bridge from setting up your validity story to addressing specific validity defenses:

V. The accused infringer had choices before being sued for infringing our patent.

A. A choice to seek a license from us.

B. A choice to design around our patented technology.

C. A choice to seek a reexamination from the Patent Office.

VI. The accused infringer instead chose to argue invalidity as a defense after we sued them for infringing.

E. Persuading by Legal Claims

1. Prior Art Validity

III.B. We worked to ensure the patented invention was novel and disclosed what came before it to show that fact.

It is critical that you communicate the patent holder's overt attempts to stay true to the requirement of novelty. When it is possible to preempt the accused infringer's obviousness or anticipation defenses, tell the jury (1) that you worked hard to ensure that the invention was novel, and (2) that the jury can expect to hear the defendant raise this issue. The good news regarding your validity responses is that jurors tend to find these concepts to be user-friendly. You call them secondary considerations, but jurors often place primary focus on behavior in the marketplace.

a. Nonobviousness

(1) Secondary Considerations for Nonobviousness

Attorney Natalie Thomas describes secondary considerations in this manner:

> Following the Supreme Court's decision in *Graham v. John Deere*, secondary considerations—also known as objective indicia of nonobviousness—have been considered when determining whether an invention is nonobvious. Secondary considerations provide tangible evidence of the economic and motivational issues relevant to the nonobviousness of an invention. Types of secondary consideration evidence include commercial success, long-felt but unmet need, and copying by competitors.[26]

When possible, fold these secondary considerations into your invention story during your infringement argument. A long-felt unmet need drives a great invention and is often accompanied by the two consequences of (positive) commercial success and (negative) copying by competitors. In the section that follows, you will see a close symbiosis between these secondary considerations and jurors' focus on how they argue nonobviousness with one another in deliberations.

(2) Nonobviousness from the Jury's Perspective

Whether or not defense counsel raises the following nonobviousness defenses, we find jurors raise these most frequently when trying to persuade their peers during deliberations:

(a) "If It Was So Obvious . . ."

". . . [T]hen why didn't someone else think of it before the patentee came up with it?!" Jurors frequently voice this sentiment when they hear the accused infringer use the word "obviousness." The word itself empowers most jurors to experience an island of familiarity in a sea of unfamiliar patent terms. Much like jurors do in other types of litigation, if they can make sense of a legal term from their own "street definitions," they often default to their own definition to the exclusion of the instructions judges read to them. In the case of obviousness defenses, patent jurors frequently go to their own street definition, as is evidenced by the following quotes from patent mock jurors in two different venues:

- "It wasn't obvious to anybody working, or else somebody would have made it years before."

26. Natalie A. Thomas, *Secondary Considerations in Nonobviousness Analysis: The Use of Objective Indicia Following* KSR v. Teleflex, 86 N.Y.U. L. Rev. 2070 (2011).

- "If it would have been obvious, then there would have been a patent beforehand, so it couldn't have been that obvious."

(b) The Greater the Perceived Effort to Develop, the Less Obvious the Invention

Again, applying their street sense of the word "obvious," jurors often look at the ease with which the patentee came to his invention. If enough is known about the effort or trial and error that went into developing the patented technology, jurors often find obviousness to be a misplaced argument. Develop well your inventor's story of development of the invention (and lay the initial groundwork in your infringement case as you describe the problem the invention was trying to solve). Jurors often look at two different elements when assessing original effort: (1) the time it took to develop the final patented technology, and (2) the number of "misfires" in getting to the final concept. As one patent juror put it: "Anything that takes three and a half years [to develop] is not obvious."

Hindsight is the enemy of a nonobviousness defense. Academic research that looks at the relationship between hindsight bias and arguments of nonobviousness finds a problem for the inventor.[27] However, nothing says nonobvious like a history of problems with early versions of the claimed invention. Do not rush this part of the invention story. The more jurors appreciate that earlier versions missed the mark, the less they are likely to find the finished concept obvious. In this regard, even small misfires and restarts matter.

Consider the story of Thomas Alva Edison's notoriously high number of failed attempts at inventing the lightbulb. (In fact, he was not the first to invent the electric lightbulb, as many think. He invented the first commercially viable incandescent light.) On January 27, 1880, Edison was granted U.S. Patent No. 223,898 for an electric lamp using "a carbon filament or strip coiled and connected to platina contact wires," but it was only after *several thousand* failed attempts. Ironically, three years later, the USPTO concluded that Edison's patent was invalid, based on its assertion that William Sawyer first invented this technology. After six years of litigation, a judge held Edison's patent valid.

If you or your patent expert are allowed to introduce this story, you can make two key points. First, failed attempts that precede the ultimate invention are proof of tenacity and nonobviousness. Second, even a well-established inventor like Edison had to weather claims of invalidity (with an ultimate finding of validity) for a famous invention.

---

27. In her article *Secondary Considerations in Nonobviousness Analysis: The Use of Objective Indicia Following* KSR v. Teleflex, author Natalie A. Thomas provides a footnote summary:

> *See Gregory N. Mandel, Patently Non-obvious: Empirical Demonstration That Hindsight Bias Renders Patent Decisions Irrational, 67 Ohio St. L.J. 1391, 1404 (2006) ("Overestimating the likelihood of a known invention occurring will tend to make the invention appear obvious. Perhaps even more powerfully, the tendency to overestimate the foreseeability of the invention will make the invention appear to have been more obvious than it actually was."); id. at 1419 (concluding from empirical studies of hindsight bias, including one of first-year law students participating as mock jurors, that hindsight bias significantly impacts nonobviousness decisions in patent law).*

Id. at 2076 n.29.

(c) The Greater the Commercial Success of the Embodiment of the Patent, the Less Obvious the Invention

Jurors' relief is almost palpable when they encounter "real-world" evidence to help them determine how to vote. When the patent holder launches commercial success as a nonobviousness defense, jurors readily understand the argument that the embodiment of the claimed invention is superior to the prior art. (They may not always ultimately agree, but they do understand.) Trial consultant George Speckart makes a similar point by contemplating the converse:

> Perceptions of whether a patent should be considered as obvious, or whether prior art should be considered as substantial or significant, are often strongly influenced by the real world market or economic impact of the related products or devices. In numerous cases, it has been observed that an idea or invention should not be considered as prior art "because he [the inventor] did not do anything with it."[28]

The following graduated timeline demonstrates the patent holder's commercial success where others in the world of prior art failed. Revealing key events on a graduated basis allows you to control what jurors learn at a pace they can absorb. The format also makes this demonstrative more memorable. No predictable horizontal lines!

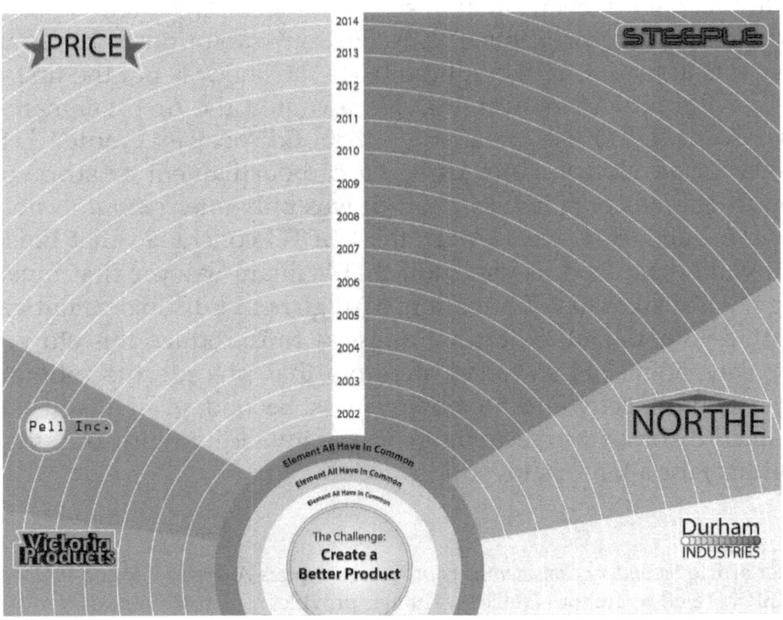

The "pseudonymed" patent holder in this example is Steeple. The first point of the timeline is to acknowledge some inherent overlap among common elements as a *starting point* in the innovation(s).

---

28. George Speckart, *Navigating the Road to a Jury Verdict*, 50 For Def. 10 (2008).

The next iteration of the timeline discloses that several competitors did patent their product versions. It is better to frame this to your advantage rather than leave it to the other side to point out.

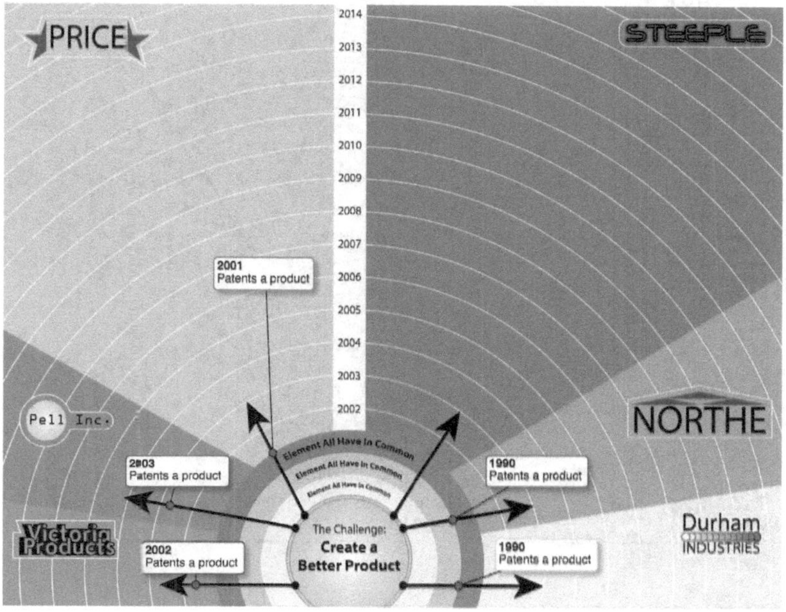

Now that you have established the prior information (including the commonalities), you are in a good position to make your case by pointing out differences. The key differences that emerge are competitors' products that either fail or are never commercialized.

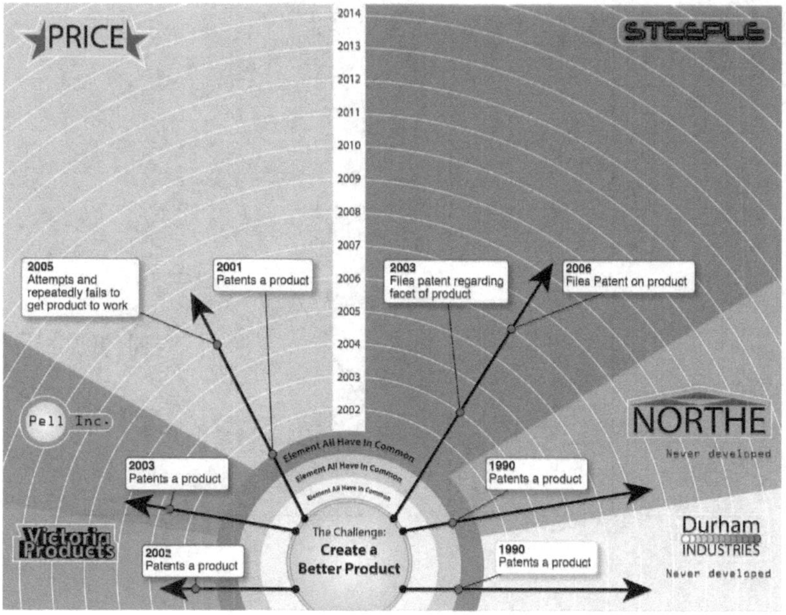

Now, the only movement occurring is for your client, Steeple.

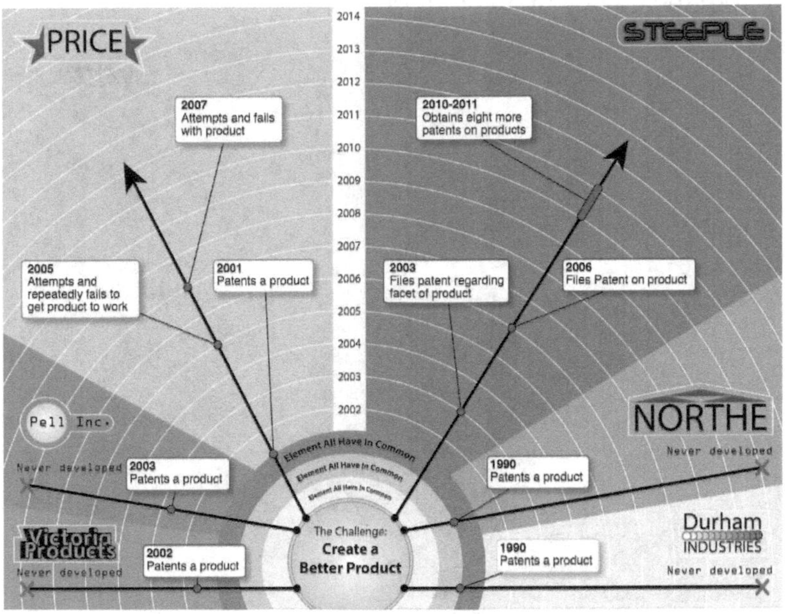

Ultimately, Steeple is the only party that succeeds in commercializing its product.

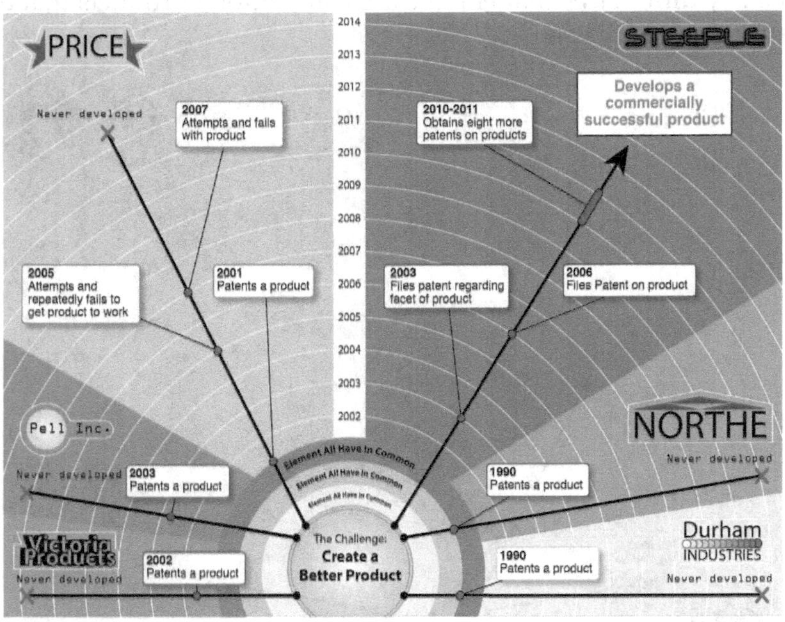

b. Lack of Anticipation

In an ironic twist of logic, there exist those jurors who are convinced that just about everything out there has been invented in someone's mind. Others believe that many patented inventions have been anticipated in some other form, even if the claims do not line up from one patent to the next. The irony lies in the fact that these almost blasé assumptions seem to more frequently help the patent holder than the accused infringer, largely because these jurors can have high standards for seeing meaningful overlap between the claimed invention and the prior art alleged to anticipate the patent at issue.

To borrow from the page of what we advised accused infringers to use when arguing for anticipation, turn their own table against them. Instead of a comparative graphic, try to show your attempt and failure to make an element-by-element comparison. A simplistic skeleton of a table is as follows:

Patent at Issue		**Prior Art**	
Element 1	[Insert your image]	[Insert your image]	Element 1
Element 2	[Insert your image]	???	Element 2
Element 3	[Insert your image]	[Insert your image]	Element 3

Make the missing element stand out. Here, a rather staid-looking table includes the *caricature of question marks* to draw the juror's attention to the misfit. Accompany this visual with a proud acknowledgment that "things often come from other things," and overlap certainly exists in Elements 1 and 3. However, one misfit (Element 2) means that anticipation does not exist here. If you can show where overlap *does* exist, you will enhance your credibility with the jury. It also allows you to focus on the missing element.

As with most legal arguments in patent cases (or other litigation for that matter), complete argumentation is necessary for jurors to comprehend and be persuaded by your position. As we noted in the infringement chapter (Chapter 6), a long-standing model of complete argumentation taught in persuasion courses throughout universities works beautifully in patent litigation. As we discussed in Chapter 6:

> *Modern-day philosopher Stephen Toulmin identified a six-part model of argumentation*[29] *(which we are simplifying here into three steps) that demonstrates the coupling of the evidence with patent law. When you read this, you may feel a reaction of "but of course." However, we caution you to take seriously the need to make the warrant (see the following image) explicit. In our experience, the biggest reason jurors lack the ability to translate the significance of the evidence or to understand an argument is because counsel believed the warrant could be left implicit.*

29. Stephen Toulmin, The Uses of Argument (2003).

For your anticipation defense, consider this simple (but complete) argument:

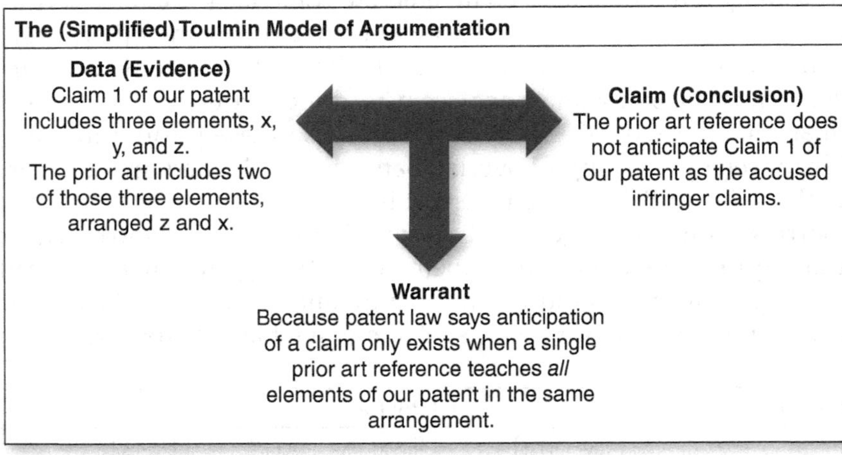

Again, the failing of most arguments is attorneys' exclusion of the warrant. What is clear to you given your knowledge of patent law is often confounding to jurors. You will not insult their intelligence by including this linking sentence. You will only make them feel smarter if they understand the warrant, and you may bring some confused jurors along who failed to follow your conclusion or evidence absent that critical sentence.

2. *Non-Prior Art Validity*

III.C. We worked hard to describe our innovation clearly in our patent application.

a. Written Description

When you want to be clear that the accused infringer fails in its burden to prove lack of written description, it can be especially helpful to persuade by contrast. For example, consider showing jurors the actual language that appears in the specification. Then, on a demonstrative next to that language, show jurors how the language would have to read for the accused infringer to be correct. (It likely entails you "striking through" or deleting the language you believe is descriptive.)

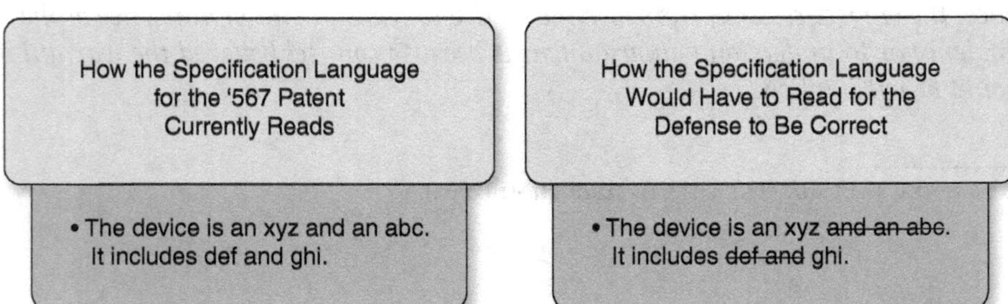

b. Enablement

If the accused infringer has argued lack of enablement, jurors will need help understanding what enablement (or, for persuasive contrast, the lack thereof) looks like. Jurors take an incredibly practical view of enablement when asked to consider this issue. As one patent mock juror synthesized it: "It's quite simple. Theirs [alleged infringer's] worked and the other's [patentee's] didn't."

As it turns out, this juror did not get it quite right. According to the USPTO:

> The enablement requirement refers to the requirement of 35 U.S.C. 112(a) . . . , first paragraph that the specification describe how to make and how to use the invention. The invention that one skilled in the art must be enabled to make and use is that defined by the claim(s) of the particular application or patent.
>
> The purpose of the requirement that the specification describe the invention in such terms that one skilled in the art can make and use the claimed invention is to ensure that the invention is communicated to the interested public in a meaningful way. The information contained in the disclosure of an application must be sufficient to inform those skilled in the relevant art how to both make and use the claimed invention.[30]

In his book *Creating Winning Trial Strategies and Graphics*,[31] G. Christopher Ritter makes a visual analogy to the Wright Brothers' invention of the airplane as a way of defining enablement in a way that helps the patentee. When the Wright Brothers succeeded in flying their airplane in 1903, they enabled their idea. Even though the idea of a flying machine had been considered and attempted for hundreds of years, no one would have been able to acquire a patent simply for the idea. His suggested demonstrative contrasts the lack of enablement from prior "would-be" inventors with the Wright Brothers' ability to inform those skilled in the relevant art how to both make and use their claimed invention.

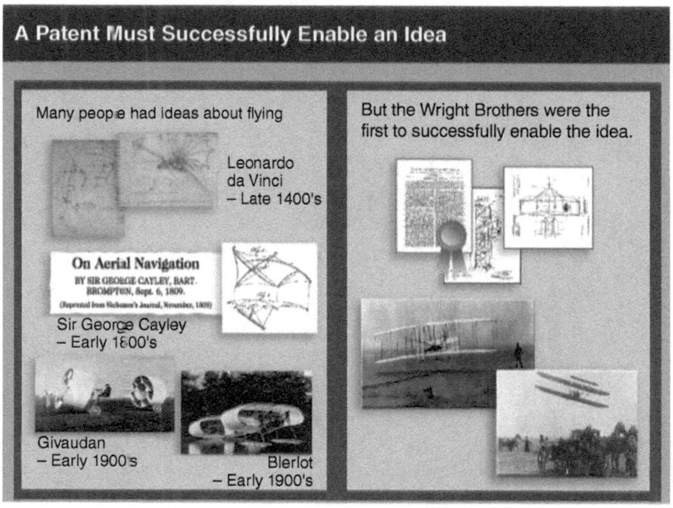

30. USPTO, Manual of Patent Examining Procedure § 2164 (9th ed. 2024), http://www.uspto.gov/web/offices/pac/mpep/s2164.html.

31. G. Christopher Ritter, Creating Winning Trial Strategies and Graphics (2004).

CHAPTER 8

Patent Damages

"Frequently, damages is treated as the poor cousin to the 'patent portion' of the case; almost as an afterthought. This is a mistake. The damages framework provides natural opportunities to reiterate the relative value (or lack of value) of an invention, and motives for the behavior of the parties. In the end, precise calculations should flow from, not stand apart from, the fabric of the overall story being presented to the jury."[1]

—Marc Cooperman, patent litigator with Banner & Witcoff

Patent cases account for many of the highest damages awards in the history of civil litigation, including awards of $2.54 billion against Gilead Sciences in the 2016 case *Idenix Pharmaceuticals v. Gilead Sciences Inc.*, $2.18 billion for VLSI Technology in a 2021 verdict against Intel, and many others in excess of $1 billion. The financial costs for a litigant taking a patent case to verdict is measured in the millions of dollars. Without question, the stakes can be high for both sides in a patent trial.

The law of patent damages is consistently in flux. We recognize that offering specific insights into juror behavior under the law current at the time of this writing can read like an offer to pay last year's prices for a brand new home. Yet jurors consistently struggle with aspects of patent damages decisions that transcend minor (and even major) changes in patent law. We leave the commentary on frequently changing patent damages law to the attorneys who know it best and focus our attention on how jurors think about patent damages regardless of the law. One of the most interesting and enlightening questions to consider is the question of how jurors handle their overwhelming uncertainty about what is reasonable and fair in order to enter a dollar amount on the verdict form.

1. Personal Communication with Marc Cooperman, Patent Litigator, Banner & Witcoff (2013).

I. Juror Perceptions of Patent Damages

> *"In this country, intellectual property deserves to be protected. My real point was that if anyone, the industry at large, if any company decides to ignore the stipulations and the rules and get too close, that they cross the line and infringe and they do it willfully, they need to understand that if they take the risk and they get caught, they should have to pay for it."*[2]
>
> —*Apple v. Samsung* juror Velvin Hogan

Consider a scenario where jury deliberations did not go the infringement defendant's way (and there was no invalidity case). The jury decides the accused infringer is at fault and now they need to determine damages. Jurors must now imagine a world that would have existed if not for the defendant's infringing behavior. They must consider a world filled with "what ifs" and "but fors." Do these assumptions and hypothetical scenarios make the jury's job easier or more difficult? The unequivocal answer is equivocal: it depends. What remains is a two-part relative constant. First, patent jurors are typically uncertain about how to make a damages decision that is both reasonable and just. Second, most jurors lack even a general familiarity with the economic analyses that often plague both sides' damages evidence. Absent some unique experience or frame of reference to inform an understanding of patent damages, most jurors are left to tackle the decision with three key ingredients: a limited ability to comprehend numbers, well-honed uncertainty reduction skills, and a healthy proportion of common sense.

Jurors face a challenging task when determining damages in complex trials,[3] and jurors admit damages decisions are difficult.[4] Many patent trial attorneys crank up their own high-powered brains, focus on spreadsheet calculations, and turn the analysis into a numbers game. The opponent does the same thing. This approach works well for brilliant attorneys who possess multiple engineering degrees. But many Americans lack proficiency when dealing with numbers, and financial numbers in particular.[5] Yet jurors are asked to reconcile conflicting evidence and arguments about what a plaintiff deserves,

2. Seth Weintraub, *Interview with* Apple-Samsung *Jury Foreman: How He Applied His Patent to Break Stalemate*, 9TO5MAC (Aug. 27, 2012), http://9to5mac.com/2012/08/27/interview-with-apple-samsung-jury-foreman-how-he-applied-his-patent-to-break-stalemate-video/.

3. *See generally* Edith Greene & Brian Bornstein, *Precious Little Guidance: Jury Instruction on Damage Awards*, 6 PSYCH. PUB. POL'Y & L. 743 (2000); Roselle L. Wissler et al., *Instructing Jurors on General Damages in Personal Injury Cases: Problems and Possibilities*, 6 PSYCH. PUB. POL'Y & L. 712 (2000).

4. *See generally* Shari Seidman Diamond, *What Jurors Think: Expectations and Reactions of Citizens Who Serve as Jurors*, *in* VERDICT: ASSESSING THE CIVIL JURY 282 (Robert F. Litan ed., 1993).

5. Valerie F. Reyna & Charles J. Brainerd, *Numeracy, Ratio Bias, and Denominator Neglect in Judgments of Risk and Probability*, 18 LEARNING & INDIVIDUAL DIFFERENCES 89 (2008).

often in multiple damages categories with multiple expert witnesses opining on what is reasonable.

Decisions under these circumstances are replete with uncertainty, and jurors do their best to reduce their uncertainty, apply the rules they are given, and return a decision that fits with their individual feelings about what is appropriate.[6] It is not an easy task. Most researchers who have carefully studied how jurors make damages decisions in civil lawsuits offer a reassuring conclusion that jurors do an effective job of reaching damages decisions in a legally appropriate manner.[7] This is the good news.

On top of the de facto uncertainty of damages determinations in the run-of-the-mill civil lawsuit, patent jurors face the additional complexities involved in patent damages, including the task of evaluating hypothetical "but for" scenarios, royalty rates "that would have been," and speculation about lost profits caused by infringement attributable to the patented elements of a given product. Even patent law commentators describe patent damages as one of the most interesting (read challenging) aspects of patent law and recognize how the law is ever-evolving.[8] Despite these challenges, researchers examining hundreds of patent trial awards have reached a reassuring conclusion that patent damages are not excessive but may even be reliably predictable.[9]

In some ways, patent cases make jurors' tasks simpler. In contrast with a personal injury case in which subjective determinations of noneconomic damages are at issue, patent cases allow jurors to focus primarily on economic losses. Instead of trying to translate the subjective perceptions of suffering into the concrete dollar amounts in a personal injury case, patent jurors are asked to understand and determine a plaintiff's financial losses—often based on hypothetical circumstances—and award a dollar amount in concert with those losses. But make no mistake: even though a category may read "economic damages," jurors' *psychological motivations* to award a little or a lot factor into the equation, even if not apparent via calculator.

---

6. *See, e.g.*, Shari Seidman Diamond et al., Damage Anchors on Real Juries (2011), http://ssrn.com/abstract=1883861.

7. *See, e.g.*, Edie Greene & Brian H. Bornstein, Determining Damages: The Psychology of Jury Awards (2003); Edith Greene et al., *The Effects of Defendant Conduct on Jury Damage Awards*, 86 J. Applied Psych. 228 (2001); Neil Vidmar & Valerie P. Hans, American Juries: The Verdict (2007).

8. *See, e.g.*, Michael J. Mazzeo et al., Excessive or Unpredictable? An Empirical Analysis of Patent Infringement Awards (June 17, 2011), http://dx.doi.org/10.2139/ssrn.1765891.

9. *See id.*

A. Juror Motivations for Awarding Patent Damages

> *"Patent damages are supposed to compensate patent owners for their losses, putting them back in the world they would have inhabited but for infringement."*[10]
>
> —Professor Mark Lemley

> *"The whole thing is about money, not humanity, about who is going to make the most money."*
>
> —Patent mock juror

Patent damages are on the rise. According to the Lex Machina *Patent Litigation Report 2024*:

> The total amount of patent damages awarded in each of the past three years surpassed $1 billion per year. In addition, the number of cases in which patent damages were awarded increased over the last four years. In 2023, the highest annual amount of total damages was awarded to the highest number of cases in any year over the ten-year period.[11]

Annual patent damages awards are measured in the billions of dollars. Regardless of what patent damages are intended to accomplish, what motivates jurors' damages decisions in patent trials? Litigation consultant Thomas O'Toole summarizes well his view of the primary motivations for patent damages awards in jury trials:

> Jury awards in patent cases stem from one of three categories: as an endorsement of the Americana principle of hard work and rewards, to punish deceptive behavior, or to punish businesses for taking a battle to the courtroom that jurors think belongs in the marketplace. Awards rarely diverge from these categories primarily because anything else ventures into the abstract and away from the everyday experiences and attitudes of the average juror.[12]

The threat of punishment is clearly the most dangerous fear for an accused infringer. It is worth talking in more detail about the distinction between jurors' motivation to compensate a patent holder and their desire to punish an infringing competitor. Once an accused infringer has been found to have infringed, most jurors view their damages decision with this "proof of copying" (or, more explicitly, theft of a profitable idea) as a primary filter. While we observe some mock jurors speaking with overt anger about damages against proven

10. Mark A. Lemley, *Distinguishing Lost Profits from Reasonable Royalties*, 51 Wm. & Mary L. Rev. 655 (2009).

11. Lex Machina, Patent Litigation Report 2024 (Lex Machina Data Team eds., 2024).

12. Personal Communication with Thomas M. O'Toole, Litigation Consultant (June 2012).

infringers, others drive damages awards through comments veiled in covert negative feelings about the infringing "thief."[13] As much as anything else, a finding of infringement can remove the brakes on damages decisions, because at least some of the jury group perceives the defendant as having lied, cheated, or stolen something that it did not rightly own.

In order to better understand how patent jurors perceive damages and how they go about making decisions regarding damages, it is helpful to examine the process of damages decision-making generally, and in patent lawsuits more specifically, starting with jurors' general approaches to damages determinations.

B. Juror Approaches to Determining Damages

There are still many unknowns and uncertainties when it comes to understanding—and especially trying to predict—how a group of jurors will reach a decision on a damages award in a civil lawsuit. Researchers like Valerie Hans, Edie Greene, and Brian Bornstein, among others, have taken the study of damages decision-making to new heights in the past few decades, and future study should only shed more light on the process.[14] The literature to date focuses on the process by which individual jurors determine damages. The following discussion of how jurors approach determining damages assumes that the case facts, jurors' evaluations of party and witness credibility, and context of the arguments and evidence lead to a judgment that the defendant is liable for the plaintiff's losses. Jurors' next task is to evaluate the plaintiff's losses and translate them into a dollar award. The overwhelming majority of mock jury and actual jury deliberations we have studied employ one (or sometimes more) of the following three approaches to damages determinations.

1. Categorical/Holistic or the "Gist" Approach

Jurors may commonly employ a subjective approach that results in a decision that "seems right."[15] There has been growing research support for this theory in the past few years, including for more subjective damages categories such as noneconomic "pain and suffering" damages. While patent litigation remedies do not include pain and suffering damages, the theory is highly instructive.

The reasons motivating this approach may vary, and scholars initially proposed and clearly described a theory by which jurors make holistic "gist" determinations about the level of damages, if any, that may be warranted in civil cases.[16] Under this "gist" theory, jurors do not base damages decisions on an

13. *See also* Martha K. Gooding & William C. Rooklidge, *The Real Problem with Patent Infringement Damages*, 91 J. PAT. & TRADEMARK OFF. SOC'Y 484 (2009).

14. *See* GREENE & BORNSTEIN, *supra* note 7; Valerie P. Hans & Valerie F. Reyna, *To Dollars from Sense: Qualitative to Quantitative Translation in Jury Damage Awards*, 8 J. EMPIRICAL LEGAL STUD. 120 (2011), https://scholarship.law.cornell.edu/cgi/viewcontent.cgi?article=2079&context=facpub.

15. GREENE & BORNSTEIN, *supra* note 7, at 159 (regarding a holistic approach: "In addition to the anchoring-adjustment and componential approaches we have alluded to a third means by which jurors may arrive at a damage award: by agreeing on a general figure that seems 'about right.'").

16. *See* Hans & Reyna, *supra* note 14.

initial anchor, or on a rigorous methodological approach that accounts for specific facts and evidence. Instead, jurors rely on their own coherent interpretation of the facts and evidence, leading them to broader conclusions about whether damages are warranted and, if so, to what extent.

As trial consultant Ken Broda-Bahm describes in "Your Trial Message," the model includes three steps after a decision of defendant liability. First, jurors make a categorical judgment ("Are damages warranted or not?"). They follow that step with an "ordinal" judgment ("Should the damages award be high, medium, or low?"). Jurors then construct a specific damages amount that comports with their own view of the ordinal gist, leading them to an opinion of the total damages award. They may do this at a macro level for the case as a whole, and also at the more specific level of requested damages categories (e.g., economic damages versus noneconomic damages versus punitive damages). In fact, research shows that in some instances juries asked to calculate multiple components of a total damages claim may do so after determining a total damages amount deemed fair and reasonable.[17] In those instances, the calculations of the individual components are simply reverse-engineered to work in concert with the total amount.

2. Anchor and Adjust

> *"In approximately 70% of the deliberations, jurors arrived at a starting number and then adjusted it because it seemed too high (frequently) or too low (infrequently)."*[18]
>
> —Edie Greene and Brian Bornstein

While the previous quote refers to a study of jury decisions in tort and contract cases, trial attorneys should recognize jurors' need for a starting point in damages determinations. The "anchor and adjustment" approach to damages determinations includes two basic tenets.[19] First, jurors begin with a damages estimate based on an *anchor*—a relevant reference point and, in the case of dollar amounts, a numerical estimate of the claimed damages. Then, jurors *adjust* their estimates based on salient information that can lead them to a final determination that is above or below, but always influenced by, the original anchor.

Jurors use anchor numbers that come from a wide variety of sources, including relevant sources like expert witness calculations and attorneys' closing arguments, as well as presumed irrelevant sources, such as jurors' own experiences ("I worked for a company that made millions on its products and

---

17. *See* Douglas J. Zickafoose & Brian H. Bornstein, *Double Discounting: The Effects of Comparative Negligence on Mock Juror Decision Making*, 23 LAW & HUM. BEHAV. 577 (1999).

18. GREENE & BORNSTEIN, *supra* note 7. This quote refers to data from a study by Nicole L. Mott et al., *What's Half a Lung Worth? Civil Jurors' Accounts of Their Award Decision Making*, 24 LAW & HUM. BEHAV. 401 (2000). Researchers examined 36 juries in tort and contract cases—not in patent cases.

19. *See* Amos Tversky & Daniel Kahneman, *Judgment Under Uncertainty: Heuristics and Biases*, 185 SCIENCE 1124 (1974).

they paid a 5% royalty") and seemingly unrelated aspects of the case (e.g., 100 million products sold, or 200 million research and development hours). In one study of 26 civil juries, 65% of jury groups began discussion of damages with a high number and adjusted downward.[20] It may sound scary to learn that jurors can begin a damages decision in your case by focusing on a high number that is completely unrelated to the damages evidence, but it happens. More commonly, however, jurors begin with and discuss the anchors provided in evidence or attorney argument.

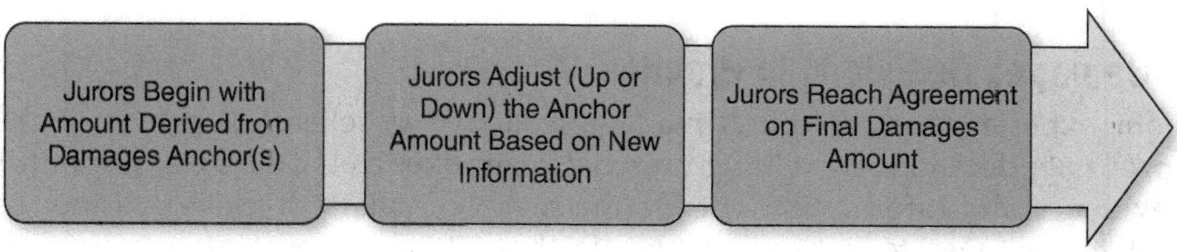

It is critical to understand that jurors can and do use anchors to reduce their own uncertainty about how to make a damages determination that achieves a fair result. As a plaintiff, your goal should be to develop evidence of high anchors (numbers) upon which jurors can base their initial damages discussion. As a defendant, your goal is often to determine an effective counter-anchor and provide jurors the information they need to adjust damages discussions downward, regardless of the chosen initial anchor. A good first step for litigators is to understand and accept that jurors' damages decisions frequently start with an initial anchor followed by adjustments resulting in a higher or, more frequently, lower final award.

3. Componential Approach

In contrast to the anchor and adjustment approach, jurors may approach damages using a componential approach that is a "ground up" calculation of the various damages components to achieve a total award. This approach, while somewhat less common, often results from a motivated jury panel with greater than average sophistication. A componential approach is more common (but certainly not guaranteed) with the use of special verdict forms that overtly ask jurors to consider the separate damages components individually. Conventional wisdom is that a special verdict form with separate interrogatory questions asking for damages decisions in a variety of categories tends to encourage a componential approach and inflates the total damages award. Mock jury research in civil lawsuits does not necessarily support this wisdom.[21] In our experience, procedural elements and aspects of a party's trial presentation (e.g., walking

20. Mott et al., *supra* note 18.

21. *See* Zickafoose & Bornstein, *supra* note 17. Researchers found that the form of damages computation (components first versus total amount first) did not much matter to the final outcome.

through the verdict questions) can encourage a componential approach, but may or may not impact the damages outcome.

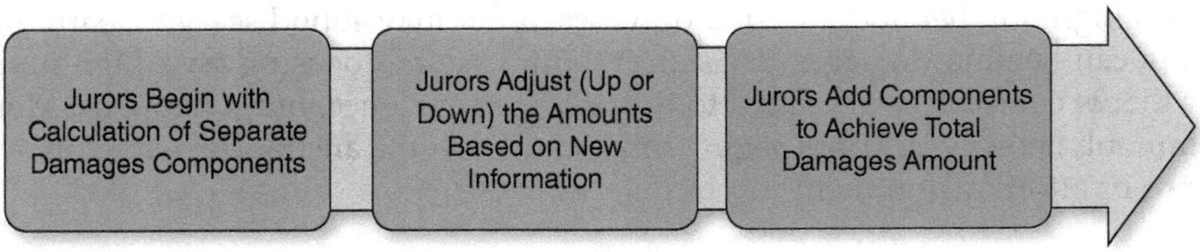

C. Damages Decisions in Practice

In our experience, jurors often manage to arrive at reliable and even legally appropriate decisions by relying on what seem like irrelevant cues. Jurors turn to evidence and information outside the realm of what attorneys consider relevant to damages to help break the tie they often perceive after seeing and hearing two opposing litigants offer thorough and comprehensive damages analyses. Both may be supported by persuasive but conflicting expert testimony, and both may "prove" the patentee plaintiff deserves an amount of money that is drastically different from the amount offered by their opponent. So, what is a juror to do? They typically break the tie by relying on available information and their collective human perceptions of what feels reasonable and just, based on three "coms" of damages decision-making: comprehension, compromise, and common sense.

1. Comprehension Is Key

"[J]uror comprehension decreases as complexity increases, even among relatively well-educated jurors with prior jury experience."[22]

—Matthew Reiber and Jill Weinberg

Nearly all sound advice on persuading patent jurors includes some reference to the importance of a simple message that jurors can understand—or to the contrary, relying on jurors' lack of comprehension to argue that if the evidence is not clear, the plaintiff failed to meet its burden.[23] After all, comprehension is a critical part of persuasion, including persuading jurors to award the damages, if any, you feel are warranted. Jurors are more likely to do what you are asking if they understand exactly what you want them to do. Jurors can struggle mightily with making damages decisions that rely on concepts fully foreign to them and their everyday lives (e.g., royalty calculations and hypothetical profits).

As with liability decisions, jurors who do not fully comprehend damages testimony and evidence will reduce their uncertainty about making a determination

22. Matthew A. Reiber & Jill D. Weinberg, *The Complexity of Complexity: An Empirical Study of Juror Competence in Civil Cases*, 78 U. Cin. L. Rev. 929 (2010).

23. Julie Blackman et al., *East Texas Jurors and Patent Litigation*, 22 Jury Expert 5 (2010).

by applying something they do understand. It happens all the time in group deliberations. While jurors do not understand how a reasonable royalty for telecommunications technology is supposed to work, they understand how their brother earned a sales commission for a percentage of steel buildings he sold to farmers in North Dakota. They understand how the local barbecue restaurant sends their cousin home with a percentage of tip money based on the food sales directly attributed to her section of tables in the dining room.

Juror comprehension is important to damages determinations. Research shows that more complex language in witness testimony (i.e., technical versus nontechnical language) can affect jurors' ability to render damages award amounts that are commensurate with a plaintiff's injuries.[24] In one study, jurors were more able to differentiate among plaintiffs with different injuries and rendered damages awards in sync with the severity of those injuries when less-complex witness language and fewer overall witnesses testified (deemed "low information load"). When witnesses used more complex language, it was more difficult for jurors to accurately assign a damages amount commensurate with the injury evidence. Interestingly, there is also research that jurors with greater "numeracy," or capability with numbers, tended to render more valid and more reliable damages in certain types of lawsuits.[25]

2. Compromise Is Common

"Let's all have our own dollar amount, write them down, then divide by the number of us and use that as a figure."

—Patent mock juror who favored patentee plaintiff

Individual jurors often enter the damages phase with widely disparate perceptions of a fair damages determination. As a result, a majority of mock jury damages determinations contain compromise that leads to a damages determination between individual jurors' highest and lowest determinations and often between both sides' best estimate at trial. Compromise (both among jurors and between the parties' damages estimates) is not unique to patent juries, but is certainly a part of how patent jurors make damages decisions. Even when instructed not to average or compromise their damages awards, many actual jurors have told us post-verdict that individuals or the entire group operated in a manner contrary to that instruction. Differing individual perceptions come from a few important sources.

First, a jury that finds liability for patent infringement against an accused infringer typically contains individual jurors who have differing levels of belief in that finding. While every juror may support the decision, some will support

24. Irwin A. Horowitz et al., *Effects of Trial Complexity on Decision Making*, 81 J. Applied Psych. 757 (1996).

25. Rebecca K. Helm et al., *Numeracy in the Jury Box: Numerical Ability, Meaningful Anchors, and Damage Award Decision Making*, 34 Applied Cognitive Psych. 434 (2019).

liability in the extreme, while others may do so with questions. Such varying levels of force behind individual jurors' belief in an infringement finding often lead to individual jurors mitigating a damages award in order to reconcile their doubts about infringement. The thinking goes, "I'm *pretty sure* the defendant infringed, but I don't think the patent holder deserves *that much* money."

A second source of jury compromise is jurors' general assumption that both sides begin from exaggerated positions about damages, particularly when the competing damages estimates offered at trial are extremely disparate (e.g., $5 million versus $100 million). The presumption of "bloat" in the plaintiff's estimate and extreme minimization in the defendant's counter-anchor frequently—and sometimes immediately—results in jurors beginning damages discussion under the assumption that their final decision should fall somewhere between the two anchors.

A third relevant source of compromise is the collaborative human interaction that jury decisions require. Jurors must manage a jury group decision by marshaling influence through information (evidence, arguments, opinions) as well as relationships (among one another). Compromise is a natural consequence and takes many forms, including trades ("I'll agree to infringement if we don't award more than 4% royalty"); caving ("I give up, I do not agree with you but I will go with the group"); acquiescing ("I will agree to infringement because I know you aren't going to change your mind"); and maintaining harmony ("I think Juror 1 and Juror 5 are both right, and the answer is in between").

As frightening as it may be, jurors rely on shortcuts and compromise to achieve a decision that is agreeable to the group. Identifying the ways that your damages can be construed as compromise is a key way to address this reality of jury decision-making.

3. Common Sense Trumps All (or Most)

> *"In approximately one third of juries the predominant strategy for determining damages was to pick an amount that seemed fair and just without explicit calculation."*[26]
>
> —Edie Greene and Brian Bornstein

Jurors want a damages decision to feel right. In order to achieve that outcome, individual jurors often begin with round numbers that make sense in their minds. It is not uncommon for jurors to say, "Let's give them 40% of what they requested," or "I think a 1 or 2% royalty rate is about right," even when those numbers are never mentioned in evidence or argument in the case. Why these numbers? In most cases, the number results in an outcome that comports with jurors' common sense and their gut feeling of what is fair and reasonable.

---

26. Greene & Bornstein, *supra* note 7. The quote refers to a study of jury damages decisions (economic and noneconomic damages) in tort and contract cases by Mott et al., *supra* note 18.

Once jurors decide on an award amount that feels right, they often engage in the relevant computations to "back into" the desired amount. In some cases, the computation includes numbers that counsel might perceive as irrelevant—anchors that give jurors a basis for making a decision that achieves a sense of fairness. For instance, a jury asked to compute a reasonable royalty percentage may decide that the plaintiff's requested percentage is too high and struggle with a way to reduce it. A juror with some business experience claims he once heard of a royalty rate in a totally unrelated industry that was about half of the plaintiff's requested percentage. Jurors accept that percentage and calculate the reasonable royalty based on it.[27] In other instances, the power of a much more relevant anchor (such as royalty percentages in comparable situations or for comparable products) helps jurors achieve the proper balance of a decision that is both evidence-based and passes the gut test.

Consider, for instance, the thorough description of how jurors in the 2012 *Apple v. Samsung* trial went about determining the damages amount:

> In the evidence, Apple had declared that Samsung had cost them in profits 35% of their revenue. On the other hand, Samsung said that it is because they took out operating costs and the value is 12%. Three of us had been through the process in our careers of dealing with financial documents. I understood [profit and loss] statements as well as the other two. What we did was look at it against our matrix of what infringed and what did not. We determined that in our experience, the percentage was not 12%, and it certainly was not 35%. It should be closer between 13% to 15%. We zeroed in on 14%. That became the magic number. Then we did our own calculations for each of the areas, adding those up with royalties that were entitled for some of the items. And we cut that value in half. When we added them together and tallied them up, that is the number we came up with.[28]

The brief description incorporates many of the elements we have observed in patent damages decision-making, including the use of anchors as a starting point, reliance on personal experience to adjust to a decision that feels fair, and calculations to achieve a final and justifiable number that fits with the legal requirements and the verdict questions. While it is not always easy to predict a jury's outcome, these are some of the common steps that many jurors follow in reaching a decision on damages.

Understanding the interactive impact of juror comprehension, compromise, and common sense on patent damages is a key part of determining how best to approach the damages evidence and arguments at trial. Whether you are a patent-holding plaintiff or a defendant found to have infringed, keeping the known and predictable aspects of jury damages decision-making in mind is

---

27. While this may seem frightening or unrealistic, we have seen it happen in mock trial deliberations.

28. *See* Weintraub, *supra* note 2.

important to your success at trial. We discuss specific strategies for plaintiffs and defendants in the remainder of this chapter.

II. Dealing Strategically with Damages Claims as Patentee Plaintiff

"I would hate to see innovation stifled. I hate to see somebody sit here and get something, then stifle major improvements on it."

—Patent mock juror who favored accused infringer

One of jurors' primary motivations for awarding damages in patent trials is to reward the patent-holding inventor's hard work and innovation. Jurors want to believe that the ingenuity and productivity that brought the patented invention to life will continue in the future, that innovation will thrive going forward, and that the potential for new and exciting improvements is uncapped. Jurors expect to see the benefits—both in society generally and in their own lives—of rewarding innovation and the patents that protect it. This positive story motivating juror awards is one part of the plaintiff's strategy for proving its patent damages.

A. Recognize General Strategies for Patent-Holding Plaintiffs

1. Trust That Infringement Evidence Influences Damages

"I don't think the [accused infringer] deserves anything from the sales because it wasn't theirs."

—Patent mock juror who favored patentee plaintiff

As in many other areas of human decision-making, supposedly "irrelevant" factors can have a powerful influence on jurors' damages determinations. Clear and persuasive evidence that a defendant copied a patent holder's idea frequently bleeds into jurors' thinking about damages and often motivates damages decisions. While solid numbers backed by economic analysis are important, the numbers rarely motivate a jury more than the perceptions of an infringer's behavior—particularly when jurors perceive that behavior as violating their sense of corporate ethics or fair play. We have observed mock jurors who argue for a damages award equal to 100% or more of a defendant's profits based solely on the belief that such a bad actor does not deserve a penny of the money it would not have made but for the infringement, despite the fact that disgorgement of profits is not a permissible remedy (for utility patents) under the Patent Act. Patent-holding plaintiffs should never underestimate the power of the infringer's conduct in driving the jury's thought processes as well as its motivation for improvising an increased damages award based on a desire to punish the defendant. There is no question that high damages numbers are an important anchor, but the argument for an award at or above the plaintiff's requested damages amount begins and ends with jurors' perceptions of the infringing conduct. In the words of one patent mock juror, "I don't just look at the trees; I look at the forest. And the forest is corporate America and corporate greed."[29]

2. Identify the Benefit in a Damages Award

> *"They could have [used their] royalties to change their product and improve it. If they're just going to [take the] royalties and not do anything to improve [the product], I'd say no [damages are warranted]."*
>
> —Patent mock juror who favored accused infringer

As discussed throughout this book, jurors' perceptions of competition and the influence of their verdict on the future of competition in the marketplace play a central role in the motivation for patent damages. When jurors see a damages award as an opportunity for advancement or improvement, they are much more likely to get behind it. As the plaintiff, be sure jurors understand the benefits of a damages award and the ramifications it will have on future innovation. Consider what jurors (and, more important, the public more broadly) may have thought about the benefits of awarding Apple hundreds of millions of dollars in its patent infringement case against Samsung. Would Apple continue to innovate as most believe it has done so effectively over decades? Would Apple sit on its laurels and bask in the victory, increasing prices and resting on its innovative past instead of continuing to offer inventive products? Shortly after a $1 billion jury verdict against Samsung in 2012, Apple released its iPhone 5, the next generation of its patent-protected smartphone. For the public, this may confirm a belief that Apple will continue to innovate and offer consumers the benefit of new products—and the story of Apple's inventions and novel idea development over time likely helped the actual jury see the benefit in a damages award.

3. Make Damages as Concrete as Possible

> *"Their claims were funny-money."*
>
> —Patent mock juror

The typical damages analysis in patent infringement jury trials includes more zeroes than most jurors will ever see behind a dollar sign. The simple fact that the money at issue may be in the tens or hundreds of millions of dollars leaves some jurors with the challenge of contemplating amounts that are far more theoretical than actual. Your job as the plaintiff is to make those dollars concrete and purposeful and to give jurors the reassurance they need to award all those zeroes. Add the following elements to your trial story to enhance jurors' perception of the concreteness of the losses and, therefore, the actual benefit to a damages award.

29. *Quoted in* Gooding & Rooklidge, *supra* note 13.

Make Damages Concrete Through Story Elements

Story Element	Narrative Description
Set the context for research and development.	As part of your invention story, be sure to highlight the plaintiff's dedication to research and development past and future to serve the dual purpose of supporting the invention story and giving jurors a concrete place to earmark many of the requested damages.
Be explicit about the infringer's undeserving gains.	Show jurors the tangible results of the infringer's profits from selling infringing products. Include photos, sales receipts, and other tangible evidence of the infringer's purchases that can be linked to the infringing sales profits. Be sure jurors understand these are the gains that would never have happened but for infringing the patents and violating the law—gains the patent holder could have and now is entitled to enjoy.
Be explicit and visual about the costs of innovation.	Show jurors tangible proof of the costs required for the patent holder to continue to innovate and develop products into the future. Seeing the investment of equipment, space, materials, and, perhaps most important, people, jurors can begin to earmark the damages award dollars for hard costs. This process of "earmarking" can help jurors feel concrete and confident about a damages award.

The Cost of Innovation

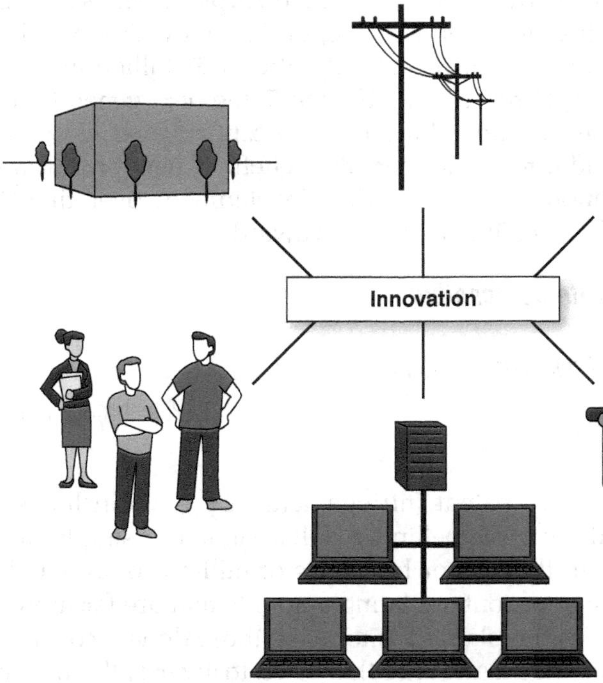

Credit: Nick Bouck

4. Account for Compromise

Jurors are humans, and humans have a tendency to choose a middle option from a spectrum of choices.[30] A tendency to compromise is increased when humans are grouped together, as they are in a jury. Litigants can take advantage of this natural tendency by accounting for it in their approach to damages. This means assuming that jurors will work with a high anchor (generally provided by the plaintiff) and a low anchor (generally provided by the defendant), and tend toward a damages award that lives in the middle of those two extremes. As a patentee plaintiff, gain an advantage by requesting a damages award that already represents a "middle" option. In practice, this means developing evidence of a high damages amount that is reasonable—a damages amount that a jury might be comfortable with—then formally requesting a lower amount that will seem even more reasonable in contrast.

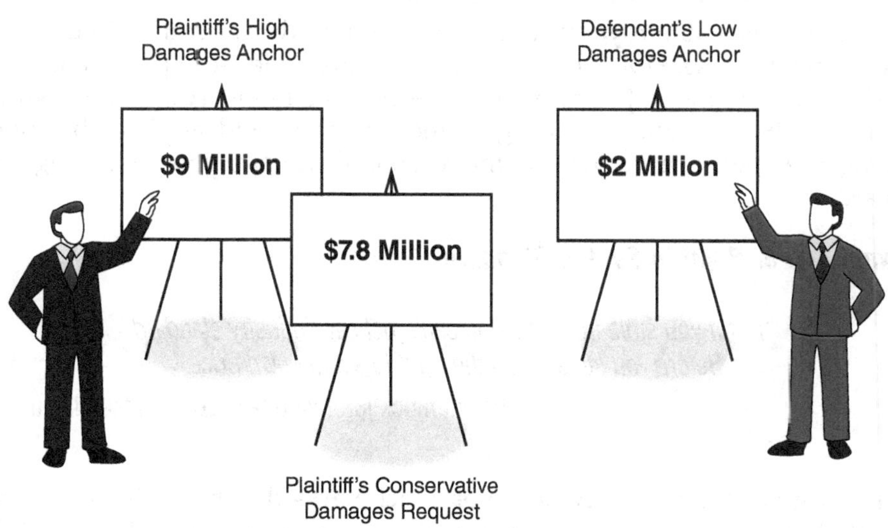

Credit: Nick Bouck

B. Strategies for Reasonable Royalty Claims

> *"I like the idea of putting a percentage of sales."*
>
> —Patent mock juror who favored patentee plaintiff

An overwhelming majority of patent damages claims are decided (at least in part) on a reasonable royalty basis, with recent statistics showing that from 2021 to 2023, $6 billion was awarded in 129 patent cases, primarily on verdict, while

30. Paul Rodway et al, *Preferring the One in the Middle: Further Evidence for the Centre-Stage Effect*, 26 Applied Cognitive Psych. 215 (2012).

$567 million was awarded for lost profits in just 40 cases over the same time period.[31] The clear trend since at least the mid-1990s is for an increasing proportion of reasonable royalty damages, due to a number of factors. Not least among them are the comparative challenges and complexities of presenting to a jury a lost-profits analysis. Nevertheless, jurors still struggle with a few issues when considering a patentee's reasonable royalty case, including:

- What profits would the patentee have enjoyed but for the infringement?
- What amount of a product's profits are derived from the patented product feature?
- What would a hypothetical negotiation have looked like?

We address plaintiff strategies for lost profits in Section II.C, but first we focus on strategies for presenting a reasonable royalty claim.

1. Know the Invention and Apply the Specifics

Evidence of reasonable royalty should be based on the facts and circumstances of the particular case.[32] Of course, this is more than a legal requirement—it is a persuasive requirement. Jurors want to see how you (and your expert witness) have established an understanding of the invention and applied that understanding to a specific argument on the reasonable royalty you are asking jurors to award.

2. Explain Your Right to Set the Standard

> *"But if you stole from me, you can't just say 'industry standard.' Before you stole, I had the right to set my own price."*
>
> —Patent mock juror who favored patentee plaintiff

Jurors put great weight on evidence of benchmarks that help give them confidence that their decisions are neither erratic nor unreasonable. They want their decisions to feel right, and for many jurors, a normative analysis that allows them to see and evaluate comparative data—such as other royalty rates or licenses agreed upon for similar products—gives them the confidence they need to make case-specific decisions about patent damages. Depending on the industry, the standard, the economic times, and many other occasionally unpredictable factors, jurors' tendency to rely heavily on benchmarks such as established royalties may benefit a patent-holding plaintiff if it gives jurors a starting place. Present the standard as the industry norm and, whenever possible, secure testimony from neutral third-party witnesses who work in the industry and are familiar with the standard. This will help avoid jurors arguing, as one of our patent mock jurors did, "I can't see any company being willing to pay that."

---

31. Lex Machina, *supra* note 11.
32. Uniloc USA, Inc. v. Microsoft Corp., 632 F.3d 1292 (Fed. Cir. 2011).

3. Lasso More Than the "Rules" of Law

Attorney argument and expert testimony in support of a plaintiff's damages often rely on the 15 factors established in *Georgia-Pacific Corp. v. United States Plywood Corp.*[33] Some jurors will certainly care about the "rules" as established by case law, and a subset of jurors will rely heavily on the persuasiveness of a visual checklist showing how plaintiff's evidence related to relevant *Georgia-Pacific* factors favors the requested royalty. Take your persuasion one step further, and reach the subset of jurors less enamored by the rules, by presenting the rationale for why a relevant *Georgia-Pacific* factor matters, and why your evidence results in a *fair outcome*.

For instance, argue that it is not just the fact that licensees in circumstances similar to the accused infringer have paid a relatively common royalty rate, but also because the going rate in the market is a common basis for how other licensees negotiate royalties, and enforcing that hypothetically negotiated royalty helps ensure a fair outcome both for the plaintiff-licensor and past licensees. Appeal to jurors' feeling that by applying the rule of the *Georgia-Pacific* factors (i.e., the 15th factor regarding hypothetical negotiation), they are also helping to achieve a fair royalty outcome for other licensees who had no choice but to operate in the same way when reaching a negotiated royalty rate with a licensor.

Note: The same approach could also be persuasive for a patent infringement defendant relying on the *Georgia-Pacific* factors in its damages analysis.

4. Reduce the Hypothetical Aspects of a "Hypothetical Negotiation"

Jurors can resist a plaintiff's damages argument based on the intuitive pause that stems from an inherently hypothetical situation wrought with uncertainties: Would a licensee agree to the plaintiff's terms? Would a licensee be able to get a better deal somewhere else? Would a competitor be willing to pay that much for a license? A patentee plaintiff can persuade by acknowledging jurors' questions about a hypothetical negotiation and systematically presenting evidence and argument that reduces jurors' uncertainties.

Help jurors see the plaintiff's requested reasonable royalty as indisputable based on the most advantageous snapshot of the parties' relevant behavior, including other royalty agreements for the patents-in-suit, other licenses and licensing habits in similar technologies, the relative importance of the patents-in-suit, and the nature of the relationship between the parties. For instance, be systematic (and visual) in building a case of past (and concurrent) behavior that supports only one juror conclusion: that the parties would have engaged in a hypothetical negotiation that has an extremely high likelihood of resulting in the plaintiffs' requested reasonable royalty.

---

33. 318 F. Supp. 1116, 1120, 166 U.S.P.Q. 235 (S.D.N.Y. 1970), *modified*, 446 F.2d 295, 170 U.S.P.Q. 369 (2d Cir.), *cert. denied*, 404 U.S. 870 (1971).

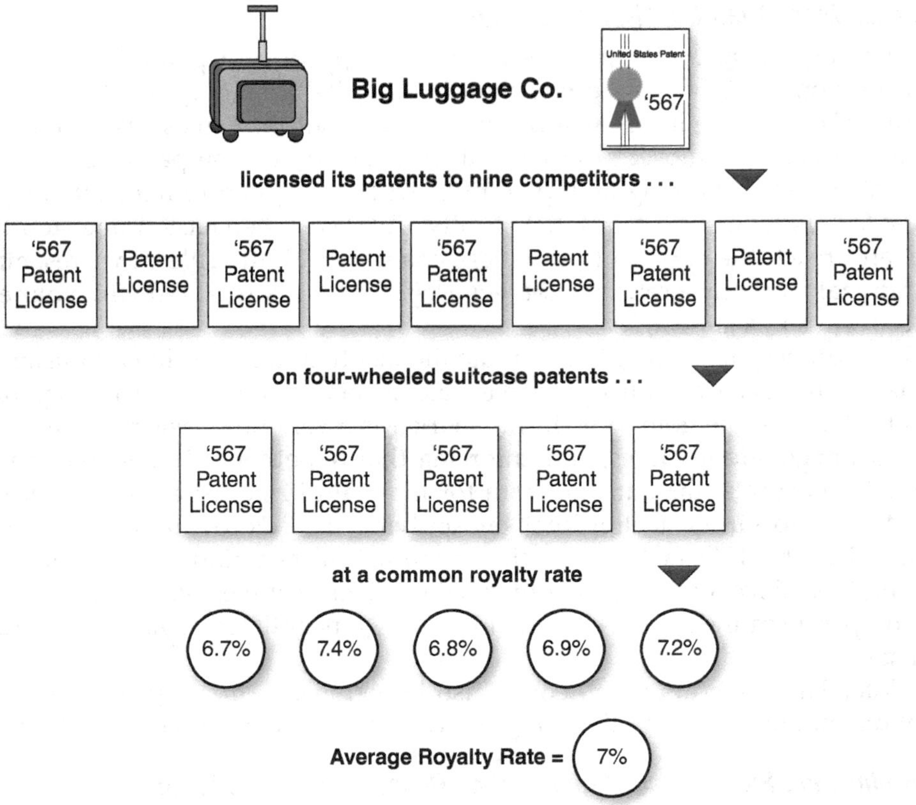

5. Embrace Intuitive Comparison

One great advantage for patentee plaintiffs in seeking reasonable royalty damages lies in jurors' relative comfort with comparing apples to apples. While so much of this book has focused on the challenges of juror comprehension, attention, and engagement with difficult technology or dense evidence, we commonly observe jurors and mock jurors enjoying the comparatively lighter lift of determining a reasonable royalty. How can that be? When they have other license agreements, past behavior, and prior royalty deals to compare and contrast with, they feel an easier path that is more intuitive to human nature than, say, an infringement analysis. Take advantage of this by embracing the simplicity of those comparisons wherever possible, and empowering jurors to recognize this part of their job as something they have been doing naturally since they were a child—eyeballing different situations and finding commonality among them.

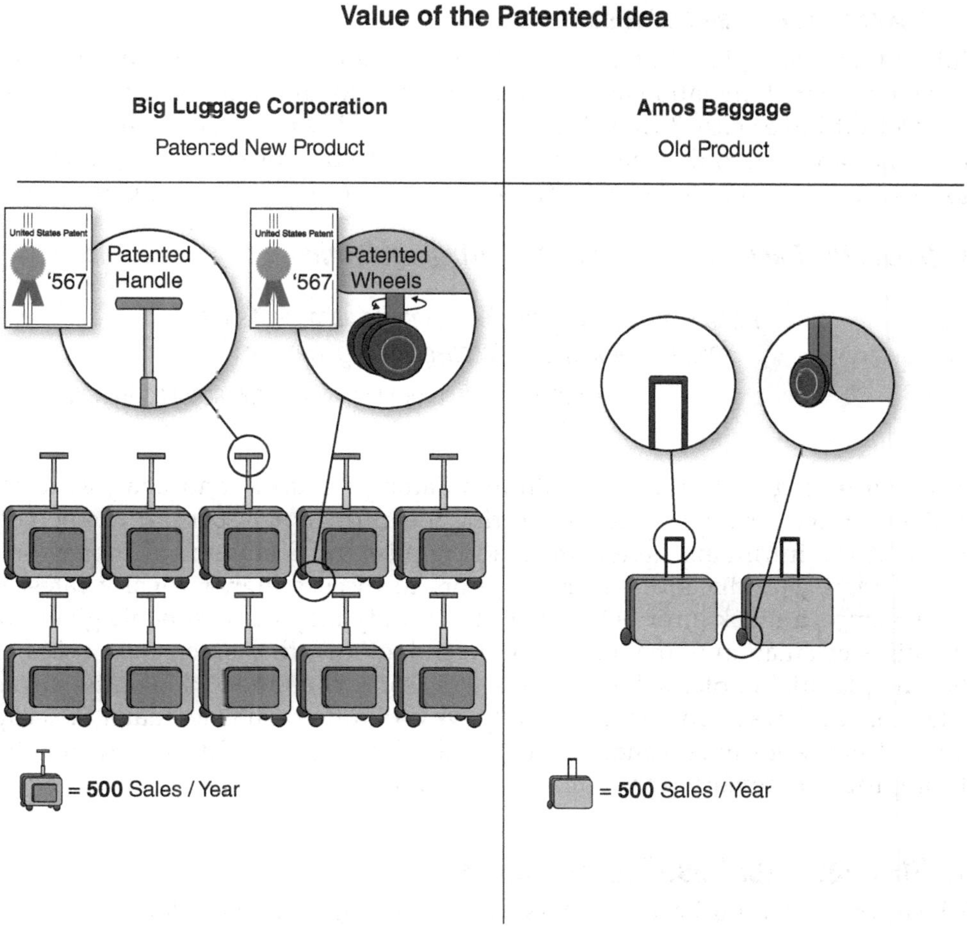

6. Visually Show the Value Added by the Patent-in-Suit

> *"[The accused infringer] was able to make a better product, and they were charging less. That made me favor [the accused infringer] a little. They are doing more to help the patients and the hospitals, and not just trying to make money."*
>
> —Patent mock juror who favored the accused infringer

Jurors learn better and more quickly when they can absorb simple visual arguments. Explore the use of creative visuals that connect the proportion of product sales attributable to the value of the patent with the actual components of the entire product. For instance, compare the number of product sales *without* the patented device to sales of products *with* the patented invention and visually align the differences with the unique aspects of the patented invention.

7. Pick the Best Horse and Ride It

Put another way, plaintiff's counsel should identify the most powerful reason that the patented invention adds meaningful and identifiable value to the product. Does it lower costs? Does it increase demand? Does it fetch a higher price for some other reason? In many instances a collection of weaker arguments is not nearly as persuasive or as memorable as a well-presented strong argument.

8. Relate the Requested Award to the Infringer's Profits

> *"I would go with what they're asking for because it's less than half of what they [accused infringer] made."*
>
> —Patent mock juror who favored the accused infringer

Mock jurors regularly relate a plaintiff's damages request and analysis to the evidence of the infringer's revenue during the infringement period. The perception that the infringing defendant made a substantial amount of money selling infringing products often drives jurors to discuss higher royalty rates. In one instance, a mock juror believed a 51% royalty may be reasonable given the plaintiff's calculation of the infringing defendant's profits. Given clear evidence that the plaintiff's potential lost profits were more than the 51% royalty, jurors' belief that 51% was a reasonable royalty was solidified. The fact that a 51% royalty did not seem unreasonable was a little shocking in light of evidence that the appropriate royalty was significantly lower.

C. Strategies for Lost-Profits Claims

A lost-profits claim is based on the goal of restoring a patent holder to the state it would have been in but for the infringement, assuming the patent holder would have earned sales and resulting profits greater than it actually earned.[34] Seems simple enough, right? Unfortunately for patent holders claiming lost-profits damages, jurors do not always see a lost-profits analysis in the same way you see it. Jurors can struggle with the theoretical bases for the lost-profits analysis and certainly struggle to understand the sophisticated economic analysis that often accompanies a lost-profits claim. Specifically, jurors toil with the threshold questions when considering lost profits.[35] For example:

- To what extent did consumer demand for the patent holder's product actually exist?
- Could consumers have purchased comparable, noninfringing products from another company?

---

34. *See, e.g.*, Lemley, *supra* note 10; Barry Grossman, *Patent Infringement Damages*, *in* PATENT LITIGATION STRATEGIES HANDBOOK (Barry L. Grossman & Gary M. Hoffman eds., 3d ed. 2010).

35. *See* Lemley, *supra* note 10; Grossman, *supra* note 34.

- How did the demand affect the price the patent holder could have gotten for its product?
- Could the patent holder manufacture enough products to meet the demand?
- How could the patent holder have made the claimed level of profits?
- How much of the product's claimed demand is attributable to the infringed patent versus the features of the product not covered by the patent?
- And, perhaps most important, do jurors understand and apply the sophisticated economic analysis required to render an accurate decision under the lost-profits analysis?

To make determinations on these questions, jurors evaluate evidence of sales figures, pros and cons of the patented product in the market at relevant time periods, the presence of third-party competitors, and the proportion of a product's value attributable to individual but often interconnected features. But more often than not, they still rely on the parties' behavior. So how can a patentee plaintiff enhance its lost-profits case?

1. Make Clear the Steps You Will Prove

Jurors respect greatly and are often persuaded more by the better teacher. Even when it comes to damages decisions, jurors appreciate counsel who clearly lays out the nature of the decision that must be made so the criteria by which the evidence should be measured can be well understood. Consider, for instance, a simple graphic explaining the distinct pieces of your lost-profits claims that prove the fuzzy legal concept of causation.[36]

Step 1	Consumers wanted the patentee plaintiff's patented three-wheeled suitcase during the infringement period.
Step 2	The patentee plaintiff was the only noninfringing seller of desired three-wheeled suitcases.
Step 3	Patentee plaintiff could have made enough three-wheeled suitcases to meet the demand.

Given this visual template, you can add layers that will give jurors the road map for your evidence and arguments for each step, helping them understand exactly how your evidence fits into their decision-making task—the critical "why does it matter" that jurors are too often left to misinterpret on their own.

Teach your expert's damages analysis through similarly clear and transparent steps. Use simple graphics to give your expert the opportunity to teach and your jury the opportunity to learn. For instance, use a preview graphic that helps jurors understand the key steps of your expert's analysis.

36. *See* Grossman, *supra* note 34.

Lost Profits In Four Steps	
1. Plaintiff's Price Per Product	
2. Number of Lost Sales	
3. Plaintiff's Price Reductions	
4. Plaintiff's Increased Costs	
Total Lost Profits	

Credit: Nick Bouck

Then, have your expert walk through the four steps and explain in greater detail the documentary and analytic evidence that supports the expert conclusions. The following sample graphic demonstrates one way to visually present one of the four steps.

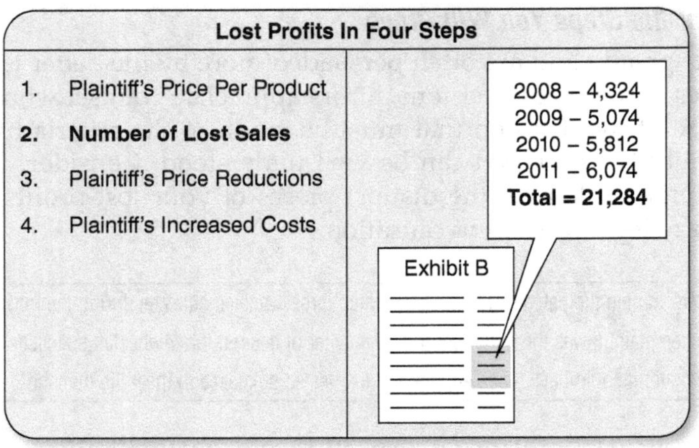

Credit: Nick Bouck

2. Paint a Vivid Picture of the "What-if" World

> *"All the profits that [accused infringer] made would have gone to the plaintiff. It could have grown like [the accused infringer] did."*
>
> —Patent mock juror who favored the patentee plaintiff

Jurors can react negatively to overdramatization. They need to imagine how things might have been (the "would have" and "could have" in the aforementioned juror quote). However, they need you to help them visualize a hypothetical world by telling a thorough story of how (and why) the patent-holding plaintiff would have enjoyed a much different reality but for the infringer's actions. Consider the following narrative elements to communicate how the innovative patent holder would have maximized profits in a market where even copiers were rewarded.

Paint a Picture Through Story

Story Element	Narrative Description
The Patent Holder's Hard Work to Achieve Its Potential	It required hard work to innovate and develop a patented product.
The Patent Holder's Known Potential in the Market	The anticipated outcome and resulting profit were substantial.
The Immediate Effect of the Infringer's Decision to Infringe	The defendant chose to infringe and prevent the anticipated outcome (without doing the hard work).
The Infringer's Temporary Enjoyment of the Patent Holder's Potential	Copying paid off in the short term, with the infringer enjoying the benefits of the patent holder's anticipated outcome.
The Patent Holder's Eventual Realization of Its Potential (above and beyond what the infringer enjoyed)	The hard-working innovator would have realized an even greater outcome than the infringer.
Empower the Jury	The jury has the power to give back to the patent holder what it would have gotten if not for the infringer's choices.

3. *Identify Boundaries in the Relevant Market*

"I think we have to assume that [patentee plaintiff] lost out on everything [accused infringer] sold, because they were the only other one there selling this type of product."

—Patent mock juror who favored the patentee plaintiff

A patent holder's clear goal in a lost-profits claim is to offer evidence that it would have made the infringing product sales if the infringer had not been able to sell its infringing product. Simpler is almost always better for jurors, so identifying meaningful ways to reduce the pool of potential product sellers in the product market is helpful. Persuade jurors that there were no other possible sellers by distinguishing the patent holder's product from other possible substitutes. The goal is to encourage jurors to reach the conclusion that this patent mock juror who favored the patentee plaintiff describes: "Had [the accused infringer] not been in existence, they would not have made anything and [patentee plaintiff] would have made it all."

Beware of one lesson when the patent holder is also a licensor. We have seen mock jurors criticize the plaintiff's claim that there were no other sellers in the relevant market based on the fact that the patentee plaintiff had license agreements with at least two other companies, making it obvious to mock jurors that at least two other companies (and maybe more) were selling product substitutes. Mock jurors concluded that sellers other than the plaintiff could have sold similar products and earned profits that neither the patentee plaintiff nor the infringer would have earned—all without concrete knowledge of what products the licensees were selling, let alone a clear understanding of whether or not the licensed products were substitutes for the infringing sales. This pitfall highlights the importance of identifying and articulating for jurors the boundaries of the relevant market using bright lines for how jurors can recognize whether a seller offered a noninfringing substitute product or not.

4. Corroborate Price Erosion Claims

> *"I wouldn't give them the price erosion. That is an 'over and above' kind of number that is not provable."*
>
> —Patent mock juror

Jurors can struggle mightily when asked to render damages decisions without any direction or boundaries.[37] While speculation permeates lost-profits claims, price erosion poses a unique challenge, since it can be based on a clear price decrease or, more ambiguously, on an inability to increase prices to the desired level as a result of the infringement. Make your price erosion claims concrete in three steps.

Step 1: Define Jurors' Power

First, jurors need a concrete understanding of their power to render evidence-based decisions on what the price would have been. Put another way, jurors need to clearly understand that they are empowered to make the decision based on the available information. Thus, plaintiff's counsel must do everything in her power to remove the perception of speculation from that equation.

Step 2: Corroborate Price Trends

Second, corroborate price trends with credible witnesses. Jurors respond positively to clear patterns and trends and may be persuaded by a visual display of increasing historical prices prior to infringement that decreased during the period of infringing sales. But jurors will question the origin of the evidence and will be particularly interested in the testimony and opinion of perceived "neutral" third-party witnesses. Securing testimony from unbiased purchasers or relevant suppliers will be a powerful way to give life and credibility to the price patterns displayed in a graph.

Step 3: Strike Jurors Resistant to Your Price Erosion Claims

Third, identify and strike jurors most likely to struggle with the inherent speculation involved in your price erosion claims. For instance, jurors who work in fields in which data verification and reverification (i.e., quality assurance, bookkeeping, mathematics, etc.) are critical are likely to be skeptical of "imaginary" numbers based on a speculative analysis. Jurors who believe a damages award

37. We have heard from actual jurors and observed mock jurors say they can struggle from feeling a lack of direction from the court and from the litigants when determining damages. This finding is also supported by research including Mott et al., *supra* note 18. At the same time, once jurors get comfortable with their ability to make a damages decision, we often observe them engaging in great speculation about the factors that may affect such a decision.

is justified only with "tangible proof" of lost profits may also be the type of people who are more literal (noncreative fields), less imaginative, and more socially and fiscally conservative. See Chapter 5 on jury selection.

D. Asserting Enhanced Damages for Willful Infringement

"I want to hit them hard. That was arrogance. Coming to our country to screw our company?"

—Patent mock juror who favored the patentee plaintiff

Patentee plaintiffs have a substantial opportunity with enhanced damages. A finding of willful infringement opens the door to treble damages and the potential that the plaintiff can recover attorneys' fees—no small potatoes in patent infringement litigation. As in other areas of patent law, enhanced damages case law evolves quickly. We will not focus as much on changes in enhanced damages law as we will on how we observe jurors understanding and reaching decisions on willful infringement and how patentee plaintiffs can present a persuasive case for enhanced damages.

1. Focus on the Defendant's Actions

The bottom line is that jurors rely on the evidence you might expect them to rely on when making decisions about an accused infringer's knowledge—the accused infringer's actions. One study of jury damages decisions concluded that juries found willful infringement at similar rates before and after the 2007 *In re Seagate Technology*[38] decision, suggesting that jurors' standard for evaluating willfulness is stable in spite of changes in the law expected to decrease willful infringement findings.[39] Changing legal standards matter less to jurors than their own feelings about a defendant's conduct and what constitutes willfulness.

2. Tell a Simple "Copycat" Story

Not surprisingly, evidence of copying is highly correlated with findings of willful infringement. According to one study, willfulness was found in 63% of cases where the patentee plaintiff presented evidence of the accused infringer's copying compared with just 29% when no such evidence was presented.[40] The fact that jurors learn in grade school that copying is "bad" and that doing their own work is a virtue makes the patentee's copycat story a simple and persuasive argument not only for infringement but also for the question of willfulness. Do

38. 497 F.3d 1360 (Fed. Cir. 2007). This 2007 Federal Circuit decision changed the requirements for a willful infringement finding by abandoning the "affirmative duty of due care" requirement and instead requiring the plaintiff to prove by clear and convincing evidence that the accused infringer was objectively reckless.

39. Christopher Seaman, *Willful Patent Infringement and Enhanced Damages After In re* Seagate*: An Empirical Study*, 97 Iowa L. Rev. 417 (2012).

40. *Id.* at 458.

not overcomplicate what jurors need to know to understand the copying story. Instead, follow the simple logic jurors need to find that copying occurred.

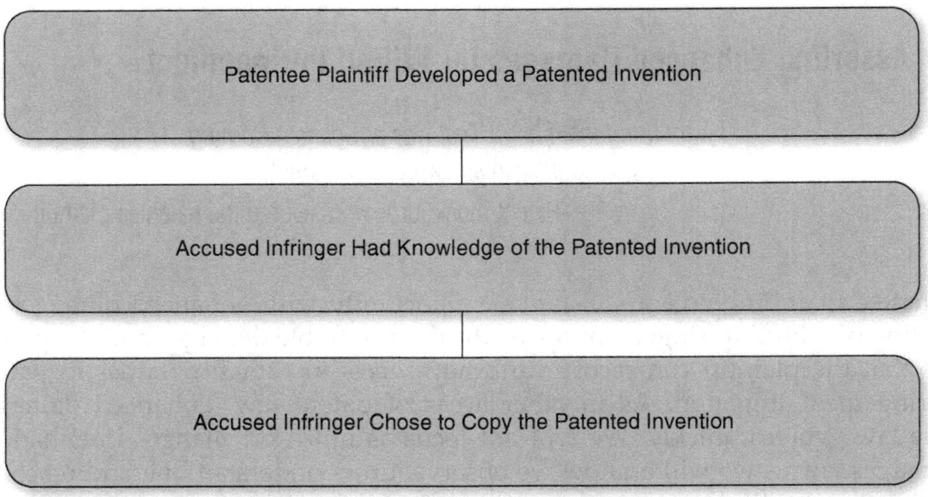

3. Use the Accused Infringer's Own Words

Counsel refers to damning internal documents as "smoking guns" for a reason. Jurors trust what a defendant company's own personnel say in the moment far more than they trust practiced testimony that comes out at trial. Jurors see the statements and motives communicated through emails and memos as candid and reflective of what people believed at the time, regardless of what they say in the courtroom. Whenever possible, emphasize the evidence of the accused infringer's words *at the time it was infringing* over just about all other evidence in the case.

III. Defending Against Damages Claims as Accused Infringer

"At first, I was for giving [the plaintiff] everything that they wanted. But over time, I saw some greediness there."

—Patent mock juror

A. General Strategies for Defending Patent Damages

1. Propose a Credible Alternate Damages Figure

Jurors frequently assume the plaintiff's damages request is exaggerated and represents more than the plaintiff actually expects to be awarded at trial. In most mock jury damages discussions, we hear at least one mock juror take the position that plaintiffs "always ask for the stars" while simultaneously acknowledging the jury's task is to find an appropriate and fair damages amount—usually an amount less than the plaintiff's request and more than the defendant's minuscule estimate. By the time jurors discuss damages, they are often already primed to compromise, and damages discussions that begin with an "exaggerated" plaintiff's request and a "low-ball" counter by the defendant only enhance the need for juror compromise. One study shows that defendants' damages anchors are more influential than plaintiffs' anchors.[41]

> *"Criticizing the plaintiff's numbers is usually not enough."*[42]
>
> —Ken Broda-Bahm, Ph.D., litigation consultant

Patent defendants must make the most of what we know about how jurors respond to both sides' damages figures by proposing a credible damages estimate that encourages compromise toward the low side of the midpoint between the plaintiff's and defendant's damages numbers.

Substantial scholarly research confirms what experienced trial lawyers already know—jury damages decisions often rely on the plaintiff's damages request—the high "anchor" in the damages negotiation.[43] But rarely do jurors ultimately decide to award the plaintiff's requested amount. They take into consideration the defendant's counter-anchor and frequently work toward something in the middle. When jurors focus on mitigating a damages award, what makes for a credible estimate by a patent defendant?

A Credible Defense Damages Estimate Should:

1. Set the low anchor.	A defendant's counter-anchor consistently helps set the parameters for juror discussions. While the goal is to set the lowest possible anchor, reasonableness must also be a criterion so as to avoid juror backlash for countering with a number so low and indefensible that it strains credibility and creates juror anger.
2. Include appropriate concessions.	Jurors appreciate appropriate concessions that help avoid the perception that you are not being reasonable. Some humility goes a long way with juries.
3. Avoid unnecessary technicalities.	The last thing you want to do at the end of a complicated patent trial is plod through an expert witness analysis that even you see as including loophole technicalities and fancy accounting gesticulations. Jurors will not like them, and the time it takes to communicate them may not be worth it.

2. Show Your Work

Help jurors track your accounting of your expert damages analysis (and potentially the flaws in the plaintiff's analysis as well) by walking them through the

41. Diamond et al., *supra* note 6.

42. Ken Broda-Bahm, *When Arguing Damages, "Drop Anchor" Even in Murky Waters*, Your Trial Message (Aug. 29, 2011), https://yourtrialmessage.com/damages-anchoring/.

43. *See, e.g.*, J. Zuehl, The Ad Damnum, Jury Instructions, and Personal Injury Damage Awards (1982) (unpublished manuscript); Greene & Bornstein, *supra* note 7, ch. 8 (providing a summary).

process and showing them the numbers. Just like your elementary school math teacher forced you to do, show the work that it takes to arrive at your damages amount. Be clear about how you are apportioning the value of the patented device in proportion to the entire product. Do not assume that less is more when it comes to providing jurors with the actual numbers behind your damages analysis. In many instances, a jury will decide to make its own calculations based on the data you have shown them, encouraging compromises and encouraging a reduction in the overall award. As cited previously, jurors rarely agree completely with the plaintiff's request, so empowering them to reduce that amount through the ability to make their own calculations is often a defendant's strength.

3. Sequence Closing Argument Strategically

Improve your damages defense and your liability defense by considering the most persuasive way to sequence your arguments on both in closing argument. In the words of litigation consultant Jeffrey Frederick:

> The defense in patent cases often argues liability and then damages in closing arguments even when it means the last words the jury hears are how much the plaintiff deserves. Tip: resist the temptation to have your argument mimic the order of proof. Switch the order of argument and gain a persuasive edge. Start with an attack on the inflated damages claim, highlighting their unreasonable nature. Transition into your liability argument by adding one last reason the plaintiff's damages are unjustified: the defendant is not liable. This structure allows you to start strong on damages and end strong on liability, win-win situation.[44]

4. Make Consumer Options Critical

> *"It's all about the bottom line. People are going to buy the cheapest one."*
>
> —Patent mock juror who favored the patentee plaintiff

An increased number of product sellers in a given market generally provides consumers with more options and pulls down product prices. As discussed in Chapter 4, a focus on consumer options can help persuade some jurors that favoring the accused infringer may result in benefits to consumers holding credit cards in the checkout line. The strength of this appeal is much stronger for a defendant's *damages* argument than it is for its *noninfringement* argument for two primary reasons. First, a majority of the jury-eligible public (nearly 70%) believes patents help competition in the marketplace. A *noninfringement* argument focusing on the need for competition and increased consumer options speaks to only about 30% of the jury pool. On the other hand, jurors are rarely motivated to put a litigant completely out of business. By citing the need for competition and consumer options as a reason to mitigate damages, a defendant

44. Personal Communication with Jeffrey Frederick, Litigation Consultant (2013). *See also Jury Research Update—Persuasion at Trial: Closing Arguments*, NAT'L LEGAL RSCH. GRP., http://www.nlrg.com/our-services/jury-research-division/our-services/case-preparation/persuasion-at-trial--closing-arguments/ (last visited Feb. 5, 2025).

does not violate jurors' need to protect patent rights, but does appeal to jurors' desire to protect competition and ensure consumer choices—especially in disputes directly or indirectly affecting the consumer products market.

5. Emphasize Plaintiff's Responsibility for Its Own Losses

> *"A lot of it is the way they're managing their company. They're not aggressive enough and there is competition out there going after their business. If [they] have to [they will] bring you to court instead of working on their own research and development and bringing their own product up to par. I think they probably could have stayed in the game better."*
>
> —Patent mock juror who favored the accused infringer

Personal responsibility bias has long been a meaningful factor in jury decision-making. We regularly hear actual and mock jurors criticize plaintiffs for bringing a lawsuit when they perceive the plaintiff as failing or refusing to take personal responsibility for mistakes. Jurors frequently evaluate whether the patentee plaintiff is deserving of the requested money damages. Jurors consider a patent holder's "worthiness" by considering a handful of factors and engaging personal responsibility bias in a few ways. Be mindful of these factors when creating your defense. Your decision point is whether to overtly note these factors or to provide jurors with just enough information to allow them to draw conclusions on their own.

a. The Patentee Was Not Honest with the Patent and Trademark Office

Evidence of a patent's invalidity based even in part on a patentee's lack of complete disclosures during the application process can influence jurors' views of whether or not the patentee is deserving of damages. As discussed in other parts of this book, jurors focus heavily on the parties' behavior, often considering behavior that is seemingly irrelevant (and sometimes legally improper) to the jury's damages determinations. Nonetheless, these perceptions matter to jurors' overall evaluation of the case and can directly impact perceptions of damages. Accused infringers should always consider how evidence of a patentee's behavior in the noninfringement or patent invalidity case may also turn into persuasive arguments if and when jurors turn to a decision on patent damages.

b. The Patentee Offered an Inferior Product

> *"My thinking is [the accused infringer has] a better product and that's what people were buying."*
>
> —Patent mock juror who favored the accused infringer

Jurors care about the patentee's product quality. In one instance, mock jurors turned their perception of poor product quality into a reason to mitigate damages against the infringing defendant. This factor helped mitigate damages not only because it caused jurors to question the patentee's contention that it would have made the sales but for the infringing sales (i.e., customers wanted the "better" product provided by the infringer, and may not have wanted the patentee's "inferior" product), but also because it left some with the impression that the patentee was not doing as much as it should have been doing to maintain a quality product. In other words, the patentee's behavior with respect to product development, manufacturing, and sales can reflect on jurors' perceptions of whether or not the patentee plaintiff deserves its requested damages.

c. The Patentee Was Not Competing Effectively

> *"[Patentee plaintiff] just isn't keeping up with times, there's competition out there."*
>
> —Patent mock juror who favored the accused infringer

In cases involving sports product companies, we have heard mock jurors make the argument in jury deliberations that "[i]f you are not pushing the envelope, you are not trying." Even a patentee's competitive (or not-so-competitive) conduct is fair game for jurors evaluating damages requests. The perception that a patentee lost out on sales due to ineffective competition in the marketplace can help a damages-mitigation juror argue against an award of substantial damages. The belief that "they weren't trying hard enough to make them deserving" can be hard for pro-damages jurors to rebut. This perception can spawn from the perception that a product maker has chosen not to remain on the cutting edge of research and development, is failing to adapt to the market, or is simply failing to meet customer needs. In the words of one mock juror, "If [the patentee plaintiff] was satisfying the customer, they wouldn't have been tanking. They were losing customers because of poor customer service."

While jurors often react negatively to a defendant's attempts to openly criticize an inventor, a defendant can effectively contrast its own efforts to research, develop, manufacture, and market its product with those of the patentee plaintiff. Instead of flatly telling jurors about the plaintiff's shortcomings, articulate the defendant's strengths in order to create a perceptual contrast in the minds of jurors. This approach helps avoid tacit resistance to the defendant's "telling" jurors what to think of the plaintiff while still providing the evidence needed for jurors to reach the desired conclusions on their own. Consider overtly (or subtly) arguing the following to achieve the desired juror conclusion about the plaintiff's damages worthiness.

Encouraging Jurors to Question the Patentee's Damages Worthiness

The Defendant's Efforts	The Plaintiff's Efforts	Juror Conclusion
The defendant consumer-tested 150 different designs before beginning manufacture.	The plaintiff tested fewer designs.	The defendant worked harder than the plaintiff.
The defendant spent $3 million a year on marketing.	The plaintiff spent less money.	The defendant competed more aggressively than the plaintiff.
The defendant has adapted to changing consumer needs.	The plaintiff is still selling its ten-year-old patented design.	The defendant adapted better to the market than the plaintiff.

B. Defending Against Reasonable Royalty Claims

1. *Emphasize the Reasonable in Reasonable Royalty*

> *"I would never award royalties—how can you prove who would have paid what?"*
>
> —Patent mock juror who favored the accused infringer

Again, asking jurors to evaluate a hypothetical negotiation of a royalty rate is a challenge plaintiffs must face. Jurors struggle with determining a reasonable royalty and discuss "typical" royalties in other industries. They need anchors and benchmarks from which to base a reasonable decision, and accused infringers must develop support for why a low number is alternatively a reasonable royalty rate. Combat the patentee plaintiff's reasonable royalty claims by encouraging jurors to focus on reasonable numbers, not perfect numbers in a make-believe scenario. Explain to jurors that speculation is not reasonable, and where the patentee plaintiff's claimed royalty rate lacks support, it fails to meet the simple criteria that a reasonable royalty must be reasonable.

2. *Recognize Jurors May Exceed an Established Royalty*

> *"The most I've ever heard was 10% to 15%."*
>
> —Patent mock juror who favored patentee plaintiff

Do not assume that the jury will unflinchingly apply a known royalty rate in a given industry. We have observed mock jurors argue in favor of an extremely high royalty rate based on a few different arguments, including the argument that a high royalty rate would be a fair compromise between the plaintiff's exaggerated suggestion of lost profits and the defendant's suggestion of a minimal royalty rate. In that instance, mock jurors believed a patentee plaintiff's requested royalty rate of 51% would be reasonable based on clear information that the plaintiff's lost profits were more than the 51% royalty. We also see mock jurors test the overall fairness of a reasonable royalty award by comparing the total damages amount based on a known royalty rate in the industry with the accused infringer's profits. If the math under that analysis seems fair, jurors can get comfortable with rates that far exceed the known industry rate. In the words of one patent mock juror, "I would go with what they're asking for because it's less than half of what they [the accused infringer] made." This opinion prevailed even though the accused infringer countered with evidence that the patentee plaintiff had issued another license using a 2% royalty rate.

> *"51% doesn't seem that unreasonable to me when considering the alternative is they would have earned $0 without infringing."*
>
> —Patent mock juror who favored patentee plaintiff

Do not underestimate the way that jurors evaluate the equities when making damages determinations. Instead of relying too heavily on the industry standard by arguing that "the standard royalty rate is 3% in the wheeled-suitcase industry," appeal to the overall fairness of an outcome produced by the industry royalty rate. For jurors, it is not the simple fact of an industry standard that makes it the proper rate, but the overall *fairness* of the outcome of applying that rate that makes it the reasonable choice for them.

3. Focus on the Concrete Questions in a Hypothetical Negotiation

While concreteness can help jurors see plaintiffs' requested damages as more tangible (and, therefore, more justified), a defendant's concrete answers to jurors' questions about a hypothetical negotiation can also push them *away* from the plaintiff's requested royalty. For instance, jurors ponder many questions when it comes to considering how a hypothetical negotiation would have transpired. Effectively pointing out the concrete variations in how the negotiation could be handled; the variety of ways it could have happened given the parties' past agreements, licenses, and behavior; the concrete ways that the patent-in-suit is different from past others; and other concrete factors can help jurors consider the multitude of possibilities and see the plaintiff's requested royalty as less likely.

When possible, defendants should also consider a visual.

C. Defending Against Lost-Profits Claims

> *"Every [product the accused infringer] sold did not mean that [the patentee plaintiff] lost a customer. . . . Those customers may not have bought from [the patentee plaintiff]."*
>
> —Patent mock juror who favored patentee plaintiff

In addition to our general advice on defending patent damages, consider these thoughts for addressing lost-profits damages in particular.

1. Point Out Bald Speculation

Patentees arguing a lost-profits case must tell a hypothetical story of what might have been. In response, accused infringers have an opportunity to focus on the factual evidence and focus jurors' attention on the patentee plaintiff's reliance on speculation of what might have been. Keep it simple by showing digestible evidence that contradicts the plaintiff's hypothetical assumptions and empowers those jurors who favor the accused infringer.

2. Stick with Tangible Evidence

In addition to pointing out the patentee plaintiff's speculation, accused infringers should consistently rely on tangible evidence that does not ask nor require jurors to make hypothetical assumptions. If possible, present a lost-profits counter-argument that derives each piece of analysis from actual numbers and actual facts in evidence as opposed to speculation. Consider the contrast based on the facts outlined in the following table and an accused infringer's focus on tangible evidence rather than speculation.

Assume the Following Facts in Evidence

1. Amos Baggage Company (ABC) sold 50,000 suitcases during three years of selling allegedly infringing products.
2. ABC profited $100 on each suitcase sold for a total of $5 million in that three-year period.

Contrast Plaintiff's Speculation with Tangible Evidence

Patentee Plaintiff's Speculation	Accused Infringer's Tangible Evidence
Dr. Lee would have sold all 50,000 of the suitcases ABC sold.	Dr. Lee has never sold a single suitcase like ABC's wheeled suitcase.
	Five other companies sell competing suitcase products, totaling 30,000 product sales in the three-year period.
Dr. Lee would have profited $5 million in the three-year period.	Dr. Lee testified that his manufacturing costs would have been "substantially greater" than ABC's.
	Four of the five other companies sell competing suitcases for lower prices than ABC sells its allegedly infringing suitcase.

3. Use Common Sense to Expand the Market

Accused infringers should encourage jurors to perceive a given product market as containing (or likely to have contained) multiple sellers of noninfringing products. Drawing this conclusion will support the accused infringer's argument that if other sellers could have filled the market demand, jurors cannot assume that the patentee plaintiff would have earned all the profits from the accused infringer's sales. Instead, other sellers would have—or at least could have—made those sales and earned those profits.

Expand the market by asking jurors to consider:

- How many companies are waiting to expand their market share in a common consumer market like wheeled suitcases?
- How many licensees does the patentee plaintiff have? How many noninfringing products could those licensors have made in the alleged infringement period?
- How broad is the allegedly infringing product market? Does it include all four-wheeled suitcases? How large is the number of noninfringing products that consumers would consider purchasing?

4. Show How the Accused Infringer Created a Larger Market

"They had a few extra things that were more advanced than [the patentee plaintiff's], so that probably caused them to get more business. It was not only that they infringed, but they had extra stuff that helped them."

—Patent mock juror who favored the accused infringer

We have observed mock jurors discount damages based on the logic that the infringing defendant offered some unique, noninfringing contribution to the market that increased the market size beyond what it would have been but for the infringer's presence. For instance, an infringer may have developed or provided special equipment, savvy marketing, or a desirable brand, or may have generated novel consumer need. These factors can lead some jurors to reduce the plaintiff's damages based on the belief that the market that would have been available to the patent holder would have been smaller if not for the infringer's presence. A smaller market that "would have been" means the patent holder would have earned fewer sales dollars.

> *"[Patentee plaintiff] probably would not have made those profits because they didn't have the equipment that [the accused infringer] had. [The accused infringer] was generating more of the market."*
>
> —Patent mock juror who favored the accused infringer

There is value in a defendant's damages approach that includes a story of the infringer's unique market contributions. Clearly, the invention story is almost always a critical part of the accused infringer's noninfringement defense, but do not assume the same type of story (a "market invention" story) has no place in the damages case. Encouraging jurors to see the unique contributions that might have helped develop a strong product market can lead to minimized damages awards and a greater motivation to protect an infringing party as a result of more positive views of the defendant's overall positive impact on the market.

D. Defending Enhanced Damages for Willful Infringement

> *"[A] 'substantial' or 'legitimate' defense to infringement is the most significant predictor of a finding of no willfulness."*[45]
>
> —Christopher Seaman

Willful infringement is a serious matter for patent defendants. Enhanced damages can as much as triple the amount of actual damages and expose defendants to the burden of paying the plaintiff's attorneys' fees. Statistics show that juries find willfulness in more than 60% of cases where willful infringement evidence is presented and do so at significantly higher rates than judges after *Seagate*.[46] As described earlier on how to make a patentee plaintiff's enhanced damages case, jurors' perceptions of whether the defendant copied the patent and whether it communicated internally about attempts to do so are critical to willful infringement findings and enhanced damages. Defendants must focus

45. *Quoted in* Seaman, *supra* note 39.

46. *See* Kimberly Moore, *Judges, Juries, and Patent Cases—An Empirical Peek Inside the Black Box*, 99 MICH. L. REV. 365 (2000); *see also* Seaman, *supra* note 39.

on the noninfringement case to help jurors see the motive behind their actions not as the easy road to profits (copying), but as the hard-earned and different path to competitive success.

1. Emphasize Noninfringement

"The outcome data indicate that juries are more easily persuaded than judges by 'bad guy' evidence."[47]

—Judge Kimberly Moore

In a unitary trial (as opposed to a bifurcated proceeding), a strong, independent invention story and evidence of noninfringement are persuasive reasons for jurors to perceive defendants' conduct as lacking willfulness. Jury research illuminates the conclusion that a strong noninfringement case has a powerful effect on jurors' views of willful infringement.

Percentage of Willful Infringement Decisions Based on Infringement Defense[48]

Substantial Noninfringement Defense	No Substantial Noninfringement Defense
13% (5 of 40 cases)	57% (55 of 96 cases)

Statistical analysis of willfulness decisions is consistent with what we see in our own work with mock jurors—details such as opinion of counsel and attempts to design around a patent are not as persuasive as contemporaneous evidence of the accused infringer's behavior and beliefs at the time the allegedly infringing actions were taking place.[49] Jurors tend to see an opinion of counsel that the defendant does not infringe as biased rather than neutral, and jurors can disbelieve such opinions if they contradict the greater noninfringement story.

2. Emphasize a Contemporaneous Belief in Noninfringement

Blunt the persuasive impact of a plaintiff's "smoking gun" memos by showing jurors the myriad ways the defendant's internal communication verifies a belief that its noninfringing approach was distinct from the patented invention. Even if the communications are subtle, a pattern of documents telling the same story (or at least belying the simple story plaintiff wants to tell) can have a persuasive impact. This approach has at least two clear persuasive goals:

(1) To contextualize any harmful internal documents within a sea of additional communication
(2) To highlight the independent invention story through the words of the defendant's own personnel

47. Moore, *supra* note 46.

48. Seaman, *supra* note 39, at 457.

49. *See id.* at 454. Seaman cites statistics showing accused infringers were found willful 43% of the time when offering an opinion of counsel defense and 44% when no such opinion was offered.

IV. Conclusion

> *"Whether you represent the patentee or the accused infringer, everything you do at trial should be directed to helping jurors conclude that it is fair—that it is the right thing—for your client to win."*[50]
>
> —Martha Gooding and William Rooklidge, patent litigators

The balance of our experience and the balance of what we have shared in this book point to an overarching conclusion about persuading in patent trials: jurors and judges need you to be tireless educators in order to be credible advocates. Focusing on how a decision for your client is both fair and legally just is a nonnegotiable combination. Every recommendation in this book is rooted in how we have observed jurors and judges reach decisions in patent disputes, and each is included to help you become not only effective in patent litigation, but also patently persuasive.

50. Gooding & Rooklidge, *supra* note 13.

APPENDIX A

Patent Infringement Case Example

Camera Anywhere Co. v. BigPhone Corp.

The plaintiff is Camera Anywhere Co. (CAC), a multinational, American-based corporation that manufactures and sells mobile phone camera technology. The defendant is BigPhone Corp. (BigPhone), a company headquartered in Palo Alto, California. CAC purchased and now owns a patent for a nine-lens microcamera that can be used in mobile phones. The patent is called the Nika '567 patent. BigPhone designs, manufactures, markets, and sells a series of mobile phones that include within the device a nine-lens camera.

CAC's Contentions

CAC contends that BigPhone is infringing the '567 patent by making, using, selling, offering to sell, or importing the BigPhone product called the BigPhone "Planet 3." This claim is for direct infringement.

CAC seeks to prove direct infringement in two ways. The first is called "literal" infringement. To prove literal infringement, CAC must prove that it is more probable than not that BigPhone's "Planet 3" mobile phone contains each and every limitation of any one or more of the CAC '567 patent claims.

CAC claims that it has suffered damages as a result of BigPhone's infringement in the form of lost profits on each of BigPhone's sales of the infringing product. CAC also claims that, at a minimum, it has lost damages in the amount of a reasonable royalty. CAC must prove by the more-probable-than-not standard the damages it has suffered as a result of BigPhone's infringement.

CAC also claims that BigPhone has knowingly and willfully infringed the '567 patent. To prove willful infringement, CAC must prove that BigPhone made, marketed, and sold the BigPhone "Planet 3" despite an objectively high likelihood that its actions constituted infringement of the CAC '567 patent. CAC's willful infringement claim requires a higher burden of proof—the highly probable standard—than CAC's other claims, which require proof by the more-probable-than-not standard.

BigPhone's Contentions

BigPhone contends that the BigPhone "Planet 3" does not infringe the '567 patent because the "Planet 3" is substantially different from what is covered by the '567 patent and the "Planet 3" lacks several of the claimed limitations or the functional equivalents.

BigPhone also contends that the CAC '567 patent is invalid for two reasons.

First, BigPhone contends that the invention covered by the CAC '567 patent is not new. An invention that is not new is said to be "anticipated" by the prior art. In order to prove that a claim is anticipated by the prior art, BigPhone must prove that it is highly probable that each and every limitation of the claim is present in a single item of prior art.

Second, BigPhone contends that the '567 patent is invalid for obviousness. A patent claim will be invalid, even if it is not anticipated by the prior art, if the claimed invention would have been obvious to a person of ordinary skill in the field of the invention at the time it was made. In order to prove invalidity based on obviousness, BigPhone must prove that it is highly probable that the invention claimed in the CAC '567 patent would have been obvious to a person of ordinary skill in the art at the time the invention was made.

CAC'S Patent Validity Responses

CAC responds to BigPhone's invalidity claims by arguing that the '567 is not anticipated by prior art and that the alignment of the nine lenses and the technology integrating images captured by the nine lenses each represent novel contributions of the '567 patent.

CAC also claims that the '567 is not invalid due to obviousness in part because prior art has long included many similar features (multiple lenses, image integration, etc.) but for all those years has never integrated the multiple captured images as done in the '567 patent.

APPENDIX B

Confidential Juror Questionnaire

Confidential Juror Questionnaire

A. The information you give in response to this questionnaire will be used only by the Court and the attorneys to select a qualified jury. Your responses to this questionnaire will be kept confidential and all parties will be under orders to maintain the confidentiality of any information they learn in the course of reviewing these questionnaires. Please answer these questions by yourself.

B. You are expected to sign your questionnaire, so your answers will have the effect of a verbal statement given to the Court under oath. What is needed is your very best, honest effort to answer the questions contained in this questionnaire.

C. You are to complete this questionnaire **on your own** and you should not discuss the questions contained here with anyone else either while completing the questionnaire or after you have finished your answers. You are a prospective juror in this case and, as such, should refrain from discussing any of the issues and/or names summarized here starting now and through completion of trial.

D. Do not conduct any research on the issues or names included in this questionnaire. This includes doing research in person, on the internet, via the media, or through any other means.

E. Please answer each question below as completely and as accurately as you reasonably can. **Please complete your answers in pen**. Please do not write on the back of the questionnaire. Your complete written answers will save a great deal of time for the Judge, for the lawyers, and for you.

F. If there is a question that you do not want to answer because of privacy concerns, then write in the blank by that question the word "privacy." You may need to visit with the Judge and the attorneys out of the presence of the other potential jurors concerning that question.

G. If you simply cannot understand a question, then write in the blank by that question the words "do not understand."
H. Some of the questions ask you to provide information on yourself or "anyone you know well." The phrase "anyone you know well" refers to family, close friends, or anyone who has ever lived in your household.
I. If you need more space to explain any of your answers, there is a blank page at the end of the questionnaire to use. When you need to do so, simply continue your answer on the blank page and write the page number and question number you are answering on the blank page.
J. Remember, there are no "right" or "wrong" answers, only complete and honest ones.

Name: ____

(Last) (First) (Maiden/Middle)

Age:_________ **Gender:**____________

Background Information

1. Place of Birth: State____________________County______________Date_____
2. Number of years you have lived in [the state or county]:_______________

Family Information

3. Marital Status:
   Single/Never Married Separated Widowed Married Divorced
4. What is/was your spouse's/partner's occupation? ____________________
5. What are/were your spouse's/partner's main job responsibilities?

____

Children: Gender Age Education Level/Major Occupation

6.a ____
6.b. ____
6.c. ____
6.d. ____

Employment History

7. What is your current employment status?
   Employed Retired Homemaker Unemployed Disabled
   Laid Off Full-time Student
8. Describe your current or most recent job:

Name of Employer: ________________Type of Business: ______________

Describe your job duties: ______________________________________

Dates of employment: ______________ Length of time at job: ______________

9. Describe your job preceding your most current one: ______________
Name of Employer: ______________Type of Business: ______________
Describe your job duties: ______________
Dates of employment: ______________ Length of time at job: ______________
10. In any of your jobs, have you ever held a management/supervisory position? Yes No
    If yes, please explain: ______________
11. In any of your jobs, have you ever worked for a company that employed over 500 employees?
    Yes No
    If yes, what was the company and what was/were your job title(s)? ______________
    ____
12. Have you or someone close to you ever worked for a government agency?
    Yes, I have Yes, someone close to me has No
    If yes, which agency and what was your/their role? ______________

Educational Background

13. What is the highest level of education you have completed?
    Less than High School Diploma High School Graduate/GED
    Technical/Business School Some College College Graduate
    Post Graduate
14. Beyond high school, what have been your degrees and your major areas of study/training? ______________
15. If you returned to school, what would you like to be your major area of study? ______________
16. Beyond high school, have you ever studied and/or specialized in:

Patents	Yes	No	Specialization?
Computers	Yes	No	Specialization?
Engineering	Yes	No	Specialization?
Product design	Yes	No	Specialization?
Marketing	Yes	No	Specialization?
Manufacturing	Yes	No	Specialization?
Legal field/Law	Yes	No	Specialization?
Product development	Yes	No	Specialization?
Economics	Yes	No	Specialization?
Mathematics	Yes	No	Specialization?
Travel	Yes	No	Specialization?
Accounting	Yes	No	Specialization?
Sales	Yes	No	Specialization?
Physical sciences	Yes	No	Specialization?

For all Yes answers, please explain: ______________

Experience with Mobile Phone or Camera Technology [i.e., Patented Technology In-Suit]

17. How often do you purchase a new mobile phone?

    Daily Weekly Rarely Never

    17a. What types of mobile phones do you typically buy? Why?

    ____

    17b. Have you ever bought or used a mobile phone without a camera?

    Yes No

    When? For What?______________________________

    17c. Have you ever seen or read anything about disputes regarding mobile phone cameras?

    Yes No

    If Yes, please briefly describe what you know. ______________

18. How often would you say you use your mobile phone camera either personally or professionally?

    Daily Weekly Rarely Never

For what purposes do you typically use your mobile phone camera?__________

____

19. Have you ever used a mobile phone camera to produce or create a photography project personally or professionally?

    Personally Professionally Neither

    If yes, briefly describe: ______________________________

20. How familiar are you with mobile phone camera technology?

    Extremely familiar Somewhat familiar Not at all familiar

    If you have any familiarity, please briefly describe what you know:_______

____

Legal Experience

21. Have you previously served on a jury? Yes No

If yes, please answer the following: Number of times you have served on jury duty:______________________________

Criminal Civil Both Which party won?

22. Have you ever been a witness in a trial or hearing? Yes No

If yes, please explain:______________________________

23. Have you or anyone close to you ever filed a lawsuit or grievance of any kind? Yes, I have Yes, someone close to me has No

If yes, briefly describe: (1) the nature of the lawsuit/claim and (2) the outcome:

____

24. Have you or anyone you know well, or any company or person you work for, ever been sued? Yes, I have Yes, someone close to me has No

If yes, briefly describe: (1) the nature of the lawsuit and (2) the outcome:______

______

25. Have you or anyone you know well ever had legal training or worked in the legal system? Yes, I have Yes, someone close to me has No

If yes, briefly describe:______

Community and Leisure Activities

26. Please list any groups or organizations of which you are a member or do volunteer work. This includes church/religious organizations, school groups, social, fraternal, service, professional, business, sporting, union, political, or community groups:

______

______

______

______

27. What, if any, newspapers or magazines do you regularly read?
28. What are your favorite television programs?
29. What are your favorite radio programs?
30. What are your favorite websites?

Patent Experience

31. Have you or has anyone you know well ever invented anything? Yes No

If yes, please explain:______

32. Have you or has anyone you know well ever applied for a U.S. patent? Yes No

If yes, please explain:______

33. Have you or has anyone you know well ever been granted a U.S. patent? Yes No

If yes, please explain:______

34. Have any of your employers ever been granted a U.S. patent? Yes No

If yes, please explain:______

35. Have you or anyone close to you ever had any experience/contact with the U.S. Patent and Trademark Office (USPTO)? Yes No

If yes, who had the experience/contact: ______

Please describe the nature of the experience/contact if you know: ______

______

Include Specific Content Areas Here

Concluding Questions

36. Do you have any philosophical or religious objection to civil lawsuits?
    Yes No

If yes, please explain:______________________________

37. Have you ever heard of BigPhone Corporation? Yes No

If yes, what is your overall opinion of BigPhone Corporation?______________

____

Very favorable   Somewhat favorable
Somewhat unfavorable   Very unfavorable

38. Have you ever heard of Camera Anywhere Company? Yes No

If yes, what is your overall opinion of Camera Anywhere Company?

Very favorable   Somewhat favorable
Somewhat unfavorable   Very unfavorable

39. Do you or does anyone you know well have any close affiliations with:
    BigPhone Corporation Yes No
    Camera Anywhere Company Yes No

If yes, please explain:______________________________

40. Below is a list of witnesses who may be called to testify in this trial. Please circle the name of any witness you recognize and note how you know of that person.

Witness	How You Know of This Person

Please explain if you have difficulty seeing, reading, hearing, or speaking the English language.

41. This trial is scheduled to last four weeks. Please explain if there exists any reason, personal or otherwise, that would make it difficult for you to serve as a juror in this case.

I declare that all of my answers to the questions contained on this questionnaire and the attached explanation sheets are true and correct to the best of my knowledge.

Signature ______________________ Date ______________

Explanation Sheet

If you feel that you were unable to sufficiently answer any questions in the spaces provided, please use this sheet to provide that information. Thank you very much for your cooperation.

____

____

____

____

____

____

____

____

____

____

____

____

APPENDIX C

Additional Supplemental Juror Questionnaire Sections for Patentee Plaintiff

Additional Background Experiences

1. Have you or has anyone you know well ever had a reason to file a lawsuit but chose not to do so? Yes No

If yes, please explain:________________________________

2. Have you or has anyone you know well ever been accused of copying an idea or method that the accuser believed was patentable? Yes No

If yes, please explain and please explain how the issue was resolved:__________

____

3. Have you or has anyone you know well ever been accused of infringing a patent? Yes No

If yes, please explain and please explain how the issue was resolved:__________

____

4. Have you or anyone you know well ever felt taken advantage of in a business deal? Yes, I have Yes, someone close to me has No

If yes, briefly describe:________________________________

Opinions of Patents

5. The patent process:
   - Strongly hurts competition
   - Somewhat hurts competition
   - Somewhat helps competition
   - Strongly helps competition
6. How do you feel about the practice of protecting inventions with patents?
   - Strongly support
   - Somewhat support
   - Somewhat oppose
   - Strongly oppose

7. How easy or difficult is it to mislead the patent office during the patent approval process?
   Very easy Somewhat easy
   Somewhat difficult Very difficult
8. Getting a patent for an invention today is:
   Very easy Somewhat easy
   Somewhat difficult Very difficult
9. When the USPTO issues an inventor a patent for an invention, it means that invention is innovative and unique.
   Almost never Rarely
   Often Almost always
10. The fact that individuals and companies can patent an idea or product:
    Strongly helps consumers Somewhat helps consumers
    Somewhat hurts consumers Strongly hurts consumers
11. The best progress comes from inventions that:
    Build on prior innovations Are completely novel and unique
    Why do you feel that way? ______________________________
12. Patent holders have exclusive rights for up to 20 years. That length of time is: Too long Just right Too short
13. What is your belief regarding how detailed the USPTO is in evaluating a typical patent application?
    Extremely detailed Somewhat detailed
    Somewhat general Extremely general
14. How often do you think the USPTO makes a mistake in granting a patent that it should not have?
    Almost never Rarely
    Often Almost always
15. How common or uncommon is it that companies use the patented ideas of others without respecting those patents?
    Extremely common Somewhat common
    Somewhat uncommon Extremely uncommon
16. How common or uncommon is it for a company that owns a patent to overstep its patent rights?
    Extremely common Somewhat common
    Somewhat uncommon Extremely uncommon
17. What feelings do you have about patents or the process by which patents are obtained?______________________________

Opinions of Business and Government

18. If a smaller company makes allegations that a larger company has done something wrong, are you more inclined to believe the smaller company or more inclined to believe the larger company?

    Smaller Company Larger Company Neither

19. Which of the following most closely mirrors your opinion about competition in business? Businesses should prioritize:

    Competing aggressively over competing fairly

    Competing fairly over competing aggressively

20. Which statement best describes your general perception about corporations?

    They tend to be ethical They tend to be unethical No opinion

Why do you feel that way?

---

21. What is your opinion of the following government agencies?

	Very Favorable	Somewhat Favorable	Somewhat Unfavorable	Very Unfavorable
The Food and Drug Administration				
The Internal Revenue Service				
The Environmental Protection Agency				
The USPTO				
The Securities and Exchange Commission				

Civil Litigation and Money Damages

22. What are your general feelings about lawsuits where a company sues for money damages for harm it claims to have received from patent infringement?
23. In general, what are your feelings or opinions about companies that bring lawsuits?

---

24. Are financial consequences the best way to encourage responsible business behavior?

    Definitely yes Probably yes

    Probably no Definitely no

If no, please tell us why you feel this way?

---

25. When personal ethics and the law conflict, I would:

    Almost always follow personal ethics Generally follow personal ethics

    Generally follow the law Almost always follow the law

APPENDIX D

Additional Supplemental Juror Questionnaire Sections for an Accused Infringer Defendant

Additional Background Experiences

1. Have you or has anyone you know well ever wanted to file a lawsuit or a grievance but could not or did not for some reason? Yes No

If yes, please explain:____

2. Have you or has anyone you know well ever felt you had an idea or invention stolen? Yes No

If yes, please explain:____

3. Have you ever worked in a job or for a company whose success depended to some extent on patents, trademarks, or copyrights? Yes No

If yes, please explain:____

4. Have you ever or has anyone you know well ever worked in a job or for a company who was harmed by the existence of a patent, trademark, or copyright? Yes No

If yes, please explain:____

5. Has anyone ever copied an idea or method of yours or of someone you know well that you/they believe was patentable? Yes No

If yes, please explain and please explain how the issue was resolved:__________

____

Opinions of Patents

6. How do you feel about developing technology through building on others' prior inventions?

Strongly support	Somewhat support
Somewhat oppose	Strongly oppose

7. How often does a case against a corporation for patent infringement have merit?

Almost never	Rarely
Often	Almost always

8. Do you prefer to purchase name-brand products or less expensive, generic products?

Always name-brand	Generally name-brand
Generally generic	Always generic

9. To what extent do you agree or disagree with the view that patents hurt innovation?

Strongly agree	Somewhat agree
Somewhat disagree	Strongly disagree

10. How do you feel about a patent granting an inventor a monopoly for a number of years?

Strongly oppose	Somewhat oppose
Somewhat support	Strongly support

11. How common or uncommon do you think it is that competitors unlawfully copy another patent?

Extremely common	Somewhat common
Somewhat uncommon	Extremely uncommon

12. How likely do you think it is that the USPTO makes mistakes in awarding patents?

Very likely	Somewhat likely
Not very likely	Not likely at all

13. Once a patent is granted, should competitors still be allowed to argue the patent is not valid?

Definitely yes	Probably yes
Probably no	Definitely no

14. Why do you feel that way?____________________________________

____

15. How common or uncommon is it that companies use the patented ideas of others without respecting those patents?

Extremely common	Somewhat common
Somewhat uncommon	Extremely uncommon

Opinions of Business and Government

16. If an inventor's competitive actions tend to reduce the number of competing companies that can sell a similar product, would you tend to believe those actions are probably:

    Definitely fair   Probably fair

    Probably unfair   Definitely unfair

Why do you feel that way?____

____

17. When common sense and a government agency's decision are in conflict, which would you tend to give greater weight?

    Definitely common sense

    Probably common sense

    Probably the government agency's decision

    Definitely the government agency's decision

18. Please indicate your level of trust in governmental/regulatory agencies.

    A great deal of trust   A slight amount of trust

    A slight amount of distrust   A great deal of distrust

19. How much should the government police large corporations?

    Much less   Somewhat less

    Somewhat more   Much more

20. How much responsibility should large corporations be held to in comparison with individuals?

    Much less   Somewhat less

    Somewhat more   Much more

21. To what extent does the government favor large corporations over ordinary Americans?

    Very little   Somewhat

    Mostly   Very much

22. When people sue large corporations, how often do the cases have some merit?

    Almost never   Rarely

    Often   Almost always

23. How often do you believe a large corporation would lie if it could benefit financially from doing so?

    Almost never   Rarely

    Often   Almost always

24. What is your opinion of the number of lawsuits against large corporations?

    Far too many   Somewhat too many

    Somewhat too few   Far too few

25. How much environmental harm, if any, do you believe is caused by large corporations?

Almost none	Very little
Some	A lot

Civil Litigation and Money Damages

26. What is your opinion of the number of lawsuits today?

Far too many	Somewhat too many
Somewhat too few	Far too few

27. Do you believe there should be limits placed on how much money a jury should be allowed to award a company claiming its patent has been infringed?

Definitely yes	Probably yes
Probably no	Definitely no

If yes, please tell us why you feel this way:______________________________

____

Index

A

About the ABA Section of Intellectual Property Law

From its strength within the American Bar Association, the ABA Section of Intellectual Property Law (ABA-IPL) advances the development and improvement of intellectual property laws and their fair and just administration. The Section furthers the goals of its members by sharing knowledge and balanced insight on the full spectrum of intellectual property law and practice, including patents, trademarks, copyright, design, and trade secrets. Providing a forum for rich perspectives and reasoned commentary, ABA-IPL serves as the ABA voice of intellectual property law within the profession, before policy makers, and with the public.

Books from the ABA Section of Intellectual Property Law (ABA-IPL)

ABA AMERICAN BAR ASSOCIATION Intellectual Property Law Section

Title	Regular Price	ABA-IPL Member Price
ADR Advocacy, Strategies, and Practices for Intellectual Property and Technology Cases, 2nd Ed. (5370231)	$149.95	**$119.95**
ANDA Litigation, 3rd Ed. (5370243)	$379.00	**$295.95**
Antitrust Issues in Intellectual Property Law, 2nd Ed. (5370263)	$149.95	**$119.95**
Arbitrating Patent Disputes (5370229)	$89.95	**$74.95**
Biosimilars Litigation and Client Counseling (5370267)	$169.95	**$139.95**
Careers in IP Law (5370204) (The ebook is complimentary with ABA-IPL Section membership)	$24.95	**$16.95**
Commercialization of IP Rights in China (5370241)	$119.95	**$95.95**
A Comprehensive Patent Practice Form Book (5370260)	$139.95	**$109.95**
Computer Games and Immersive Entertainment, 2nd Ed. (5370239)	$89.95	**$69.95**
Copyright Litigation Strategies (5370228)	$369.00	**$285.00**
Copyright Remedies (5370208)	$89.95	**$74.95**
Crash Course on U.S. Patent Law (5370221)	$39.95	**$34.95**
The DMCA Handbook, 2nd Ed. (5370234)	$79.95	**$64.95**
The Essential Case Law Guide to PTAB Trials (5370233)	$249.95	**$199.95**
The Essentials of Japanese Patent Prosecution (5370245)	$149.95	**$119.95**
Intellectual Property and Technology Due Diligence (5370236)	$219.95	**$179.95**
The Intellectual Property Law Handbook, 2nd Ed. (5620154)	$139.95	**$109.95**
IP Protection in China, 2nd Ed. (5370270)	$149.95	**$119.95**
IP Strategies for Medical Device Technologies (5370238)	$149.95	**$119.95**
IP Valuation for the Future (5370237)	$89.95	**$59.95**
The Law of Trade Secret Litigation Under the Uniform Trade Secrets Act, 2nd Ed. (5370242)	$369.95	**$295.95**
A Lawyer's Guide to Section 337 Investigations before the U.S. International Trade Commission, 5th Ed. (5370266)	$139.95	**$109.95**
Legal Guide to Video Game Development, 2nd Ed. (5370227)	$74.95	**$59.95**
A Legal Strategist's Guide to Trademark Trial and Appeal Board Practice, 4th Ed. (5370247)	$179.95	**$144.95**
Marketing Your Invention, Product, or Journey, 4th Ed. (5370271)	$59.95	**$47.95**
New Practitioner's Guide to Intellectual Property (5370198)	$89.95	**$69.95**
Patent Claim Drafting Practice (5370259)	$179.95	**$144.95**
Patent Freedom to Operate Searches, Opinions, Techniques, and Studies (5370230)	$139.95	**$109.95**

Title	Regular Price	ABA-IPL Member Price
Patent Litigation Strategies Handbook, 5th Ed. (5370269)	$425.00	**$340.00**
Patent Trial Advocacy Casebook, 3rd Ed. (5370124)	$149.95	**$119.95**
Patently Persuasive (5370206)	$129.95	**$99.95**
The Practitioner's Guide to the PCT, 2nd Ed. (5370261)	$139.95	**$109.95**
The Practitioner's Guide to Trials Before the Patent Trial and Appeal Board, 3rd Ed. (5370258)	$169.95	**$139.95**
Pre-ANDA Litigation, 3rd Ed. (5370256)	$349.00	**$259.00**
Preliminary Relief in Patent Infringement Disputes (5370194)	$119.95	**$94.95**
Principles of Patent Claim Drafting and Patent Claim Analysis (5370268)	$159.95	**$127.95**
Right of Publicity (5370215)	$89.95	**$74.95**
Settlement of Patent Litigation and Disputes (5370192)	$179.95	**$144.95**
Starting an IP Law Practice (5370202)	$54.95	**$34.95**
Summary of Covenants Not to Compete (5370244)	$179.95	**$144.95**
The Tech Contracts Handbook, 3rd Ed. (5370248)	$42.95	**$33.95**
Trademark and Deceptive Advertising Surveys, 2nd Ed. (5370255)	$189.95	**$151.95**
What Is a Copyright, 4th Ed. (5370257)	$19.95	**$16.95**
What Is a Patent, 4th Ed. (5370262)	$19.95	**$16.95**
What Is a Trademark, 5th Ed. (5370254)	$19.95	**$16.95**
What Is a Trade Secret (5370265)	$19.95	**$16.95**

Find these and other ABA-IPL books at ShopABA.com

Thank you for your order!

Jeff Salyards
Executive Editor, ABA Publishing
jeff.salyards@americanbar.org

Tax, shipping and handling charges may apply.
See web store for complete details and current shipping and handling rates and information.

2 EASY WAYS TO ORDER **ShopABA.org** OR **(800) 285-2221**